THE SOCIAL MEANING OF CIVIC SPACE

Studying Political Authority through Architecture

CHARLES T. GOODSELL

University Press of Kansas

Published by the University Press of Kansas
(Lawrence, Kansas 66045), which was organized by
the Kansas Board of Regents and is operated and
funded by Emporia State University, Fort Hays State
University, Kansas State University, Pittsburg State
University, the University of Kansas, and Wichita
State University

Library of Congress Cataloging-in-Publication Data
Goodsell, Charles T.
    The social meaning of civic space: studying po-
  litical authority through architecture/Charles T.
  Goodsell.
      p. cm.—(Studies in government and public
  policy)
    Bibliography: p.
    Includes index.
    ISBN 0-7006-0347-6
    1. Political leadership. 2. Authority. 3. Local
  government. 4. Architecture and state. 5. Public
  architecture. I. Title. II. Series.
  JF1525.L4G66 1988
  320.2—dc19   87-21466

British Library Cataloguing-in-Publication Data is
available.

Printed in the United States of America

10 9 8 7 6 5 4 3 2 1

*To the person in
photograph IV.5, with
love and devotion*

Thrones may be out of fashion, and pageantry too; but political authority still requires a cultural frame in which to define itself and advance its claims, and so does opposition to it. —Clifford Geertz

Contents

Photographs, Figures, and Tables

PHOTOGRAPHS

FIGURES

TABLES

Preface

This book is unusual in that it is a book on architecture written by a political scientist and predicated on the assumptions that architecture and politics have much to do with each other and that new insights can be gained in each realm by transcending the disciplinary boundaries that normally separate the two. In this book, I study architecture to learn what it "says" about political life, and I deliberately do not follow customary lines of politico-architectural inquiry. Such inquiry tends to fall into three categories: (1) generalized "power" diagnoses of the façades of governmental buildings; (2) detailed descriptions of the history of styles in public architecture; and (3) survey research into the behavioral and attitudinal effects of public space on occupants and users. Rather, following the lead of Paul Goodman, John N. Hazard, Allan Greenberg, and Harold D. Lasswell, I look at governmental architecture as an expression of political ideas. I examine the design of buildings, built (and rebuilt) under the aegis of political authority, as a nonverbal statement emanating from the political culture of the time. Architecture is used as a physical and therefore durable "readout" of common tendencies in political life prevailing at the time of construction. Because those in power inevitably made an imprint on the huge public investments that are represented by governmental buildings, this interpretation reflects the shared values of political regimes and elites. In this study we focus on such values with specific reference to the evolving concepts of political authority.

To my knowledge, the present project is the first to pursue this topic by means of a detailed, widespread, comparative field study. In accordance with a methodological approach that Amos Rapoport advocated for studying the social meanings of physical settings, I have restricted the analysis to a single functional class of space. This step makes the comparisons both possible and revealing. The class that I chose is the city-council chamber. I have studied firsthand seventy-five such chambers located throughout the continental United States and also in Hawaii and Ontario. The city-council chamber was selected for this purpose because it represents a varied and significant example of what I call civic space, defined as enclosures within governmental buildings designed for the performance of political rituals before audiences. I argue that the architecture of this kind of space is particularly revealing with respect to regime-accepted notions of political authority.

In developing the project it became clear that while not much has been written on the expressive content of civic space per se, enormous bodies of literature relate to this subject in one way or another. These literatures are found in several academic disciplines and sometimes within more than one school of thought in those disciplines. As a result, in order to lay an adequate conceptual foundation for the study, I had to gather and integrate much material. This material was too voluminous to incorporate in the first chapter of the book, and hence a separate chapter (II) is given over wholly to this task. I hope that the integrated schema drawn from this disparate material will assist future scholars who wish to examine the fascinating phenomenon of civic space. (Readers who are not concerned with the theoretical basis of my interpretations may wish to skip chapter II.)

The purpose of the book is to explicate trends in underlying concepts of political authority as they have unfolded over time in North America from the Civil War to the 1980s. A large quantity of empirical data provides the basis for this explication, and a consistent methodology is employed in collecting and analyzing these data. Further, many of the concepts used in "decoding" meaning are widely used by others. Nonetheless, despite this systematic approach, I am the first to admit that my personal interpretations permeate the work throughout. Subjectivity is inevitable in a study of this kind. Still, the photographs and floor plans that are included in the book should assist the reader in checking my interpretations and arriving at an independent judgment.

I conclude that city-council chambers built since 1865 fall into three categories, each identified with a time period: (1) Traditional, 1865 to 1920; (2) Midcentury, 1920 to 1960; and (3) Contemporary, 1960 to the mid 1980s. I argue that essential and largely prevailing design features of the chambers in these categories express distinctive and meaningful concepts of political authority. The Traditional room is characterized by large, boxlike spatial composition, exalted building placement, an intimidating rostrum, and strict separation of officials and spectators. Its design stresses the superiority of the governors over the governed. The Midcentury chamber, which is smaller, longer, and lower and which employs a corporate dais that directly faces ground-floor public seating, states an oppositional relationship between the governors and the governed and allows for notions of checked power and democratic accountability. Finally, the Contemporary space possesses a rounded floor plan, curved surfaces, amphitheater seating, and obscured means of segregation; it expresses values of community and integration, albeit in often manipulative ways. The progression of ideas that is represented by these three ideas about authority—blatant assertion, faced confrontation, and skillful encapsulation—are seen as also

being evidenced in other realms of society where power is exercised.

With respect to the organization of the book, chapter I introduces the reader to the topic of civic space and describes the scope and the methodology in the study. Chapter II summarizes pertinent literatures from many disciplines and draws from them a theoretical framework to guide interpretation and organize the analysis. Chapters III through V then analyze, successively, the three chamber types of Traditional, Midcentury, and Contemporary. In each chapter, attention is given to (1) the social and architectural setting, (2) the composition of space, (3) the arrangement of furniture and allied features, (4) interior decoration and display, and (5) the overall aura of the space. Chapter VI concludes the main body of the text by summarizing the interpretations and by considering the implications of the study for future research on architecture and society. The Appendix contains my personal recommendations for the design and redesign of legislative meeting rooms.

Numerous people have assisted me with this project. In 1981, Edward Loucks first turned my attention to city-council chambers, with the Dallas chamber as an example of one filled with social meaning. In 1982, Edwin Pease, currently an architect in the firm of Carlton Abbott and Partners, Williamsburg, Virginia, helped me begin the actual work via guidance to the literature of architecture and through training in the art of photography. William L. Lebovich, architectural historian with the Historic American Buildings Survey in Washington, also assisted at that early stage by allowing me to consult the raw files of the America's City Halls exhibition project, then in the process of being put together. Later he was kind enough to review the manuscript.

During the summer of 1984 I had the pleasure of being a visiting senior fellow at the Center for Advanced Study in the Visual

Arts of the National Gallery of Arts in Washington. This opportunity allowed me to conduct further research, have prints and slides prepared, and write the first half of the book. I am especially indebted to Deborah A. Gómez and Andrea Gibbs of the gallery's staff for the progress that I made during that period.

Several friends and acquaintances from academia helped over the course of the project. At an early stage, Amos Rapoport of the Department of Architecture of the University of Wisconsin disabused me of several unsound ideas; at the end, he wrote a careful critique of the manuscript. John A. Rohr, my colleague at the Center for Public Administration and Policy of Virginia Polytechnic Institute and State University, also read the manuscript in full and made hundreds of helpful suggestions. Others who helped in multiple ways are Orion F. White, Jr., another colleague at Virginia Tech; Cynthia J. McSwain of the Department of Public Administration of George Washington University; William L. Whitwell and William G. White of the Department of Art at Hollins College; Clarence N. Stone of the Department of Government and Politics of the University of Maryland; Joseph F. Freeman of the Department of Political Science at Lynchburg College; and Robert B. Denhardt of the Department of Public Administration of the University of Missouri.

While I was doing research in the field, a great many people were especially helpful, among whom were many architects: J. Norman Pease of J. N. Pease Associates, Charlotte, North Carolina; Leslie H. Kenyon of Kenyon and Associates, Peoria, Illinois; Bennie M. Gonzales of Bennie M. Gonzales Associates, Scottsdale, Arizona; Jack T. Hofmann of Ahern, MacVittie and Hofmann, Tempe, Arizona; Eugene W. Betz of Eugene W. Betz Architects, Dayton, Ohio; Robert W. Hawley of Hawley, Stowers and Associates, San Jose, California; Preston M.

Geren of Geren Associates, Fort Worth, Texas; and William Scott of Setter, Leach and Lindstrom, Minneapolis, Minnesota.

Many city officials were generous with their time and insights during the field research. These included several mayors: Richard Lazer Hillman of Annapolis, Maryland; Anne R. Hachtel of Bay City, Michigan; Joseph P. Riley, Jr., of Charleston, South Carolina; Gary Falati of Fairfield, California; Al Gunia of La Salle, Illinois; Elliott L. Shearer of Lynchburg, Virginia; Elizabeth G. Baumgartner of Madison, New Jersey; Frank J. Duci of Schenectady, New York; and Arthur J. Holland of Trenton, New Jersey. Other especially helpful officials were city clerks John J. Lyons of Brockton, Massachusetts; Albert B. Olson of Saint Paul, Minnesota; and Donald L. De Ment of Tucson, Arizona; council members Patsy T. Mink of Honolulu, Hawaii; Arthur K. Snyder of Los Angeles, California; William Russell Robinson of Pittsburgh, Pennsylvania; and Miriam P. Block of Raleigh, North Carolina; and city managers Douglas Harmon of Alexandria, Virginia; Ross Calhoun of Arlington, Texas; Leon F. Shore of College Park, Maryland; Charles K. McClain of Fremont, California; and Thomas G. Dunne of Walnut Creek, California.

In site visits, certain city staff members would often take a special interest in my project and go out of their way to help. They include John J. Rosettie, Albany, New York; V. Glenn Cootes, Austin, Texas; Vicki Porter, Baltimore, Maryland; Phillip F. Nasca, Buffalo, New York; Paul Bockelman, Cambridge, Massachusetts; Edward N. Sizer, Charlotte, North Carolina; Joseph W. Casserly, Chicago, Illinois; Walter Hahn, Cleveland, Ohio; James Fountain, Dallas, Texas; William B. Bradley, Denver, Colorado; Charles O'Connor, Des Moines, Iowa; Roger Kurrle, Duluth, Minnesota; Susan E. Sparks, Greensboro, North Carolina; J. Edward Tewes, Long Beach, California;

Elizabeth Jones, Louisville, Kentucky;
Orville H. Soffa, Milwaukee, Wisconsin;
Frank J. Sudol, Newark, New Jersey; George
Dini, Oakland, California; Richard Tyler,
Philadelphia, Pennsylvania; Carl Craig,
Phoenix, Arizona; Charles R. Mansolillo,
Providence, Rhode Island; Connie Miottel,
Sacramento, California; Arthur Morris, San
Francisco, California; Margaret A. Lynch,
Springfield, Massachusetts; Maryanne C.
Corder, Tempe, Arizona; Donald L. Frazer,
Toronto, Canada; and Edna S. Lundin,
Worcester, Massachusetts.

Finally, I would like to thank Judith C.
Hoover and Carol J. Lanphear-Cook for
clerical services; Andrew R. Lewis, Gregory
B. Hunsaker, and Victoria Stone Price for
graphic-design services; and Amanda C.
Sandell for translation services. Two family
members, my daughter Holly D. Goodsell
and my sister Barbara C. Clark, made an important
contribution by reading the manuscript
for errors.

Permission has been received from James
Austin of Cambridge, England, to publish
his photograph of the French Chamber of
Deputies (photograph I.1) and from the National
Gallery of Art for publishing a photograph
of Giovanni Paolo Pannini's "The
Interior of the Pantheon" (II.1). I took all of
the other photographs.

I The Notion of Civic Space

Studying political authority through architecture is too fascinating to begin with cold concepts and lifeless abstractions. Let us start instead with four concrete examples, taken from different times and places in history, of built environments that are imbued with political ideas. Together these scenes demonstrate the intimate association of architecture and politics. Also they provide subject matter that will later be of use in presenting the notion of civic space.

FOUR SCENES
Versailles

The place is the royal palace at Versailles; the time is the spring of 1789. A vast meeting hall had been constructed at the palace under the orders of Louis XVI to accommodate a convening of France's Estates General, which had not assembled for 175 years. The reason for the long delay was resistance by a succession of Bourbon monarchs—including Louis XIV—to considering the demands that each of the three great orders of French society was making against the crown. The first estate, the clergy, was seeking a number of ecclesiastical and social reforms. The second estate, the nobility, was demanding greater protection for its privileges, which were being increasingly challenged as the forces of revolution mounted. The third estate, a diverse body composed of town officials, guild representatives, merchants, lawyers, magistrates, physicians, and academicians, was calling for a variety of profound changes in the prevailing system of concentrated power and wealth.

The hall that had been constructed for the Estates General was temporary but sumptuous—a large rectangular room called the Salle des menus plaisirs du roi (the hall of the king's pocket money, or the hall of the privy purse). It featured massive side colonnades and a richly decorated vaulted ceiling. At one end, on a raised platform, was mounted the king's throne, surmounted by a high canopy, or baldachin. On the king's right, in rectangular sectors of chairs, was seated one estate, the clergy. On his left was another block of chairs for the nobility. At the end of the room, facing the monarch and farthest from him, was a third seating area, reserved for the third estate. This last bank of chairs was especially large, because Louis had reluctantly agreed to a doubling of bourgeois representation; the third estate's delegation now numbered six hundred, compared to three hundred each for the privileged estates, a critical point, because it meant that the clergy and the nobility could not join together to defeat the bourgeoisie.[1]

For six weeks in May and June 1789 the estates deliberated, although separately, with only the enlarged third estate meeting in the Salle des menus plaisirs. From the standpoint of the monarch and other conservative interests, the new voting proportions were too dangerous to permit a plenary session. Unimpeded, the rebellious third estate voted to take the drastic step of transforming itself from a corporate delegation into a combined assembly of individually voting members who represented the nation, a drastic political idea at the time.

When on June seventeenth the third estate unilaterally took this radical step, the vacillating Louis abruptly ordered the hall closed. Its members thereupon removed to the famous tennis court of Versailles. The king, finding his support rapidly disappearing in many quarters, reluctantly called a joint meeting of all three estates. They met in the Salle des menus plaisirs on June twenty-seventh, becoming in effect France's first national assembly. Significantly, when the members filed into the hall, they did not sit in their regular estate seating blocks but at various individual positions in the room, depending on their personal political views and aims. The more conservative, promonarch clergymen and nobles took chairs on the king's right hand, while the clerics and aristocrats who were sympathetic to the bourgeoisie seated themselves either in the back of the room or on his left.[2]

Thus began the parliamentary tradition—common today in many countries and particularly on the Continent—of seating the ideologically "Right" and "Left" factions of an assembly on the presiding officer's right and left hand, respectively. These seating relationships eventually became, of course, key terms in political nomenclature, with the Right meaning conservative and the Left, radical. In 1793 the architectural basis for an ideological seating spectrum along these lines was solidified when a hall was prepared for the National Convention by the architect J. P. Gisors. He converted a theater at the Palace of the Tuileries in Paris for this purpose, and its pattern of semicircular banked rows, copied from ancient Greek and Roman amphitheater concepts, has become a model for deliberative assemblies ever since. Gisors's palace no longer exists, but his architectural achievement does: a marriage of the classic amphitheater, meant for dramatic visual and oral presentation, and the modern representative assembly, with its actions springing from the ideological mix of members as spatially seated. The idea is today perfectly exemplified by the Salles des séances (meeting hall) of France's Chamber of Deputies at the Bourbon Palace, Paris (photo I.1).[3]

Berlin

Our second scene is in Berlin in the twentieth century. The central figure of this tableau is Adolf Hitler. Intrigued throughout his life with the details of architecture, Hitler sought consciously to express the values and aspirations of the Third Reich in vast public buildings and sprawling urban plans. Stylistically, Nazi architecture was monumental, neoclassical, blocky, and executed in massive stone. Façades were decorated with vertical elements, heavy cornices, and political emblems. Governmental buildings not only provided official space but also expressed the power and glory of the state, as well as the greatness, permanence, and "clarity" of the German nation.[4]

Students of Nazi architecture agree that the prototypical Hitlerian building is the "New" Reich Chancellery, built in 1939 under the skillful direction of Albert Speer. This enormous structure, erected quickly and at great cost, was over a quarter-mile long and covered most of a city block in the heart of Berlin. The lengthwise façade, with its deep-set windows, square columns, and eagle astride a swastika, constituted what can only be regarded as a brutal symbol of fascist power. The building was badly damaged during the war and was systematically destroyed by the Soviets after they entered Berlin in 1945.[5]

The interior of the Reich Chancellery is what interests us here. It utilized incredible linear distance and spatial progression, coupled with profuse symbolic decoration, to mold the visitor's impression of the Third Reich and its Führer (see fig. I.1). The foreign diplomat or other dignitary who called on Hitler entered the building through 17-foot double doors at the Wilhelm Strasse portal. Instead of being thereupon "inside" the building, the visitor found himself in the open Court of Honor, 240 feet long and 110 feet wide. At the end of this courtyard was a flight of steps, flanked by statues represent-

Photo I.1. *Salle des séances, France's Chamber of Deputies (courtesy of James Austin, Cambridge, England)*

ing the two powers of coercion at Hitler's command, "The Party" and "The Army." The visitor's next spatial encounter was with a sizeable antechamber featuring vases brimming with flowers, a typical Hitlerian touch. After this was the Hall of Mosaics, an empty and massive vaulted chamber exe-

cuted in contrasting colors of marble. Its walls were covered with mosaics of eagles, oak leaves, torches, and other symbols of the Nazi movement.

The route to Hitler's office, still far from concluded, continued on, with passage through the high Round Room, which was

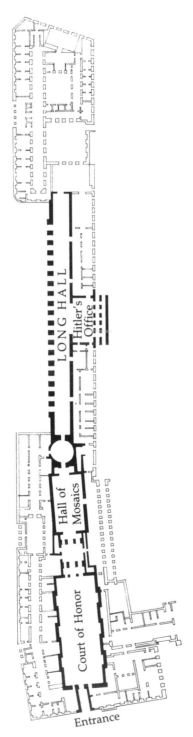

LONG HALL

Hitler's Office

Hall of Mosaics

Court of Honor

Entrance

Figure I.1.   *Ground plan of the "new" Reich Chancellery, showing the route to Hitler's office*

lit from above by a glass cupola and was decorated underfoot by a swastika inlaid in the floor. From here one entered the Marble Gallery of the Long Hall, which at 479 feet was twice the length of the Hall of Mirrors at Versailles. To the visitor's left in this enormous room were nineteen windows opening to the building's lengthwise front façade. To the right were five massive doors, the center one being the entrance to Hitler's office. This was defended by two Schutzstaffel (SS) guards, whose perfect silent immobility transformed them into living sculpture. The office inside, 55 by 92 feet, was lavishly hung with tapestries and paintings but was almost devoid of furniture. Only a large but barren desk and a few stuffed chairs and incidental tables could be seen; its purpose was not the conduct of business but the expression of grandeur.

If one adds up all the distance traversed, the journey to reach Hitler took the visitor some 725 feet. This architectural preparation for visiting the Führer was exactly what he wanted: "When one enters the Reich Chancellery," he once said, "one should have the feeling that one is visiting the master of the world." In the eyes of this remarkable megalomaniac, only such distance and monumentality could adequately express the greatness of himself and his role:

> I stand here as representative of the German people. And whenever I receive anyone in the Chancellery, it is not the private individual Adolf Hitler who receives him, but the Leader of the German nation—and therefore it is not I who receive him, but Germany through me. For that reason I want these rooms to be in keeping with their high mission.[6]

London

We turn now to a third scene. The place is the Palace of Westminster at London, a Gothic complex that is monumental in size, like the Reich Chancellery, but at the opposite pole in terms of what it stands for governmentally and ideologically. The time is 28 October 1943. Hitler's great adversary, Winston Churchill, was addressing the House of Commons. The prime minister was speaking, however, in the chamber of the House of Lords.

This anomaly is explained by Churchill's topic—the reconstruction of the Commons chamber. During a Luftwaffe air raid on the night of 10 May 1941, the Commons chamber and its adjoining division lobbies had been, after direct incendiary hits, gutted by fire. Although several other parts of the palace were also damaged, the House of Lords and most of the other major ceremonial rooms of Sir Charles Barry's magnificent structure were preserved. Immediately after the fire, the House of Lords moved out of its chamber to the Queen's Robing Room, allowing the Commons to occupy its space. Now, more than two years later, the Battle of Britain was over, and Churchill could turn his attention from saving the nation to the rebuilding of Westminster.

In his speech of October twenty-eighth, Churchill told the Commons that the government was firmly committed to returning the chamber essentially to a reproduction of its former condition. The House had met here for almost one hundred years, and the room had had, Churchill believed, an important influence on the development of British parliamentary and political traditions. The preservation of these democratic traditions was critical, Churchill went on, because of the worldwide political uncertainty that was bound to come after the war. In what has become a famous sentence, he declared: "We shape our buildings, and afterwards our buildings shape us."[7]

Two characteristics of the Commons chamber had been particularly influential upon British political traditions, Churchill believed. The first was its general shape and layout. Most parliamentary chambers, he

observed, are semicircular in form, with an assigned seat for each member according to ideological or party position. This encourages multiple parties and furthermore allows each member to have a desk lid to bang during tumultuous sessions. The Commons chamber, by contrast, is rectangular (68 by 45.5 feet), has no assigned seats (except for the Speaker, the prime minister, and a few others), and provides benches for members, not individual seats. The benches are, furthermore, arranged in two opposing sets of double blocks of seating, with five rows of benches in each (photo I.2).

Between the opposing benches is a space a dozen feet wide, known as "the Floor." Woven into the carpet in front of the foremost bench on each side is a red "sword line," across which no debating member is to step. The distance between the lines (9' 3") assures, it is said, that two opposing swordmen could touch tips but not draw blood. This arrangement of furniture, Churchill felt, had helped to shape the two-party system in Britain; crossing the Floor and thereby switching parties constitutes a very serious political act, as Churchill himself could well testify.

The second key feature of the chamber, according to the prime minister, is its size. The 3,904 square feet of floorspace is, as we shall see later in this book, less than that found in the council chambers of many American city halls. It is much smaller than Hitler's office. This small size, to Churchill, was not a sign of weakness or lack of English grandeur; rather, it was a way of creating an intimate debating atmosphere. To him, "a small chamber and a sense of intimacy are indispensable." Furthermore, since the benches can accommodate only about two-thirds of the membership, drama as well as intimacy is possible: "If the House is big enough to contain all its Members, nine-tenths of its debates will be conducted in the depressing atmosphere of an almost empty or half-empty chamber." In a smaller room,

Photo I.2. *British House of Commons*

on momentous occasions all members will come to hear, creating a "sense of crowd and urgency."

After seven years of reconstruction, Churchill's wishes were carried out. When the members of Parliament returned to their chamber in 1950, the floor was exactly the same dimensions as before, although some thousand square feet had been added in the upper gallery, to provide more seating for spectators and the press. Some details of ceiling construction, windows, woodwork, and amplification had been changed, but the Floor and the furniture on it had been faithfully recreated. All was not new, however; in accordance with Sir Winston's wishes, the arched lobby portal to the Commons, left only partly standing after the 1941 raid, had not been replaced—to serve as a memorial to those who "kept the bridge in the brave days of old."[8]

Paris

Our final scene is in Paris, at 19 avenue Kleber, a few blocks from the Étoile. At this address is located what was once the Hotel Majestic and is today the International Conference Center of the French Foreign Ministry. In January 1969 a historic incident occurred in the grand ballroom, or Grand salle des fêtes, of this former hotel: a breakthrough in the opening round of the Paris Peace Talks, which eventually ended the Vietnam War. In this hall, which is 70 feet long and is decorated with Gobelin tapestries and crystal chandeliers, representatives of the United States, South Vietnam, North Vietnam, and the Vietnamese National Liberation Front negotiated for seventy-seven days, at a cost of more than eight thousand additional American lives, about the shape of the conference table.[9]

This *ébénisterie diplomatique*, or diplomatic cabinet work, as the French press labeled it, had its basis in the issue of whether the National Liberation Front was or was not politically distinguishable from the government of North Vietnam. The Americans and their Saigon allies took the position that the members of the Viet Cong were mere agents of Hanoi, and thus should be seated with them. The North Vietnamese, by contrast, argued that the Front was independently fighting a civil war in South Vietnam and thus should sit apart from Hanoi.

At first, the United States' South Vietnamese allies preferred a clearly two-sided table format, such as a long rectangle, with themselves and the Americans on one side and the Communists on the other. Washington was willing to consider a rounded table, but nonetheless wanted it split somehow into two halves so that dichotomization would be displayed. Possibilities discussed along this line were an almond shape, two crescents, a halved round table, and a bifurcated "doughnut," with its center cut out. One variation of the doughnut idea was to divide a round table into halves by a transverse strip of green baize; other variations placed green baize at opposite points on the doughnut, inserted a long table inside the doughnut, or attached two tables to its outer rim.

All of these proposals were initially rejected by the Communists, who argued for a simple square table, with one side per negotiating team, each marked by the delegation's nameplate and flag. The deadlock was ended when the North Vietnam–Viet Cong negotiators suddenly modified their position and accepted a solid round table, along the lines of Washington's original suggestions, minus nameplates and flags. They also agreed to the Americans' desire for bifurcation by allowing a set of two tables, for conference secretaries and stenographers, to be placed on opposite sides. These side tables were stipulated to be exactly 45 centi-

meters away from the main table, so as not to give in fully to the American notion of bisection.

Overnight, French carpenters produced the three tables: the round one was 26 feet in diameter, and the two rectangular tables were 45 centimeters distant (fig. I.2). Eight Americans and eight South Vietnamese sat on one side; eight North Vietnamese and seven Viet Cong sat on the other. In view of their claims of separation, the two Communist delegations positioned themselves slightly apart. With the *ébénisterie diplomatique* thus finally concluded, one of the longest wars in modern history could now be negotiated to a close.

THE CONCEPTS OF CIVIC SPACE

In all four of these scenes the phenomenon of physical space was prominent. Bounded, three-dimensional cubic capacity—in other words, differentiated volume—was the focus of events in each instance. Moreover these cubic capacities were not just any physical volumes, they were places—domains that were specifically identifiable by human beings as having some purpose or meaning. These places did not occur in nature but were built, that is, they were humanly conceived, designed, and constructed. Furthermore, each had a distinctly political meaning, in that they were all used by kings, dictators, prime ministers, legislators, and diplomats for the exercise of governmental power.

What Is Social Meaning?

This book inquires into what is called here the social meaning of such space. By this term we refer to two distinct matters, although they are often intermingled.

One kind of social meaning of architectural space is what it "says" about those who inspired, built, arranged, and use it. This is

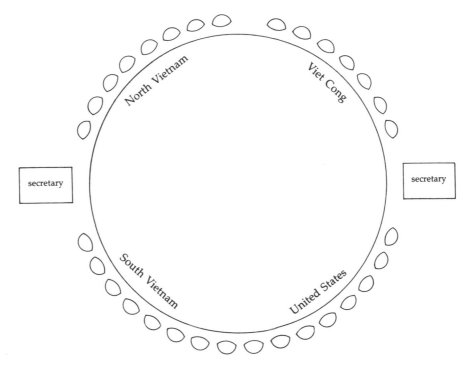

Figure I.2.   *Table design for the Paris Peace Talks, 1969*

the expressive function of architecture. Political places, for example, are not randomly or casually brought into existence; they reflect various antecedents and predispositions, including architectural conventions of the day, the conscious preferences of those in power at the time, underlying characteristics of the prevailing system of political authority, and—perhaps—certain universal human tendencies regarding spatial relationship. Thus, such space and the objects within it become what might be thought of as nonverbal commentary about people, politics, culture, and civilization.

Because our interest in this book is primarily concerned with the interrelationships between architecture and politics, the emphasis here will be on what these statements say about political culture. In political science the topic of political culture has customarily been associated with the prevailing political attitudes held by individual members of a population. I depart from this

custom by using it to refer to the prevailing habits of mind and practice on the part of governing elites. We seek to discover how successive elites, over time, think and have thought about a key ingredient in their respective cultures—namely, the concept of political authority.

Indeed, using architecture to "read" the past is an especially attractive aspect of its expressive function. Buildings, rooms, and objects are constructed of durable materials; hence they can last a long time. We can use them as vivid and embracing portrayals of the past; walking into old spaces is, perhaps, the closest we can come to entering a time machine. At the same time, the expressive meaning of an architectural past must be interpreted with care, since it cannot be understood except by appreciating the sociocultural context in which it was built. Even then, we are never sure that a given reading accurately states what is being said. Ironically, even though architectural phenomena are "hard" and objective, their meanings are by necessity "soft" and ambiguous. Thus the interpretations of specific civic spaces in this book are my own and therefore can be warmly disputed by others. Nevertheless, I would argue that a rigorous comparative methodology, on the one hand, and a careful use of widely accepted interpretive guidelines, on the other, can elevate such interpretations from sheer conjecture to justifiable inference.

Let me illustrate my approach to interpreting social meaning by briefly drawing on the four scenes described above. If we think for a moment of the layout of the Salle des menus plaisirs, for example, we notice that (1) the king was given a prominent, central, and unique seating position, consisting of a throne and an overhead baldachin; (2) this assemblage of furniture was placed on a high podium, with all other persons being seated on a flat floor below; (3) the more privileged estates were located closest to the king, with the clergy on his right and the nobility on his left; and (4) the bourgeoisie was situated at the rear of the room, farthest from the king.

Now let us consider the following well-accepted notions about the human use of space: (1) greater height is almost always associated with higher status; (2) centrality of position is typically given to the most important persons; (3) physical distance often correlates with social distance; and (4) in most cultures, items on the right hand are considered superior to items on the left.[10] It seems possible then, to interpret the Salle des menus plaisirs as an expression of the unique power status of the crown in the French *ancien régime* and the successive importance, at that time, of the first, the second, and the third estates. This political order was, of course, crumbling in 1789; hence in this case, architecture provided a primarily retrospective view. Yet, significantly, the new space built for the French National Assembly by Gisors proceeded to

express the changed constitution: (1) seating was no longer in blocks, but was in curved rows, with seating position by ideology, not estate; (2) the delegates were themselves elevated; and (3) the republican presiding officer was provided a raised bench, or tribune, but not a throne—indeed, he was not given a chair of any kind, let alone a baldachin.

Without interpreting them in comparable detail here, suffice it to say that the other three scenes described above also express aspects of the particular political cultures involved. The Reich Chancellery, with its incredible longitudinal dimensions and blatant symbolism, speaks volumes about the imperious nature of the Nazi state and the megalomania of its head. Just as articulately, the dimensions and the intimacy of the House of Commons say much about the British penchant for face-to-face political debate. The fact that the bombed-out chamber was lovingly rebuilt, except for the Churchill Arch, also underscores the reverence for political continuity and tradition found in the British ruling establishment. The conference furniture at the Hotel Majestic, for its part, was of such significance in expressing the negotiating parties' political aims and desired images of reality that it was haggled over for months. While architecture may not always be as politically expressive as is true in these examples, it is clearly capable of telling us much about the nature of the rules and the rulers of a given political order. Perhaps, in fact, it can give us occasional insights that are even more penetrating than what we can glean from the written and spoken record.

Architecture has social meaning beyond cultural expression. Physical space, as Churchill reminded us, also affects its present occupants. As we shall see in chapter II, controversies rage among various schools of thought as to whether physical environments (1) determine human behavior, (2) affect it negligibly, or (3) condition or influence behavior to an intermediate degree.[11] We cannot settle this argument here, nor do I intend to try. The problem of conducting adequate research on environmental influence is very difficult, and methodological complications abound. Individuals vary greatly in how they receive, perceive, and decode incoming stimuli. It is technically difficult to measure and validate behavioral or attitudinal responses to physical variables. Moreover, responses shift over time; repeated exposure to a given physical environment leads to a habituated frame of mind that lessens the effect of the environment.

In this study we do not dismiss the issue of behavioral impact simply because it is hard to investigate. However, we limit ourselves to certain basic assumptions and do not move beyond these. First, it is assumed that physical space can have an important influence on the attitudes and behavior of its occupants, especially if they are first-time or occasional visitors. It would seem to be impossible, for example, to dismiss the ability that the 725-foot walk to Hitler's office would have to humble, or even terrify, a first-time visitor to the Reich Chancellery. Second, this influence is assumed to be the product of complex and individualized interactions between spaces, persons, and occasions and hence not to be subject to generalization beyond the obvious. There is a certain intuitive appeal in Churchill's observation that the opposing and insufficient seating in the House of Commons encourages two-party politics and dramatizes national crises, but one would be hard put to prove this empirically.

Finally, it is accepted that one investigation, such as this one, cannot deal adequately with both the expressive and the behavioral aspects of architecture's social meaning. The comparative method that is needed in order to explore expressive meaning would be most difficult to combine with the experimental design needed to plumb the depths of behavioral causation. In short, two studies, not one, would be required in order to cover both aspects. In the present work, I examine architectural expression systematically. Comments on behavioral impacts do not go beyond impressionistic statements by users and an occasional broad and largely self-evident generalization.

What Is Civic Space?

Let us now make what I am calling civic space more explicit. I do so by distinguishing it from other kinds of architectural space. This can be done by reference to four categorizing dimensions: (1) ownership or control, (2) accessibility to outsiders, (3) purpose or use, and (4) degree of enclosure.

We mentioned earlier that the four scenes described above have a political nature because they are populated by kings, dictators, prime ministers, and the like. We now articulate this idea more carefully by restricting civic space to places that are owned by the state or are normally controlled by official agents of the state, such as heads of state, members of parliaments, and governmental bureaucrats. This includes spaces owned or controlled by subunits of a national government, such as provinces or municipalities. Among our four cases, Versailles was the property of the crown, while the Reich Chancellery and Westminster were governmental buildings. The Hotel Majestic, originally a private structure, now belongs to the French Foreign Ministry.

What is the significance of such "state" space? It is that the space is under the control of that overriding presence in the modern polity, duly legitimated government. Location, design, and layout have received the state's imprimatur. Ideas of authority and status, as reflected in the space, are either officially endorsed or at least are not in conflict with accepted regime values. Among our examples, the configuration of the National Assembly's amphitheater was implicitly accepted by the republican revolutionaries, just as the Paris conference's furniture design was explicitly approved by the negotiators involved.

Moreover, state spaces are places wherein matters of great moment occur. The ultimate coercive power that rests in the hands of state authorities is exercised in them. Here, matters of treasure, life, freedom, war, and peace are decided. This is why a place such as the Reich Chancellery can be so frightening and a place such as the House of Commons is treated with such reverence.

By comparison, privately owned and controlled space, such as the executive suite or directors' board room of a business corporation, is quite different. In a capitalist society, company buildings tell us much about the intended corporate image and the latest fads in office design, but they say practically nothing about the values of the political regime. Furthermore we are likely to enter such space in a comparatively relaxed and instrumental frame of mind— one's treasure or job may be at stake here, but not one's life or freedom from imprisonment. Then, too, the ownership of private space passes easily from one investor to the next, while state space tends to endure in its hallowed status over time.

The second categorizing dimension of civic space pertains to accessibility. Architects and urban planners refer to public space. By this they mean terrain that is open to any passer-by, without permission or monitoring. Examples are parks, streets, squares, shopping malls, and the like. Civic space is a subcategory of public space, in that it is relatively accessible but not entirely unguarded. The House of Commons, for example, can be visited by any person, but strict rules state when and where this can occur. Civic spaces such as the Reich Chancellery's chambers or the Hotel Majestic's ballroom are open only to official visitors,

aside from internal staff and the authorities themselves.

The crucial characteristic of civic space from the standpoint of accessibility is it is built with the realization that outsiders may be present on auspicious occasions. Civic space is not a "back room" where occupants are automatically out of sight and hence can behave in an uninhibited manner, away from the prying eyes of those who may judge them. Instead, it is a "front room," where acts of officials will be conducted within full view of those who may evaluate them from a perspective other than the officials'. The literature that I review in the next chapter will explain how, in such space, people often perform before others in a calculated manner, in what might be thought of as a form of staged presentation. This presentation extends not only to speech, bodily movements, and personal appearance but also to the physical surroundings that are arranged to set off the action. Hence, civic space can be thought of as a kind of stage, with scenery and props designed and selected to convey a certain impression. By studying that stage, we can in effect study those who designed it and those for whom it was designed. Hitler's public office, with its vast size, lavish tapestries, and absence of clutter, was a deliberate depiction of awesome power. It was on this stage that he held audiences with outside visitors, including foreigners. Consequently it was managed carefully.

The third definitional criterion for civic space has to do with its purpose and use. Civic space is not employed for mundane purposes. It is not simply a work floor on which everyday tasks are accomplished. The chambers at Westminster, for example, are national shrines, not conference space. Civic space is also not multipurpose; it is reserved for special activities, such as the proceedings of a given body or the conduct of a specific activity. As a result of its nonutilitarian and specialized use, then, civic space acquires a designated, particularized character and cannot be treated casually or frivolously.

We can describe such space as ceremonial. That is, ritual is performed in it. The rites of governance, while usually less dramatic than religious or magical rites, nonetheless invoke their own sanctity. Their formalistic, solemn format reminds those who are present of the grand and even mysterious compulsion of state authority. At Westminster the endlessly repeated processions, divisions, and stylized debate reinforce every day an acceptance of a commitment to the roots and the rightness of English parliamentary life. While the work of legislative bodies is profane in the sense that it addresses the most immediate and pressing problems of the day, it possesses also the sacred aura of a great public activity being conducted in behalf of the entire society.

Ceremonial ritual achieves its power over the human mind and heart through the manipulation of symbols. These are words and artifacts that invoke, in an indirect and emotional way, ideas or beliefs, apart from the immediate substance of the symbol itself. For example, a national flag is far more than a piece of cloth—it stands for the nation as a whole, as conceived by the individuals who are contemplating their banner. By the careful manipulation of symbols, vaguely articulated but deeply felt beliefs can be mobilized at a given time and place. Because of its dedication to ritual, civic space is, not surprisingly, replete with symbols; in fact, the space as a whole can perform symbolically.

To illustrate, the backdrop wall of France's Chamber of Deputies, with its tapestry, columns, classical frieze, statuary, and vast verticality, symbolizes the grandeur of the French nation, the cultural richness of French society, and the republican nature of the French constitutional tradition (photo I.1). In Commons, the Bar of the House (telescoped in the foreground of photo I.2) symbolizes the sanctity of the Floor, while the canopied Speaker's chair suggests the immense prestige of its occupant. The referents of these symbols are, needless to say, intimately associated with the values and the belief structures that constitute the very foundations of political authority in France and in Great Britain. Hence, studying them closely helps us to understand those foundations.

The final dimension by which we are defining civic space is the degree of enclosure. A space that is strongly demarcated presents a clear definitional image. Space that is bounded in all horizontal and vertical directions is particularly well defined, as is the case with an interior room.

Wholly enclosed space also surrounds completely. This point is crucial if we are concerned with the behavioral impact of physical settings. In enclosed spaces the opportunity exists to embrace the occupant from all directions, to monopolize the occupant's attention, and to immerse the occupant in a fully controlled set of physical symbols and mood cues. At the same time, perforation opportunities may be afforded into this inner environment by such openings as windows and doors.

In this study, I regard civic space as differentiated volume that is relatively well enclosed. That is, it is essentially inside and usually refers to rooms. The space is either wholly bounded by walls, floors, and ceiling, or it is exterior space that is well demarcated. The Reich Chancellery's Court of Honor, for example, had no ceiling, but it was enclosed to the point of being well protected from the outside.

Civic space, then, possesses four characteristics. It is (1) state owned, (2) publicly accessible, (3) ceremonial, and (4) enclosed. Figure I.3 graphically summarizes the delimitations involved. In order to portray all four dimensions, two matrices are shown, the right-hand one of which subdivides the

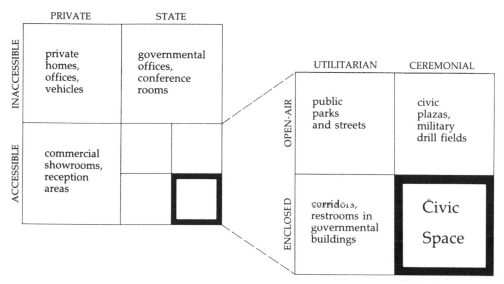

Figure I.3.   *Delimiting civic space*

state-accessible cell. Examples of space that by definition fall outside of civic space are given for purposes of clarification. Examples that fall inside are parliamentary chambers; throne rooms; public offices; ceremonial circulation spaces, such as decorated lobbies and rotundas; chambered monuments; courtrooms; legislative committee rooms; the hearing rooms of governmental bodies; and—in anticipation of the rest of this book —city-council chambers.

THIS STUDY OF CIVIC SPACE

Civic space is a relatively enclosed physical volume that is controlled by the state and in which ceremonies are performed before outsiders. Let us now turn to the specifics of this study of civic space. First, I outline the scope and the premises of the study and then turn to its research design and methodology.

Scope and Premises

I have already stated that in this book I concentrate attention on interpreting the expressive statements of civic space. These expressions relate specifically to changing concepts of political authority. By political authority I refer to more than the formal or legal powers that are granted to governmental officials by constitutions, statutes, ordinances, and the like. I mean also the informal and underlying attitudes and beliefs that support and make possible the exercise of power. Laws alone, not to mention coercion, are inadequate for the task of ruling in the modern polity; what makes governance possible is the widespread acceptance of that rule, in the form of the habits, customs, and norms that undergird it.

The seminal political scientist Charles E. Merriam distinguished between the *miranda* and the *credenda* of power, both of which foster the popular acceptance needed to legitimize power. Miranda do this by invoking admiration or even adoration, via such instruments as the national flag and the founding hero. Credenda create the basis for rationalizing belief in the rightness of power by imputing the presence of ordained authority, expertise, or reasonableness.[12]

Both miranda and credenda are necessary to a system of political belief. Such a system is not unilaterally invented by the ruling elite to hoodwink the masses, although certainly much conscious manipulation does take place. Rather, the belief system emerges over time and in myriad ways, and it forms an integral part of the culture, or shared assumptions, of a given polity. Its nature reflects the historical heritage and the ongoing challenges of current times, including those imposed by external events. The deeply ingrained character of the political belief system means that it cannot be adequately studied by survey research alone; it also requires the analysis of a polity's symbols, myths, heroes, and rituals.

Civic space, I maintain, is an indicator of the political miranda and credenda that can significantly supplement other cultural indicators, such as conduct, language, rules, sagas, songs, art, uniforms, and rhetorical style.[13] For it is in civic space that the authorities, or those who possess formal authority, promulgate and sometimes determine the public policies that they currently declare to be authoritative. Furthermore, civic space is where authorities perform the rituals of entry, consecration, and enactment that both verify their own status as bonafide officials and legitimize their decisions and promulgations.

In totalitarian societies, such rituals may be regarded as meaningless in that the confirmation or approval of official appointments and initiatives have a preordained conclusion. Even totalitarian societies, however, must attempt to shore up the exercise of raw power by affecting the minds of its citizens. This is done chiefly through miranda. In democratic societies, it can be said that the rituals of governance take on a special importance: they become an opportunity for the contemplation of and the participation in the governance process by those outside the immediate ruling circle. Such activities as public debate, open and recorded voting, the hearing of public statements, the explanation of official purpose, and the petitioning for redress of grievances become opportunities for the system to show itself as not merely legal and powerful but also reasonable, judicious, accountable, and well intentioned. In other words, credenda can be added to miranda.

Lest I be accused of blindly defending official power because I study efforts to legitimate it, an open declaration of some personal values is in order. First, I perceive the existence of a legitimated political order as being essential to a liveable society; yet, needless to say, I prefer a regime that is democratically responsive to its citizens as opposed to one that is not. Second, I would hope that miranda and credenda can operate as much as possible through inducement and attraction rather than through awe or fear. Third, I favor legitimation techniques that convince populations through honest confrontation and discourse rather than deception or hidden manipulation. These statements are not meant merely to disarm critics or to burden the reader with my personal opinions. They form the normative bases of prescriptive conclusions concerning civic space that are offered in the Appendix of this book.

By employing architecture as an indicator of the miranda and credenda of power, we are using lifeless stone, wood, steel, and glass to speak to us about intensely human phenomena. Further, we are using the durability of those materials to tell us about attitudes and beliefs of the past, even though their use and placement were integral to that time and cannot be understood without considering it.

As Bill Kinser and Neil Kleinman have pointed out, buildings, clothing, and other material objects are not discursive or logical as communicators. When "reading" architecture, we do not, as in reading a verbal text, accumulate understanding by a linear exposure to an expanding base of information. Moreover we are not provided a sequential logic of ideas, as in speech or writing. Architecture is presentational and holistic: we receive all our information at once and cannot enter into a dialogue with the builders, except rarely.[14]

Thus, care must be taken in deciphering what architecture says to us about political culture. We must proceed cautiously, not leaping quickly to conclusions, and be prepared to accept the fallibility of our interpretations. We are not simply uncoding the signals of dead minds by mechanistically consulting a code book to the past. We are attempting instead to understand the human but impersonal messages inherent in what Juan Pablo Bonta calls indexes—that is, direct emissions of past or present cultural reality that are not deliberately sent or even intended. At bottom, we are attempting to get at what might be thought of as the underlying essence (or, as some would prefer, structure) of political culture, whose nature is very likely not even understood by contemporaries. This is done by examining the manifestations of this culture that are (or were) natural outgrowths of its content, created not by anyone's formative act but by the general character of the culture itself.[15]

Buildings are, however, designed by individual architects. How does the political culture get transmitted to the architect's sketches, models, and blueprints? This happens at two levels. The more superficial level is a conscious interaction between governmental officials and architects. Hitler commissions Albert Speer to build the Reich Chancellery and tells him what he wants. Or, more typically today, the mayor of a city describes to the architect of a planned city hall the kind of building that is generally desired. The architect shows sketches and plans to the official and, perhaps, a building committee, and the two sides interact over time as the structure is being designed and built. Sometimes, employee groups and community organizations also attempt to influence various features of a new edifice. The media, too, are not ignored; press complaints about high costs and a feared white

elephant may lead to the modification of plans.

The second level of cultural transmission is deeper and more significant. It is the level of the common cultural milieu that encompasses both officials and architects and includes contemporary third parties as well. As Amos Rapoport points out, a common world view into which members of a culture have been socialized shapes shared concepts of space, form, and communication. Those who have been thus acculturated attempt to fashion their built world in ways that reflect these ideals. Rapoport goes on to argue that primitive or vernacular architecture communicates the cognitive schema of culture even more effectively than does self-conscious architecture, because the former is less affected.[16]

The authenticity and the freshness of vernacular architecture lead us to the important realization that professionalized architecture adheres to style. Styles follow artistic conventions that seem to get in the way of authentic cultural determinations of form. Moreover, architectural styles are often international in scope, thus creating a possibly exogenous cultural influence.

Nonetheless the contaminating influence of architectural style can be countered if we proceed with care and recognize our limits. First, architectural styles may be exogenous and elitist, but they are also integral to the generalized cultural milieu of an era. Fashion in styles may lead popular taste, but they are not independent of it. Second, we can take care to interpret meaning on a broad, sweeping basis and not to make the mistake of attaching significance to the idiosyncrasies of stylistic detail. This breadth of focus should also be both temporal and spatial: we should look for trends that transcend individual stylistic periods, and we should examine patterns that are reflected in numerous examples, rather than in single structures. Finally, we can study aspects of architecture that are less studied, in the vernacular sense. Exterior façades are historically the most stylistically affected portions of buildings. In this study, I draw conclusions, not from façades, but from interior spaces. The furnishings of these interiors would seem particularly expressive of lay culture, because they are intimately used by officials and therefore adjusted by them.

Design and Methods

The design of this study is comparative. The heart of the comparative method is the examination of multiple examples of a category of phenomenon so that contrasts between them will highlight features that would be overlooked in examining any one case. The concreteness of architectural forms allows us to make comparisons in very tangible, even exact, ways. The durability of physical structures over time permits us to compare historical eras.

In light of the inherent complexities of architectural interpretation, we follow Rapoport's suggestion of holding social function constant when making comparisons. That is, we examine only one type of civic space, the rooms in which formal meetings are held by the governing bodies of municipalities, such as city councils, city commissions, or boards of supervisors. By eliminating from our purview parliamentary chambers, courtrooms, the public offices of elected officials, chambered monuments, and the many other interesting kinds of civic space, we avoid apples-versus-oranges comparisons that introduce differences created by function alone. For example, the usefulness of comparing courtrooms and parliamentary chambers would be substantially lessened by the fact that the rendering of justice and the passing of laws are different governmental activities involving varied official roles. By holding function constant, the contrasts that do emerge are registered in variables that have counterparts in all ex-

amples, thus increasing the potential for uncovering meaningful variation.

City-council chambers were chosen as the type of civic space to study. I did this for several reasons. First, such spaces are numerous. Some nineteen thousand incorporated municipalities exist in the United States alone, although not all of them possess council chambers. Second, city halls in which council chambers are located vary conveniently in age. They range from historic buildings built two centuries ago to newly completed structures, thus providing a long cultural record for analysis over time. Third, council chambers are quite easily accessible for study, more so, for example, than are courtrooms or the executive offices of elected officials. One can usually gain entrance to a council chamber with little or no prior clearance, whereas judges and mayors are often unenthusiastic about having strangers prowl around their courts or offices.

A final reason for studying council chambers is that in a very clear way they pose the issue of how official authority relates to the ordinary citizen. When visiting offices or reception rooms, members of the public are mere guests; when in courtrooms, they appear as defendants, witnesses, jurors, and in other specialized capacities. Yet in legislative space they are voters who elect the legislators, taxpayers who supply the treasure that legislators disburse, and residents who receive the public services that legislators authorize. Hence we have before us a relatively clean and simple relationship between the governors and the governed. One of my central arguments is that the architectural evolution of the city-council chamber reveals important changes over time in this elemental and profound relationship.

For this book, I studied seventy-five council chambers, housed in seventy-four city halls located in the United States and Canada (I analyzed two chambers in one building). To anticipate the outcome of the analysis, comparisons of these seventy-five rooms from the standpoints of spatial composition, furniture design and placement, and decor and objects yielded three prototypical models: Traditional (represented by twenty-five chambers), Midcentury (twenty-two) and Contemporary (twenty-seven), with one restored early chamber being categorized as Pretraditional. While the chambers within each model are by no means of uniform design, this trichotomy of types emerged gradually but unmistakably from the empirical realities of the rooms themselves as I studied them, and was not hypothesized at the beginning of the project.

No attempt was made to make the sample of seventy-five chambers scientifically random. Leading and significant examples, not a random set, were sought out for study. The logic of this approach is the same as that which would compel a scholar studying a culture's literary manifestations to search out classic and superior books. At the same time, the seventy-five examples that I selected represent a very diverse, widespread, and probably quite representative sampling. The buildings that I studied are located in all parts of the United States, plus the Toronto metropolitan area in Canada. Cities of all sizes are included, from small towns to giant metropolises. Also, the age of the structures varies from quite old (from a New World perspective) to brand new, with a fairly continuous distribution of the time of construction from the 1860s to the 1980s. I also examined council chambers in city halls in Australia, Britain, France, Newfoundland, and New Zealand to enhance my breadth of outlook on the topic.

The sample was drawn as follows. First, information was solicited by mail from the 150 largest United States cities regarding their city halls. The resulting documentary and photographic material then became the basis for many discriminating choices. A second step was to examine, in the offices of the National Park Service in Washington, D.C., the voluminous files on city halls possessed by the Historic American Buildings Survey. These files had been developed for the purpose of an exhibiting and publishing project directed by William Lebovich called *America's City Halls*.[17] Third, public notices were placed in several periodicals that cover local governmental matters in the United States and circulate to city officials throughout the country. These notices asked for nominations of distinctive chambers for study by readers; several suggestions were received. A fourth step was consultation, in the course of field work, with architects, city officials, and historical preservationists. Quite often they were aware of other buildings that they perceived as significant. A fifth and final step was to search the directories that index the standard architectural magazines; journal articles that were thus uncovered furnished an added basis for choice.

Field visits were conducted between July 1982 and July 1985. I personally studied and photographed each of the seventy-five spaces at length. Distances, heights, and angles were meticulously recorded by using a tape measure and a sighting protractor developed for this purpose. I took copious notes, and I sketched floor plans, an effort that not only provided a field record but also forced me to comprehend more fully the details of the complicated visual scenes that I encountered. Also, general spatial relationships were observed, and the sense of the room was felt. To appreciate how others saw the space, I interviewed as many pertinent people as possible. These included city officials, elected members of councils, architects who had designed the rooms or had been involved in their modification or restoration, and reporters and attorneys who frequented the space. Then, too, I sought out workers and craftsmen who were intimately familiar with the physical aspects of the rooms, such as clerical personnel, janitors, painters, and carpenters. Also, when possible, I attended and observed council meetings that were held in the spaces. When architectural and historical records were available, I obtained them from municipal files, libraries, and archives. In all of this field effort, I made a sincere attempt to achieve what Edward Relph has called "emphatic insidedness"—that is, immersing oneself physically and emotionally in the space, trying to accept it on its own terms, appreciating the meanings endowed on the place by its habitual users, and being attuned to the room's symbolization.[18]

Yet, as Relph assures us, our interpretation of that space springs from our own personal experiences as well. The very nature of symbolism is that its meaning is vague and undefined, not clear and unequivocal. The noncontemporary nature of many of the examined spaces and artifacts meant that they were being interpreted outside their original social contexts. Moreover, I could not question the stone, wood, steel, and glass. True, I could ask contemporaries how they saw these settings, but it was impossible to place myself fully within their subjective worlds.

I argue, nonetheless, that four features of the research procedure enabled me to make considered judgments about the social meaning of these civic spaces. First, I studied the phenomena at first hand, systematically and in great detail, including and recording as much data as the resources permitted. Second, I made rigorous comparisons across a large number of examples, drawn from throughout a temporal range and a geographical area. Third, the conceptual tools of interpretation that I employed—to be presented in the following chapter—were not invented by me but are based on the literatures of numerous disciplines. Finally, the conclusions that I draw

have an overarching character that does not depend on the details of individualized subjective interpretation. I generalize sparingly from vast quantities of data, rather than build elaborate conclusions from a few cases.

PREVIOUS STUDIES OF CIVIC SPACE

Although a vast amount of literature has been published that touches on civic space, little has been done directly on the topic.

Students of the ancient world tell us that civic space is nothing new. In fact, we have recently learned that it is perhaps ten thousand years old, far more ancient than had previously been thought. An anthropological team led by Robert J. Braidwood of the University of Chicago has analyzed the remains of a complex of buildings in Turkey that dates from about 8000 B.C. and yet includes space that clearly extends beyond a sheltering or agricultural function. The buildings were architecturally elaborate, located on the eastern side of the settlement, and had adjoining plazas. Inside they had been decorated with plaster, painting, pilasters, and upright stones. Interestingly enough, the ground plans of the oldest of the spaces were round or ovoid in configuration, while later ones were rectilinear.[19]

Civic space was a matter of great moment in the ancient Greek and Roman worlds, and in chapter II, I draw from the scholarship on antiquity several classical architectural ideas that become important for modern civic space. We will find, for example, that in Greece the amphitheater form was preferred for council houses, or bouleuteria. Members of the public were often not admitted to this space, however, and hence the use of the amphitheater form for general audiences must be traced to early theaters, not to council or legislative space. As for the Roman world, it was the practice in the Roman Senate not to admit the public but to leave the doors to the chamber open; this permitted the citizens outside to catch the drift of what was going on, and they often reacted in noisy ways that permitted the senators to know whether their speeches met with approval or disapproval.[20]

With respect to more recent civic space, Clifford Geertz's study of the theater state in nineteenth-century Bali includes an extensive analysis of space in the king's palace. Its floor plan is intricately divided into inner sacred areas, at one pole, and outer impure areas, at the other, with public assembly areas such as courts and kitchens at an intermediate degree of accessibility.[21]

The earliest discussion of civic space that I have come across which employs a perspective similar to mine is some limited comments by the essayist Paul Goodman. In a book published in 1952 entitled *Utopian Essays and Practical Proposals*, he devotes several pages to the seating implications of legislative bodies. Goodman discusses the oppositional pattern in the House of Commons, the semicircular design of France's Chamber of Deputies, the separate desks of the United States Senate, and the raised front bench of the Soviet Presidium. Goodman interprets the House of Commons as a set of opposing teams of individualists. The French chamber is seen as a spectrum of viewpoints that have little common ground. As for the United States Senate, its desks are viewed as casting its members in the role of regional ambassadors. The severe, straight Presidium bench is said to state a concept of unassailable expertise and undemocratic central planning.[22]

Another relatively early work on civic space deals with the symbolism of courtroom design. In 1962, John N. Hazard published an article in which he compared the furniture arrangement in Anglo-American and European courtrooms. He noted that, unlike the U.S. pattern of similar tables for the prosecution and for the defense, Swiss courts place the prosecutor in a position superior to that occupied by the defense by seating the prosecutor at the judge's own bench. In Soviet Russia the prosecutor is placed apart from the judge and on the same level as the defense attorney but is positioned favorably in the room, so as to be able to face the court without rising. In Poland the prosecutor sits at the same level as the judge, but their desks are separated by a narrow space devised to assert autonomy. Also Hazard contends that when certain officials are furnished with ornate or high-backed chairs, this designates them as possessing special status; the placement of juries in separate boxes suggests that they possess more independence from the judge than would otherwise be the case; and the provision of up-front tables or well-placed galleries for newspaper reporters indicates relatively more interest in (or tolerance of) press coverage.[23]

In a more recent discussion of courtroom symbolism, Allan Greenberg points out that the positioning of the judge on a raised central podium recognizes this person's role as an impartial arbiter. Members of the audience are portrayed as silent observers, facing the judge from the rear of the room. In older courthouses, outsized public spaces convey an aura of dignity and a sense of order. The shape and the placement of foyers, lobbies, windows, stairs, and other elements provide a sense of orientation and suggest the hierarchical importance of destinations. It is Greenberg's contention that desired symbolic relationships should, in courtroom design, be considered along with the values of efficiency and convenience.[24]

Some empirical studies have been conducted of the design of legislative chambers. Michel Ameller conducted a comparative study of national parliaments and concluded that whereas chamber design is sometimes a mere historical circumstance, it may also "reflect a state of mind, a particular outlook or an unusual political situation." In another comparative study, Valentine Herman covers more than fifty countries and finds the floor plans of legislative chambers to be about equally divided between rectilinear and curvilinear form: twenty-five are rectangular; twenty-six, semicircular; one, quarter circular (in Sweden); one, octagonal (in Sri Lanka); and two, round (in Brazil and Finland). Claiming that "seating arrangements are more important than the shape of the chamber," Herman found thirty-eight parliamentary rooms with curved concave rows, like the French Chamber of Deputies; ten with opposing rows, like the House of Commons; and eight with straight rows facing the residing officer in classroom style.[25]

In a behavioral study of state legislative seating in the United States, Samuel C. Patterson found that members of the same political party sit together in 49 percent of the lower houses and in 58 percent of the upper ones. Also he discovered that seating propinquity seems to be related to both personal friendships and voting behavior. In another article on seating, a tongue-in-cheek piece entitled "The Administration of Chairs," Donald Stone and Alice Stone maintain that circular chair patterns facilitate interaction and symbolize equality, whereas classroom-style rows are inhibiting, austere, and repelling to participants. A center aisle has two defects, say the Stones: from the front-table perspective, it forces speakers to look down a chasm; and from the audience perspective, few observers have the temerity to go forward up it.[26]

Very few scholars have examined the design implications of city-council chambers as civic space. In an article that only peripherally describes physical features, Irene S. Rubin found in the chamber of a midwestern city that the council sat at a raised semicircular dais but that the city staff sat at separate tables located below that level, reflecting an inferior status.[27] Cortus T. Koehler specifically studied the behavioral conse-

quences of council-chamber design, however. Employing rigorous observational techniques, he examined communication patterns in nine council chambers in small towns in the San Gabriel Valley of California. Koehler differentiated the rooms on two bases: (1) those that did or did not possess a divided barrier or elevation difference separating officials and public and (2) those that had rectangular floor plans, as opposed to a curvilinear configuration. He found that verbal communication activity and public participation seemed greater in the rectangular rooms and in those that did not have a barrier or separation.[28]

NOTES ON THE HISTORY OF PUBLIC BUILDINGS

Because the conclusions of this study rest on comparisons of civic space over time, it is useful to end this introductory chapter by offering some limited background on the history of public buildings. Readers who are familiar with architectural history will find these notes to be a mere introduction to the subject.

In the ancient world, structures existed solely for governmental purposes, such as the Greek bouleuteria. But for centuries after the collapse of classical antiquity, governmental bodies met in multiple-use buildings, at least in the West. The oldest dated governmental building in Europe is said to be the Palazzo del Broletto at Como, Italy, which dates from A.D. 1215. It, like most medieval town halls, consists of a two-story structure with an arcaded open market downstairs and official enclosed space upstairs. Beginning about 1250 the town halls of Tuscany had the downstairs closed off, indicating that the market function was being performed elsewhere. Throughout the Middle Ages the town-hall structure incorporated a high tower, originally for defense and signaling and later to symbolize independence from feudal control. Great town-hall towers can still be seen in the cities of northern Europe, especially the former members of the Hanseatic League.[29]

In England, town halls developed later than in Europe and were less pretentious. There, too, governmental bodies met in upstairs rooms above the market; yet even these spaces served also as a guildhall, a corn exchange, or a salon for public entertainments. Eventually, as concepts of political representation emerged in the British Isles, specialized houses became needed not only for town governments but also for parliamentary bodies. Ireland's Parliament House was built between 1729 and 1739. The British House of Commons, which initially sat in the royal chapel at Westminster (this is probably the reason for the oppositional seating), was not permanently settled in its own chamber until Sir Charles Barry completed the "new" Houses of Parliament in 1852. As for English town councils, they typically did not begin to have their own meeting spaces until after the Municipal Reform Act of 1835. The chambers were often accessible by means of a grand foyer, of double ceiling height so as to accommodate upstairs public galleries, and furnished with opposing benches or tables, as at Westminster.[30]

As for American parliamentary space, the colonial capitol at Williamsburg, built between 1699 and 1705 and restored from 1929 to 1931, served as an important precedent for the New World. Its House of Burgesses contained opposing benches, in the Commons style, while the more elitist colonial council met with the governor general in an upper room, around an oval table. The ground plan of the Williamsburg capitol is H-shaped, with the cross bar of the H serving as an interior passageway between the two sections of the building, each of which contained its chamber. This bridge connecting the sections thus visibly expresses the idea of bicameralism in the building's exterior. Such external visibility for bicam-

eralism subsequently became pervasive in the architecture of U.S. capitols, for example in separate wings for the House and the Senate in Washington.

Stylistically, U.S. capitols turned mainly to classical antiquity or to European grand styles for inspiration. Thomas Jefferson, a close student of French architecture, consciously invoked the republican spirit of Rome by using the Maison Carré at Nîmes for inspiration in designing the Virginia state capitol at Richmond. Also he brought the Roman Pantheon to the New World as the rotunda of the University of Virginia's library. The classic porticos of these buildings, with their fluted columns topped by a triangular pediment, became the permanent graphic symbol of government in American cartoons and illustrative art. Other early state capitols emulated *au courant* European styles: for example, the Greek Revival Statehouse in Kentucky and the Renaissance Gothic one in Connecticut. Within these buildings one tends to find massive rotundas, dramatic grand staircases, and sets of bicameral chambers. Although their legislative chambers are usually semicircular in arrangement, some upper houses met around circular or oval tables, as at Williamsburg.[31]

American courthouses and city halls of the nineteenth century were often monumental in size and elaborate in style, expressing community pride and faith in future economic expansion. Although these buildings were often overdone versions of neoclassical, Gothic, or Renaissance structures of Europe, the pervasive influence of the architect Henry Hobson Richardson eventually led to the distinctly American style of Richardsonian Romanesque, which features rounded arches and heavy stonework (as an example, note the Cincinnati City Hall in photo I.3). Civic space within nineteenth-century city halls tended to be monumental, although chambers that were specifically designed for meetings of an

Photo I.3. *City hall, Cincinnati, Ohio*

elected council did not generally emerge until after the Civil War.[32]

During the late nineteenth and the early twentieth centuries a wave of public building occurred in American cities and county seats, most of it inspired by the French Beaux-Arts tradition. Leading American architects invariably received schooling at the École des Beaux-Arts in Paris, whose ideal public building contained a pictorially decorated façade with receding planes; symmetry along major and minor axes; monumental interior space dominated by grand stair-cases; figurative sculpture inside and out; and progressive successions of space. Thus, American civic architecture was both highly conventionalized and artistically conservative, even long after the Modernist movement in architecture had begun. Government and politicians resisted experimentation, and buildings rarely strayed from Neoclassicism (as exemplified at Des Moines in photo I.4).[33]

Not until the late 1920s did American public buildings begin to break significantly from this orthodoxy by accepting art deco,

Photo I.4. *City hall, Des Moines, Iowa*

Photo I.5. *City hall, Dallas, Texas*

revivalist, or eclectic designs. Only after about 1960 were governmental jurisdictions willing to risk such Modernist techniques as the elimination of figurative ornamentation, the extensive use of glass or unfinished concrete, and the free sculpting of interior space. Yet when the dam of governmental conservatism finally broke, architects began to apply liberated imaginations and new ideas and technologies to civic space in an exploding variety of ways. This did not mean that the new architecture was now "American," but it did mean that its variety was greater and its predictability was far less (as illustrated by the Dallas City Hall in photo I.5).

Contemporary architectural criticism does not universally approve of these developments. Commentators such as Ada Louise Huxtable, Lois Craig, Robert Peck, and Daniel Patrick Moynihan decry the stark functionalism that is commonly found in American public buildings built after the Modernist revolution. They urge architects to strive for more creative and humane designs and to return to some degree of decoration and appropriate symbolism. Although this criticism is usually not directed to interior spaces as such, it is sometimes relevant to civic space. Huxtable, for example, denounces public buildings that seem to be designed for "an exploding office bureaucracy," rather than for "the large deeds of statesmen." Moynihan says that buildings should not "make private citizens realize how unimportant they are" but instead should create "a public architecture of intimacy, one that brings people together in an experience of confidence and trust."[34] These comments foreshadow many of the issues to be posed in this book.

II Ideas Pertinent to Civic Space

Many academic disciplines and intellectual perspectives offer ideas pertinent to the study of civic space. Rather than restrict ourselves to just one of these disciplines or perspectives and thereby place the book securely in a single academic niche, I range widely among various scholarly literatures to establish a theoretical basis for this work. Although some may consider the resultant theoretical orientation to be eclectic, the position I take is that the relevant intellectual threads weave together surprisingly well. On the subject of social interpretation of physical space we may have far more conceptual agreement and overlap among the separate disciplines and schools of thought than one could have any reason to expect. It is from this agreement and overlap that I fashion a conceptual framework for my study of civic space. This framework, provided at the end of the chapter, consists of (1) a series of conceptual lodestars by which the social interpretation of architecture can be guided and (2) a set of categories of analysis by which I organize the subsequent chapters.

The survey of pertinent theory starts with ideas from sociology, anthropology, history, and political science and then moves on to psychology, linguistics, and art history. Additional ideas are gathered from architectural theory and architectural history, followed by environmental psychology and environmental design.

IDEAS FROM STUDIES OF SOCIETY

Disciplines that study the nature of the society as a whole, such as anthropology and sociology, offer a series of broad notions that serve as conceptual building blocks for our purposes. These notions relate to ritual in general and to symbolic aspects of physical space and political life.

Rituals and Symbols

A ritual may be thought of as a formal procedure or solemn observance whose purpose is sacred to some extent. In any case, ritual is more than utilitarian behavior. Religious rituals invoke supernatural blessing or intervention. Nonreligious rituals invoke and perpetuate secular authority, such as that of the state. Some students of the subject regard ceremony as a more generic category than ritual, embracing it but also including wholly nonsacred observances.[1]

Ceremonial and ritualistic behavior is marked by stylized formalism, regularity, repetitiveness, and solemnity. Rituals enact basic beliefs, reinforce order and continuity, and create bonds between the celebrants. Participants in ritual transcend cognitive rationality and enter a realm in which belief is fortified by the inner psychological experience of the event itself. This experience is imparted to a substantial degree by elaborate staging, since what is communicated is more presentational than discursive. Embodied in the staging are, not objective facts, but our deepest understandings of the world and the underlying values with which we engage it.[2]

Ceremonial ritualism involves the manipulation of symbols. A symbol is something that stands for something else. Unlike the sign, which directly points us to a referent, and unlike the icon, which may literally depict the referent in pictorial fashion, the symbol only suggests, indirectly and vaguely. The referent so suggested is emotionally felt, rather than rationally known; it exists beyond the confines of simple description; and it stands quite apart from the manifest message or instrumental meaning of the symbol itself. The very inarticulateness of symbols makes us interpret, not understand, their meaning.[3]

A central debate regarding symbols has always been whether they are culture specific, thus making symbolic interpretation subject to strict limitations of time and place, or whether certain basic symbols are cross cultural and possess universal meaning for all peoples. The culture-specific school of thought asks us to engage in a "deep description" of a given culture before interpreting; the universalist school calls for analysis derived from the underlying structures of the unconscious human mind. One theorist of symbolism, Dan Sperber, sensibly proposes that relativism and universalism are both possible in symbolic interpretation. He contends that human beings possess innate, unconsciously held codes or rules for symbolic expression, yet the cognitive process of deriving actual meanings from the codes rests on the tacitly held, intuitive knowledge that is common to only one cultural group.[4]

The "dramatist" paradigm of sociology, founded by Kenneth D. Burke, maintains that all human life can be thought of in terms of ceremonies and symbols. Burke contends that human beings are distinguished from other animals in that they derive all meaning symbolically and behave only in staged performance. His disciple, Hugh D. Duncan, has applied the dramatist point of view to community life. Duncan argues that civic ceremonies are a presentation both to members of the public and to the community as a whole. Their purpose is to confer status and to locate authority. Such indication of superiors and inferiors is especially important in a democracy, because in such a system, everyone theoretically possesses the right to seek and hold

office. Studying civic ceremonies and spectacles thus tells us much about the distribution of power. To Duncan the physical setting of the presentation is especially revealing in this regard: "Since architecture creates the spatial environment, the scene for social staging, its forms offer many clues to the hierarchical patterns of the community."[5]

Sociology's "symbolic interactionism" school of thought originated with George Herbert Mead, who pointed out that the individual does not act in response to inner drives alone but also in relation to the role and the place that he views himself as occupying. That is, a person recognizes who and where he is in relation to the outside world and then behaves accordingly. Extending this logic to territorial settings, E. Gordon Ericksen notes that human beings do not react passively to locations but endow them with specific meanings. These meanings, often drawn from past associations, then become integral to the effects that those places exert on behavior.[6]

Another symbolic interactionist, Erving Goffman, has analyzed the microbehavior of individuals in institutions and in public from a presentationist perspective. He stresses that physical settings are skillfully manipulated by those who control them so as to "present" a certain image. He describes, as an example, governmental offices or reception areas where the public comes for services; these function as a kind of stage set, where "scenery" and "stage props" are arranged in the "front region" to impress visitors. Meanwhile the "back region" is reserved as a refuge to which the officials can escape and shed their front-stage roles. The "outside region," such as external corridors, is where visitors circulate beyond the gaze of officials.[7]

Symbols and Space

One of the founders of sociology, Émile Durkheim, proposed an influential dichotomy that has relevance to civic space: sacred versus profane. Dividing the world into these two realms is *the* distinctive feature of all religious thought, said Durkheim, regardless of church doctrine or cultural setting. The two spheres are radically different both in religious belief and in ritual action, and for both realms the essential point is that the preciously sacred must be protected from the contaminated profane. Hence, sharp interdiction between the two worlds is essential.[8]

The religious historian Mircea Eliade has elaborated this distinction. Physically the sacred world is expressed by the temple, which is shut off from the familiar, ordinary world. In many cultures, he points out, the temple is regarded as a microcosm of the celestial realm. The entry threshold of the temple is, thus, not a mere doorway but also a boundary between the sacred and the profane. Also, the topographically central point in the temple's floor often takes on an especially sacred meaning. It serves symbolically as a point of origin for the founding of human existence. A vertical space or shaft may intersect this spot, pointing vertically upwards to an aperture in the ceiling and downwards to a depression in the floor. The resulting verticality constitutes an *axis mundi* that connects the underworld below with the celestial realm above, symbolizing the integration of all realms of existence.[9]

In another relevant treatise on religious anthropology, Paul Wheatley describes the square plan of ancient Chinese temple cities. These cities symbolize the universe in microcosm: walls surround on all four sides, with each side facing a cardinal point of the compass. Accompanying this cardinal orientation is cardinal axiality; axial pathways connect the midpoint of each side to its opposite, with the two intersecting axes dividing the city into four quarters. Each axis passes through a symbolic threshold gate, with the north/south axis forming the main processional thoroughfare. Governmental

buildings in the city, such as the royal palace, are located near the center of the city, Wheatley says, and usually face south.[10]

Lord Raglan offers a provocative interpretation of the origins of ancient temples, palaces, and houses. The temple, which is reserved for the gods or their images, symbolizes the cosmos. Made of indestructible stone, its floor represents the earth, and the ceiling represents the sky. Generally the temple faces south, because this is the direction in which many peoples, such as the Etruscans, believed that the gods direct their threatening or protective glances. The palace, for its part, is the dwelling place for the king. As a divine yet mortal being, the king is provided a less permanent house than that given to the gods, and hence his edifice can be made of wood, rather than stone. Within the palace, the king sits upon an elevated throne covered with a canopy or baldachin, which represents heaven. The entry threshold of these cosmic buildings is sanctified and protected by sacred symbols around the doors. In earliest times, Raglan says, cosmic structures were round because the universe was considered spherical. The floor was ideally a concave pit, and the ceiling was a dome. Later, after the emergence of the concept of the four pillars of heaven, cosmic buildings had flat floors and were built as squares or rectangles. In ancient theocratic societies the temple and the palace were often combined into one, and in modern times these two are in effect reunited as the public building.[11]

Anthropologists and students of religion stress that the sky or heavens have always been associated with divinity. Edwyn Bevan points out that in all cultures, God is considered to "live in the sky." Hence we associate height with superiority. In fact the word *superior* comes from the Latin word meaning higher. It follows that holy places are often sited on high elevations and that church steeples and ziggurats constitute sacred architecture.[12]

In a survey of sixteen civilizations and sixty cultures, the political scientist J. A. Laponce notes that all but a handful of cultures depict "up" as more valued and more divine than "down." This appears to be a universal construct in the human psyche, he says, probably because our sense organs and brain are concentrated at the top of the body. By contrast, our feet, which obey our mind's commands in a subordinate way, are located at the lower extremities of the body. Another student of the subject, Barry Schwartz, believes that the association of height with superiority stems from the apparent tendency of the brain to think in binary combinations; "up" is superior to "down" because children must look up to taller parents. Another possibility he entertains is that those in power deliberately perpetuate the notion of the superiority of height as a way to maintain the legitimacy of the symbols by which they rule.[13]

Another spatial construct that seems to be well embedded in the human psyche is the assignment of superior value to the right hand as opposed to the left. This notion, which was first explored seriously at the turn of the century by Robert Hertz, is considered another basic polarity of human nature, paralleling the up/down differentiation. Hertz pointed out that in many languages the word *right* has a number of favorable meanings, such as "correct," "straight ahead," and "the law." The word *left*, by contrast, often suggests deviation from a pure or accepted state. A widespread religious image in Indo-European cultures, Hertz observes, is the community of believers formed in a closed circle with a radiating godhead at the center. Outside of this circle lies the "blackness" of chaos and disbelief. Within the circle, worshippers keep the exterior chaos to their left and the central godhead to their right. Laponce, whose directionality studies also include the right/left distinction, points out that the Christian cultures of Europe universally associate the "right" with privilege, dominance, and sacredness (e.g., in the Nicene Creed, Christ "sitteth on the right hand of the Father"). Laponce says the right-handed bias is a worldwide cultural pattern except among the ancient Chinese, who did not strongly favor either direction.[14]

Symbols and Politics

A relatively new movement in historiography is to examine public rites and political ceremonies as a means of studying political history. Great ceremonies, such as the coronation of kings or the triumphal entry into the city of the victors, are seen as "mini dramas" in which are inscribed the tacit assumptions that legitimize a political order. Historians of this school seek to analyze the rhetoric of these rites so as to uncover the "master fictions" that uphold particular political orders. A more traditional viewpoint would dismiss these ceremonies as constituting the mere clothing of power. But Sean Wilentz asks, "Could it be . . . that if people find some sort of meaning in the symbols of power, the clothing, then these mystifications might truly represent the deeper human reality that they are supposed to mask?"[15]

In political science, the premier theorist of symbolism and politics, Murray Edelman, has discussed political stage setting in general terms. The physical characteristics of political stages, he says, invariably include massiveness, ornateness, and formality. The degree to which the physical setting is emphasized in political performances depends on (1) the importance of impressing large audiences, (2) the need for legitimizing acts and for securing compliance, and (3) the need to establish or reinforce an official's definition of self. Clearly, all three requirements are frequently critical in modern political life.[16]

One of the founders of modern political science, the late Harold D. Lasswell, wrote his last book on architectural symbolism and politics. In *The Signature of Power*, he considered how buildings as a whole, in addition to being features of urban design, express political values. Lasswell concluded, among other things, that the height of individual buildings on a city skyline serves as an index of the relative power of various sectors of society in that city. Business is powerful, for example, when office skyscrapers dominate, whereas government is strong when a capitol's dome or a city hall's tower stands out. As for Lasswell's ideas about enclosed space, he speculates that the degree to which governmental authority wishes to share power with outsiders is expressed in the extent that it operates in closed, versus open, spaces. Democratic governments allow perforation (Lasswell uses the term *permeation*) by large windows and doors, while despotic regimes favor exclusion. Moreover, in comparison to broad-based leaders, those who are protecting a concentrated base of power tend to withdraw from the body politic, both vertically and horizontally—for example, to remote mountaintop strongholds.[17]

Another point of interest in Lasswell's discussion is the relationship between what he calls "deciding places" and "sacred places." The former are exemplified by governmental space; the latter by religious space. Despite Durkheim's insistence that the sacred and the profane must remain divided, Lasswell maintains that the two kinds of place often interpenetrate or even coincide. An illustration that he gives is the kiva, the partially underground chamber of the Pueblo Indians, which is used for sacred rites and council deliberations. This thought parallels Raglan's position that the contemporary public building combines both temple and palace.

Other writers on politics and architecture stress how structures that governments build express the values and ideology of the prevailing political regime. These authors

refer principally to façades but do not exclude interior space from their analysis. David Milne contends that public buildings enshrine each civilization's code of law and order and thus perform a conservative, stabilizing function for the society. At its most superficial level, architecture merely houses established institutions; but at a deeper level, a political demand is exerted. "The political demand," states Milne, "is that architecture shall make edifices befitting the importance and power of these institutions, that it shall make these institutions appear mighty and durable, and that it shall, in its symbolism and expressive form, state dramatically something of these institutions' 'idea' of the world."[18]

Other authors develop Milne's point by offering concrete examples. Flavio Conti describes "shrines of power" in various countries and cultures. He analyzes royal throne rooms as a particularly compelling type of power-oriented space. Richard C. Trexler, describing the nature of public life in Renaissance Florence, comments on the symbolic function of the city hall: "The sacramentals of political power—the myriad of flags, the high tower, seals, chairs, and batons—functioned in one sense to 'frame' the exercisers of power, to define and limit communicable power without extinguishing it."[19]

In a discussion of ideology and language in the architecture of power, Helio Piñón contends that the geometry, the proportions, and the hierarchical organization of interior space are capable of inferring a divine order, which in turn legitimizes systems of corrupt authority and social control. From a less ominous perspective, a book on Denmark's castles, fortresses, town halls, and other public buildings examines them as "dwellings of power." Its authors point out, for example, that the wing of Copenhagen's city hall that is devoted to the council chamber is an especially prominent element of the building, stressing the council's importance vis-à-vis the municipal bureaucracy.[20]

"STRUCTURALIST" NOTIONS

Ideas pertinent to civic space are also found in various bodies of literature that I loosely refer to as "structuralist." Quotation marks are used because the word has become almost too fashionable in recent years and has not stabilized in meaning. I employ it here as a convenient collective label for a number of ideas that stress innate or underlying imperatives that drive the human encounter with physical space and material objects.

Structuralism in Psychology

I first examine ideas that derive from the theories of Carl G. Jung. Jung believed that down through the ages, humankind has possessed a collective unconscious composed of archetypes, or basic primordial images, inherited from the earliest human past. These then mold the thinking of the conscious mind in all cultures.[21]

A foremost Jungian archetype is the notion of self, symbolized by the form of the human body. The body performs two functions psychologically: it envelops and protects an inner being, on the one hand, and it makes a presentation to the outside world on the other. Clare C. Cooper has applied this notion to architecture by suggesting that the house functions as an enveloping and presenting structure that is analogous to the body. The house defines an inner world known only to ourselves and intimates; yet it also constitutes a mask by which we present ourselves externally. In the latter case, it becomes—in Jungian terms— a "persona," or protecting façade presented to the outside world.[22]

Jungians, as well as symbolists in general, attach great significance to various geometric forms. The circle is regarded as representing wholeness, eternity, perfection, the universe. The circle is rotary, dynamic; it has no beginning or end; it points in all directions; and it is found in nature. The Sioux Indians, noting the circular nature of the sky, the sun, the moon, and birds' nests, constructed round tepees in conformity to what they considered a cosmic form. The Indian kiva that Lasswell mentioned is often circular and partly underground, with holes in the ceiling and the floor, in the manner of an *axis mundi*. These features in combination represent, according to anthropologists, a microcosm of the universe and a symbol of creation.[23]

The geometric form of the square, by contrast, symbolizes the earth, man, and terrestrial reality. When the square, or quaternary, is overlaid symmetrically on the circle, the sacred mandala is produced, which many Eastern religions consider to be a symbolic representation of the cosmos (fig. II.1). If the mandala consists of a circle within a square, rather than the reverse, it is considered a more developed structure, the reason being that in this configuration, the superior form of the two, the circle, is closer to the sacred center. Some Jungians believe that the archetypal significance of the mandala explains why ancient cities and basilicas were sometimes laid out in this form.[24]

Another geometric form, the triangle, is considered by some to be a symbol of aspiration and ascension. When upright, the triangle is the means by which man can attempt to leave earth and reach heaven. This notion, it has been argued, underlies the sacred meaning that numerous ancient civilizations attached to the pyramid. Applying triangular symbolism to house design, the Jungian psychologist Olivier Marc contends that in house architecture, both the gabled roof and the inclined stairway constitute unconscious attempts to ascend to a higher reality.[25] Marc further connects Jungian thought to architecture by reminding us that many churches have a cross-shaped floor plan. The cross, itself representing the

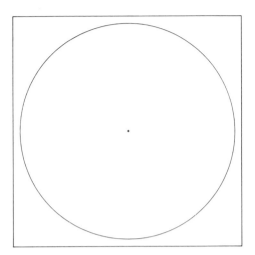

Figure II.1. *A simplified mandala*

human body, consists of a vertical stake, which symbolizes our desire to reach the eternal, and a horizontal crossbeam, which reaches out to the secular world. Another Jungian, Aniela Jaffe, theorizes that the Latin cross has a longer stake than crossbeam because it conveys the idea that the believer has succeeded to some extent in reaching God.[26]

Jung also attached archetypal significance to color. He thought that blackness represents the primal darkness from which man longs to escape. Whiteness and light in general symbolize redemption and release. In almost all cultures of the world (Japan is an exception), black is consistently associated with negative values, and white is associated with positive ones. Colors that have longer wavelengths—such as yellow, orange, and red—tend to be associated with warmth, while colors that have shorter wavelengths—such as green and blue—are considered cool. Since ancient times, individual colors have symbolized facets of nature as well as abstract ideas: red represents blood and power; yellow, the sun and warmth; green, spring and hopefulness; and brown, autumn and despair.[27]

Cognitive psychology differs from the Jungian perspective in that it concerns, not

archetypes, but the processes by which the human mind draws meaning from the world. Although for many years cognitive psychologists concentrated on such matters as eye movements and the act of perception, they have recently taken a more holistic approach to environmental comprehension. Cognitive psychology has also moved away from experimentalist positivism toward a "constructivist" position that emphasizes the subjective nature of cognition. In a recent survey of this literature, Gary T. Moore has proposed that we give more attention to the symbolic meaning that various environments have for individuals.[28]

The urban theorist Kevin Lynch, although not himself a psychologist, has developed a construct that has been utilized by cognitive psychologists in a way that is applicable to civic space. His notion concerns the way in which residents of a city view the layout of the city in their minds. The image that we have of cities, he maintains, is fashioned from five elements: *paths*, or linear channels, such as streets; *edges*, or boundaries, such as walls or elevated highways; *districts*, or territorial areas—neighborhoods, precincts; *nodes*, or strategic spots occupied by people—traffic circles, key buildings; and *landmarks*, or unoccupied strategic points—monuments, hillsides.[29]

Charles H. Burnette suggests, drawing upon the child-psychology tradition of Jean Piaget, that the infant learns about the world by experiencing Lynch's five elements. The baby's driving ego center can be viewed as a node. This initiates action, with the result that the child moves along a path and eventually encounters an edge. These experiences in turn become the basis for knowing a district, whose meaning in the child's mind takes the form of a landmark. In short, Burnette believes, these elements are archetypal to the human learning process and consequently are deeply implanted in the human mind. In the adult world they take on the character of universal symbols:

the house or the cave is a node, the road or the river of life is the path, the wall or the horizon is the edge, the field or the plain of life is the region, and the tower or the mountain is a landmark.[30]

The Gestalt tradition within cognitive psychology provides us with other pertinent ideas. Gestalt theorists contend that cognition grows from certain structural forms that are imprinted on the human mind. One strand of Gestalt thinking is body-image theory, which says that the experiences of life are importantly dependent on the unique form of the human body. As we experience mobility—that is, as we move through spatial contexts—we unconsciously carry in our mind an image of how our body is physically positioned at each moment in time. Because of the importance of the body's location to us, then, spatial coordinates are central to our thinking. Body-image theorists draw conclusions that are parallel to those mentioned earlier, such as the universality of the right/left and up/down distinctions. The position of the head determines what is right or left to the individual, and the center of the body's trunk is the reference point for what is up or down. Another universal distinction is front versus back; its basis, according to body-image theory, is the physiological fact that most of our sensory apparatus is located on one side of the upper body. Furthermore, the body is more mobile in the same direction in which the senses largely point.[31]

Structuralism in Linguistics

I turn now from structuralist notions associated with psychology to those in linguistics, where concern is less with the structure of the human mind per se and more with the structure of communication. At the turn of the century, when Charles Sanders Peirce developed his general theory of signs, he called it *semiotics*, using a word originally coined by John Locke. The Swiss linguist

Ferdinand de Saussure, a contemporary of Peirce's but working independently of him, introduced the word *semiology* to refer to his own quite different theories of sign communication. The field has been characterized ever since by multiple vocabularies and doctrinal squabbling. Even so, semiotics (as we shall call it) contributes ideas that are germane to civic space.[32]

The core concept of semiotic theory is the sign. The sign makes a direct, intentional reference to a specified other "thing," as opposed to the symbol, which refers only vaguely. Saussure called the sign a signifier and what is denoted the signified. "Natural" signs point innately to the signified, as when the human cry of pain points to acute discomfort. Most signs are arbitrary, however, in that only an agreed-upon convention of the sign's "language" (or *parole*, as Saussure called it) links signifier and signified.

To understand arbitrary signs we must possess an appropriate translation code. This code is grounded in one's particular cultural milieu. At the same time, linguists who adhere to the structuralist school maintain that beneath this cultural intermediation lies a series of basic syntactical relationships that are universal to all signs. This "deep structure" consists, for example, of underlying principles of signification, such as contiguity (relationships of contextually adjacent signs), association (similarities or correlations among signs), and opposition (contrasts between dualities of signs).

In recent years, several writers on architecture have been attracted to semiotic theory. A building or city is considered a "text," which can be "read" through application of appropriate deciphering codes. Although architectural meaning remains culture specific, hopes for universalistic structural analysis are nonetheless entertained. Peter Eisenman, for example, envisions a notational system for analyzing architecture that can be applied across time. Present and prior

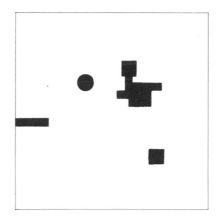

Figure II.2. *Continuous solids with figurative voids (left), and figurative solids with continuous voids (right)*

conditions can then be compared in order to discern the "state of shear" between the two.[33] Another theorist who applies semiotics to architecture, Donald Preziosi, contends that a universal unit of analysis in architecture can be discerned; he calls it the "space-cell." Such cells consist either of formations of mass or of formations of volume. Their distinctions, disjunctions, and oppositions to each other are the basis of architectonic communication.[34]

James Holston applies the mass/volume distinction to the macrodesign of urban architecture, which he regards as an "inscription of political order." He makes a distinction between cities in which buildings occupy most of the space and those in which relatively few buildings are scattered in open areas. In the first case, which is the typical grid-organized city, the "continuous solids" of the buildings are separated by the "figurative voids" of the streets. In the second plan, exemplified by Brazilia, the "figurative solids" of occasional buildings appear against the background of "continuous voids" of wide-open space (fig. II.2).[35]

Dennis Doxtater has pointed out that the specific notion of opposition, which is so integral to much semiotic theory, can be isolated as an important theme in spatial arrangements. He gives examples of where

structural anthropologists have analyzed traditional societies in oppositional terms with respect to architecture. For example, primitive houses have been divided into opposing rooms, one male and the other female. Circular villages have winter and summer hemispheres. One end of elliptical grounds on which rituals are performed is devoted to life and the other to death. Doxtater associates spatiosymbolic oppositions with the twin human tendencies for territoriality and hierarchy; in combination, these create a drive physically to separate the strong and the weak, the superior and the subordinate, the structure and the antistructure.[36]

The application of semiotic theory to architecture is not without its critics. Diana Agrest and Mario Gandelsonas have argued that architecture and verbal language differ so greatly as forms of expression that a linguistic style of analysis must be of limited value to architecture. They and others also point out that the spoken word is continuous, while any built edifice is a one-time creation. Language follows a stable convention, but architecture must be interpreted by differing, ephemeral codes that are variously devised by the architect, the critic, the user, and the casual observer. Architecture is, moreover, more readily affected than is speech by extratextual considerations such as taste and economics.[37]

Structuralism in Art History

The field of art history is my final source of ideas for structuralist notions that are applicable to civic space. Here the area of iconography is of interest. The key theorist in this field, Erwin Panofsky, regards iconographic study as aiming to understand the subject matter of art, rather than analyzing or criticizing its form. He maintains that three strata exist in iconographic meaning: (1) the natural subject matter, such as content motifs; (2) the conventional subject matter of thematic imagery; and (3) the Third Stratum, where "synthetic intuition" comes into play. At this third and deepest level, iconographic interpretation requires familiarity with the essential tendencies of the human mind and a search for what Panofsky calls intrinsic meaning.[38]

A nineteenth-century Dutch theorist of painting, Humbert de Superville, insisted that "absolute signs in art" do exist. One of these is the verticality of man. When standing erect, the human figure is aligned on a vertical axis that extends outward from the center of the earth, noted de Superville. Thus, unlike other animals, man's vertical stance turns him toward heaven in a sublime bodily attitude.[39]

Another relevant iconographic idea relates to the issue of directionality in paintings. A longstanding conundrum on what is right and left in pictorial art was resolved when critics realized that the directionality of the person who is looking at a painting does not necessarily correspond to the directionality that the painter had in mind. In many early icon paintings, directionality derives from the positions of figures in the pictures, rather than from those who are looking at them, with the result that the observer's right is the painting's left.[40]

Related to iconographic study is the study of material culture, which is the examination of the meaning of physical artifacts made by human manufacture, such as pieces of furniture. Material-culture specialists see artifacts as cultural statements from the past, which can be used to enlighten cultural history and, perhaps, to decipher a subconscious grammar that cuts across cultures and eras. E. McClung Fleming speaks about four levels in the investigation of artifacts: (1) the identification of objects, (2) the evaluation of their aesthetic quality or workmanship, (3) the content analysis of the artifact's meaning in its own originating culture, and (4) the interpretation of the item from the standpoint of our own contemporary value system. At this fourth level the interpreter creatively seeks intersections between disciplines and cultural constructs that can throw light on the larger meaning of the artifact. This meaning derives from comparing values that are manifest in the object at its time of manufacture with contemporary values. Such interpretation, says Fleming, is not objective or documentable, but it nonetheless yields demonstrable meaning for today.[41]

IDEAS FROM ARCHITECTURE

I turn next to literature from the field of architecture itself for ideas bearing on civic space. My discussion begins at the level of relatively abstract architectural theory, then turns to ideas about applied design, and finally to architectural history.

Space and Place

To architects the notion of space is central: its long history extends back to the ancient Chinese. Down through the ages, various philosophers, such as Plato, Newton, Hegel, and Einstein, have conceived of physical space in many different ways. In classical antiquity, buildings were thought of in terms of solids rather than voids—that is, as piles of masonry, rather than as enclosed space. The idea of interior space became architecturally important only in the Middle Ages, with the exception of such revolutionary buildings as the Pantheon in Rome. By the time of the Gothic cathedral, however, interior space and light were prime objects of architectural attention; moreover, solids and voids now interpenetrated each other to an elaborate degree in the form of decorative protuberances, worked façades, sculpture, and fenestration.[42]

Still, interior spaces remain a definable reality, although the degree to which they enclose varies. Philip Thiel maintains that the degree of enclosure is a product of three factors: (1) explicitness, by which he means the clarity of space definition; (2) spatial volume (immense spaces seem to enclose less than intimate ones do); and (3) the relative size of space-establishing elements, such as screens, railings, and furniture. Rikard Küller argues, in relation to this third factor, that more intense enclosure occurs in either relatively empty rooms or in rooms that are overfurnished; the empty room draws our attention to the area itself, while excess furniture creates a sense of crowdedness.[43]

Louis Hammer insists that the significance of architectural space for human experience can hardly be exaggerated. Although we usually think of life's experiences as being punctuated by time, they are also framed by space. This is due, he points out, to the simultaneous nature of spatial presence: all elements of a particular orientation to the symbolic universe are pressed in on us at one time. Entry into this space, with a sudden immersion into sensory stimuli that are received from all directions at one temporal instant, sets off a potentially profound registering of experience. The doorway, as the entry point into this simultaneous presentation of surrounding stimuli, becomes a passageway to that experience and, hence, a source of values by which to process it. The

portal, argues Hammer, "makes values possible, indeed suggests and invents them."[44]

Steven K. Peterson states that the architect has traditionally conceived of space as differentiated: it is defined, discontinuous, static, and serial in composition. But a tendency has emerged in modern architecture to view space as undifferentiated, ideally formless, continuous, open, and flowing—a piece of the limitless continuum of natural space that is outdoors and that has been only temporarily captured indoors. The result, in Peterson's eyes, is the phenomenon of antispace, by which he means space that is not seen as amenable to deliberate, manmade molding within a fixed context. Peterson urges that antispace be rejected in architectural design and that we return to more defined space.[45]

The architectural theorist Rudolf Arnheim implicitly disagrees. To him, we do not appreciate how a building "speaks to us" symbolically if we conceive of it as a mere static statement. Conceived of as a dynamic, visual form, however, it is capable of revealing its true meaning. He contends: "There is nothing expressive, and therefore nothing symbolic, in a set of stairs or a staircase as long as it is seen as a mere geometrical configuration. Only when one perceives the gradual rising of the steps from the ground as a dynamic crescendo does the configuration exhibit an expressive quality, which carries a self-evident symbolism." Furthermore, Arnheim argues, this symbolism is not merely a subjective phenomenon, it is innate in the architectural dynamics as given. For example, a building that is nearly devoid of windows conveys, inherently, a "quality of closedness," a "tightness of mind."[46]

Putting architecture into explicitly human terms, Charles Moore and Gerald Allen have written that the generic construct of building is of notable importance to humankind because it creates not only a space but also a place. It does so by "dividing what is inside from what is outside, then somehow arranging the inside things in some order." To create a place, Moore and Allen say, is "to make a domain that helps people know where they are and, by extension, know who they are."[47]

To know a place, architects are fond of pointing out, the user or observer cannot merely stand outside and look—as in the case of painting and sculpture. Rather, one must go inside. Steen E. Rasmussen tells us that in order to know a building, one must enter rooms, feel them close about, and be attuned to the concept of the architectural creation as a whole. This knowing must be done phenomenologically, argues Christian Norberg-Schulz; we understand a place, not as a cold abstraction, but as a totality of concreteness with respect to the intimate details of substance, shape, texture, and color.[48] We should further recognize, he says, how the place gathers symbols that encapsulate subjective meanings, which are in turn gathered from other places and times. These are visually displayed, along with motifs that condense the character of the place. The consequence is a microcosmic world, or *imago mundi*, which possesses a particular "spirit of the place," or as he terms it, *genius loci*. He categorizes four types of *genius loci*: (1) the Classic—an articulated, conscious composition; (2) the Romantic—an irrational, mysterious and idyllic spirit; (3) the Cosmic—an integrated, rational system; and (4) the Complex—a synthesis of the other three.[49]

If we are challenged to apply Norberg-Schultz's typology to civic space, we should appreciate the distinction that he makes between the solidity of a mass center and the hollow character of an enclosure. In a kind of solid/void dichotomy, he regards the mass center as defining place by the principles of proximity, organization, and concentration. Hence the mass center is effective in expressing abstract ideals. The enclosure, however, defines place by creating a separa-

tion from the area; hence it is superior to the mass center as a site for social interaction, psychological protection, and the performance of ritual:

> Whereas the mass-center has an abstract, ideal character, the enclosure has strong social implications. Basically it expresses a coming together, the forming of a ring for a common purpose. Most cultures have such enclosures where rituals or theatrical performances take place. The essential architectural property is a clearly defined boundary, which secures physical as well as psychic protection.[50]

Choices of Design

James Marston Fitch points out that buildings and spaces differ greatly in the degree to which the architect does or does not possess a latitude to exercise artistic freedom. In designing such spaces as surgical theaters and the control rooms of power stations, function overwhelmingly dictates form. For monuments and mortuaries, by contrast, practical usefulness is not an issue, and the designer can be freely creative. Churches and playhouses, Fitch says, fall between these two poles, although more toward the creative side than toward the practical; offices and factories are biased in the opposite direction. Using this frame of reference, we can anticipate that the design of civic space—which is not unlike church sanctuaries and theater auditoriums in its point on Fitch's continuum—will exhibit ample variation and creativity.[51] Hence the many ranges of design options that are discussed in the architectural literature are often pertinent to civic space. Norberg-Schulz, for example, speaks of a window that is a mere hole in the wall, as opposed to a window that "dematerializes" the wall. Indeed, the difference between perforating apertures and expansive window walls is not merely a technical issue but also a conceptual one; the difference between the two takes us to the very essence of what constitutes an enclosure.[52]

Variation also occurs in the techniques that are used to achieve what architects call scale. Despite the human being's capacity for depth perception, the eye-mind combination has difficulty in absorbing large spatial volumes without assistance. To provide help in this, articulating elements are often incorporated to break up and organize the space, thus making it comprehensible. Orthodox methods of achieving scale include symmetry, balance, proportion, decoration, ceiling coffers, placing columns in open space, and focusing lines on a central point, such as a podium. Modern architects include in their repertoire of scaling methods such concepts as contrasts in ceiling height, the exposure of trusses or modular ceiling vaults, the sculpting of walls, the manipulation of surface texture, and the intentional use of patterns of light and shadow.[53]

Floor-plan configuration is a highly important design variable. Rectangular plans achieve a dominating lateral, or major, axis which provides directionality to attention and creates spatial distance between the ends, or between front and back. Arnheim contends that round rooms give occupants the feeling that they are the focal point of attention; radial vectors seem to extend from their bodies outward to the surrounding surfaces. If domed ceilings are then added in a kind of vertical-axis spatial sculpting, a degree of concavity obtains, thus forming a comforting hollow into which the occupants can fit.[54]

Decoration can range from the faithful duplication of classical orders to experimentation with unique and varied effects. René Smeets finds that the rhythmic repetition in classical ornament is itself a symbol of order. Arnheim suggests that symmetry in decoration inherently conveys a sense of stability and permanence; it is not coincidental that monumental images of gods and rulers are usually symmetrical in form.[55] In a characteristically iconoclastic vein, the famous architect Robert Venturi criticizes what he calls "heroic and original" architecture, whose decoration is integral to its conception. He caustically labels this type as a "duck," named for a poultry store he once encountered whose building was shaped like a duck. Venturi defends as a contrary approach the "decorated shed," where ornamentation is casual, cumulative, and tied to utility. His prototype here is the Las Vegas commercial strip, whose glorification by Venturi brought cries of outrage from the architectural profession.[56]

Still another design variation of importance is building materials. As we have seen, ancient peoples are said to have built their temples of stone and their palaces of wood so as to reveal the relative importance of each. Similarly, contemporary architectural theory makes distinctions between the messages that various construction materials send. Charles Jencks states that whereas steel and glass convey coldness, precision, and rational planning, wood suggests warmth, naturalness, pliability, and organic emergence.[57] Other interpretations identify plastic with artificiality and superficiality; marble with solidity and permanence; textured surfaces with touchability and interest; dark-stained wood with formality; and light-stained or natural wood with informality.

A final variable of pertinence to civic space is what Joseph R. Gusfield has called symbolic gestures. To him, "cohesive" symbolic gestures embrace, in a unifying way, all persons who are present, whereas "differentiating" symbolic gestures divide people according to status or subgroup. Examples of unifying symbols are flags and emblems that represent the whole community or polity. Differentiating gestures are illustrated by establishing a throne for the king but requiring commoners to sit in ordinary chairs.[58]

Audience seating patterns can also be analyzed by means of the cohesive/differentiating distinction. Arnheim contends that when all chairs are facing in the same direction, as in a classroom or lecture hall, a "parallelism of purpose" on the part of the seated occupants is suggested. Moreover, the audience is clearly symbolized as being differentiated from the lecturer. When, however, seating rows are rounded and raked, as in a Greek amphitheater, members of the audience can see each other. Hence they are capable of thinking of themselves as a corporate body. Goethe thus described the occupants of the theater at Verona: "The wobbling, roaming animal of the many heads and the many senses sees itself unified in a noble body, shaped into unison, fused in one mass and stabilized as one form, and animated by one spirit."[59]

Concepts from History

The remaining architectural ideas to be reviewed for our study are not so much a product of concepts of architectural theory as they are the legacy of architectural practice. Particularly germane to civic space are certain notions inherent in the building practices of classical antiquity and the Middle Ages.

Cultural historians such as Phyllis Ackerman and William R. Lethaby remind us that in the ancient world, symbolism in architecture was not an artistic affectation but a cosmic imperative. Just as the ordinary mortal unthinkingly incorporated the symbols of the known universe into his everyday life, the builder automatically celebrated cosmic reality in the design and the decoration of buildings. Temples were covered with rounded domes because, it was unhesitatingly felt, they represented the heavens. Pyramidal forms, whether in angled roof lines or in triangular pediments, symbolized cosmic mountains reaching to

the sky. Sacred buildings were placed atop elevations because this would place them in conformity with the perceived natural order. The same is true with architecturally elaborated portals, nonfunctional gates of passage, and free-standing pillars and columns that seem to support the sky.[60]

With architecture constituting an uncontrived extension of belief systems, then, we should not be surprised to discover revealing differences between the public buildings of, say, classical Greece and those of ancient Rome. In the agora, or political discussion arena, of the Greek city state, high podiums or tribunes were not common. In the Roman forum, however, Caesar addressed the multitude from an elevated platform. Whereas benches were provided in Greek amphitheaters, Roman voting assemblies during the Republican period furnished no seats to their members. Allowing delegates to sit down was considered Greeklike and conducive to seditious, rash, and unrestrained action.[61]

The layout of what is equivalent to the council chambers of antiquity is similarly revealing. The first bouleuterion of Athens was a quite intimate gathering place; its members sat on three sides of the room. Stone steps rose upward from the floor in successive elevations to accommodate the members (fig. II.3). In the later council house that was built on the same spot, the steps were curved in amphitheater form. In both spaces, no evidence exists of podiums, lecterns, thrones, or pulpits; apparently the speakers merely stood in the well before their peers, with entryways to their back.[62]

By contrast, the Curia Julia of Imperial Rome, whose construction was begun by Caesar shortly before his assassination and which was later named after him, was laid out so that the senators sat in opposing rows of parallel benches, again raised on successive steps (fig. II.3). The consuls and the emperor sat at the end of the room on a raised platform, or *suggestus*. The impor-

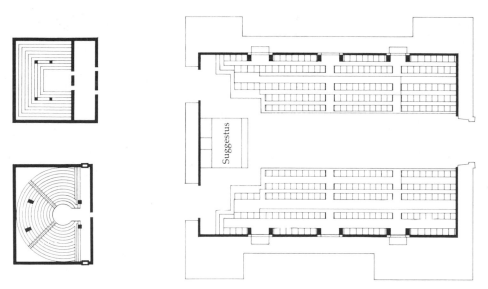

Figure II.3.   *Ground plans for an early bouleuterion in Athens (top left), its successor (bottom left), and the Curia Julia in Rome (right)*

tance of this podium is revealed by the passage in A.D. 40 of a decree that required that the emperor should be given a sufficiently lofty elevation in the curia so that no senator could physically touch him. Unlike the squarish ground plans of the bouleuterion, the curia's was rectangular, with a broad aisle more than 17 feet wide leading down the major axis to the *suggestus*. This permitted the visual accentuation of the emperor from the side benches as well as from the large front portal, whose doors had to be kept open during sessions, as previously noted.[63]

Even in ancient times, technology had its impact on architecture. The Romans opened the way to the first sizeable interiors of antiquity by inventing concrete. This material permitted the construction of overhead enclosures that were not possible with stone or timbers. It is often argued that their greatest achievement in this regard is the Pantheon, which architectural historians look upon as a veritable revolution in the treatment of enclosure (see photo II.1). The Pantheon in Rome encloses a round, domed space 164 feet in diameter and 150 feet high. An oculus, or circular opening, to the sky at the top of the dome permits natural daylight to fill the massive and magnificently formed void. For architectural historian William MacDonald, the Pantheon captures perfectly the unity and the stability of the Roman politico-religious order.[64]

Adolf Reinle, a German student of architectural symbolism, has examined the expressive qualities of public buildings from the early Middle Ages forward. Two of his conclusions are of particular interest. First he states that buildings, together with their equipment, are generally "an expression of their age—self presentations of specific cultures." Taking what might be considered an extreme position on this point, he adds: "They do not simply express the mood of an epoch, but rather give a seismographically exact portrait of their epoch." Reinle also insists that architectural symbols can possess remarkable similarities across cultures and epochs, at least within the Occident. Among the transcendent symbols he mentions are the dome, the portal, the tower, the staircase, and the baldachin.[65]

Of particular interest to us here are the

Photo II.1. The Interior of the Pantheon, *by Giovanni Paolo Pannini (1691–1765; courtesy of the National Gallery of Art, Washington, D.C., Samuel H. Kress Collection)*

staircase and the baldachin. The staircase, although physically necessary for human beings to elevate themselves to higher planes, is in addition a symbol of honor for the place or the person reached by the steps. Those who ascend the stairs thereby rise to a higher place of dignity. The baldachin, for its part, is an interior roof, or canopy, that bestows honor on the person beneath. The idea can be traced to portable umbrellas or tents used to protect ancient kings or other privileged persons from the elements when out of doors. Later, possibly in Egypt, this canopy became a symbol of royal authority. The Greeks erected a canopy above an idol when it was brought outside for public appearances—the so-called Tent of Appearances. Similarly, Roman generals were accustomed to being seated beneath a ciborium while in the field. Later the concept was transferred to the medieval Christian church, where it became customary to construct a permanent internal roof of great decorative elaborateness over the bishop's throne, pulpit, or altar.[66]

Indeed, after the decline of Rome, the church became the most important source and transmitter of architectural ideas for civic space. As Anthony Vidler has pointed out, church buildings during the Middle Ages were not only inspiring to the faithful but were also explicitly instructional; they constituted, in effect, "stone books" that taught theological and moral lessons in a commonly understood symbolic language. This transparent iconographic function lasted until the invention of printing in the fifteenth century, Vidler argues, when architecture stopped "speaking" literally.[67]

Architectural symbolism could also be quite esoteric. During the Middle Ages and the Renaissance, mathematical relationships of symbolic significance were often deliberately incorporated into buildings. The numbers three, four, five, seven, and ten in particular were regarded as sacred. If one analyzes the plans of Romanesque churches, one finds that their dimensions are frequently multiples of these numbers, if the nonstandard lengths of the Roman foot are accounted for.[68]

Also the proportions of the human body were believed to provide sacred relationships that could then be transferred to architecture. Leonardo da Vinci decided that the relationship of the height of a standing man's navel to his overall height is in accordance with the so-called golden section. This mathematical relationship stems from what is known as the Fibonacci sequence, a series of integers in which each number is equal to the sum of the preceding two (i.e., 1, 1, 2, 3, 5, 8, 13, 21, 34, 55, 89, 144, etc.). The farther this series is extended, the closer it attains the relationship of the golden section, which is approximately 1:1.618. Hence when the golden section's proportions are applied to the dimensions of a rectangular room, the length of the room is about 62 percent greater than its width. Stating this principle verbally, a room is proportioned according to the golden section when its width is to its length as its length is to the sum of its width and length (for example 89 x 144 feet).[69]

The ground plans of churches in particular were symbolic during the Middle Ages. They tended to be cruciform in shape, with the long nave placed on the axis of the symbolic stake of Christ's cross and the shorter transept placed on the axis of the crossbeam. Traditionally the Gothic cathedral faces east, with the short end of the stake pointing toward Calvary. While cathedrals built before 1500 tended to be longer than they were wide, after that time a more compact central ground plan became popular.[70]

Within the Gothic cathedral the public generally circulates in the nave, the transept, or the ambulatory, sometimes referred to as the Church Militant part of the cathedral (fig. II.4). The chancel, a protected and

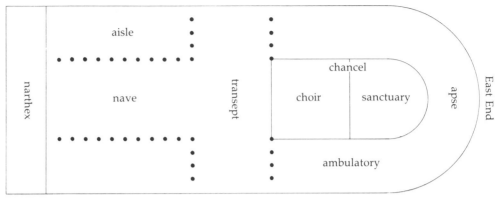

Figure II.4. *Cathedral nomenclature*

raised area in the East End, is thought of as the Church Triumphant. An especially sacred area, the chancel is sometimes entered only by clergy, by means of special portals and steps. A balustrade, or altar rail, often divides the two "churches," with a rood screen overhead sometimes adding to the demarcation. To enter the chancel is, symbolically, to enter the heavenly life, transported by the nave (*navis*, meaning ship, is also the root word for navy). This passageway is dramatized further by using aisle colonnades, to narrow the nave, and high vaulted ceilings, to give it verticality.[71]

High-church liturgical tradition requires a deep chancel—or one that is relatively long and is divided into the choir, or foremost portion, and the sanctuary, a rear section (fig. II.4). While lesser offices are celebrated in the choir, in the strictest tradition the Eucharist can be administered only in the sanctuary. The symbolic centerpiece of the church, the altar, is preferably constructed of solid stone and is often situated far back in the chancel, so as to augment its holiness. Behind the altar a reredos, or decorated screen, is sometimes found. The purpose of the reredos is dual: to set the altar off properly from the front and to protect it from profane eyes at the back. Sedilia, or especially designated chairs for priest and deacons, line the south wall of the chancel. According to orthodox tradition the orna-mentation of the walls and the ceiling grows richer as the sacred East End of the space is approached. At the extreme end of the cathedral a half-rounded apse is frequently found, lit by what are often the building's most splendid stained-glass windows.[72]

IDEAS FROM ENVIRONMENTAL STUDIES

Literature in the environmental tradition is concerned with the human behavioral response to the physical setting. Some of this material is concerned with acquiring knowledge about the response itself and belongs to the subfield of environmental psychology. Other components of it seek to use such knowledge as an aid in environmental design.

Environmental Psychology

A pioneer in what we today call environmental psychology is Roger G. Barker, although he termed it ecological psychology. At the heart of Barker's approach is the concept of the "behavioral setting," which includes not merely the physical setting itself but group behavior associated with that setting. To him, this duality of setting and behavior forms a "nesting structure" that induces recurring patterns of human behavior. These are "standing" patterns, in that they are repeated over time, despite the presence of different individuals as time passes. Hence the physical setting, together with the regularized behavior associated with it, forms a stabilizing influence in social life.[73]

Many environmental psychologists have been inspired to conduct empirical research on the behavioral effects of physical settings. Guy C. Ankerl believes that because of the concrete, objective character of such settings, a scientifically respectable sociology of architecture can be developed in which independent variables are appropriately manipulated.[74] Although Ankerl's expectations may be overly optimistic, a few results have emerged from such work. An experimental study involving the size and reverberation characteristics of rooms showed that speakers tend to speak more slowly in larger and more reverberant rooms. In regard to color, when the same lecture is given in two theaters, one decorated in red and the other in blue, the audience in the red room feels that time has passed faster than in the blue hall. Generally, red seems to have an exciting influence on people by raising muscle tension, among other physiological effects; but to accomplish this effect the red color must be bright and well illuminated.[75]

Other environmental studies concern the arrangement of furniture. Students' reactions to slide photographs of faculty offices suggest that visitors to such places feel more comfortable and welcome if the teacher's desk faces the wall, rather than facing the visitors themselves. The presence of art work and potted plants also seems to disarm the respondents. Duncan Joiner's observations of furniture arrangements in business and governmental offices revealed what he calls private zones and public zones, with the former areas being near the executive's desk and the latter apart from it. The highest zone definition seems to be when the front of the desk faces the room, with the skirt of the desk forming the zonal frontier. Clovis Heimsath has noted a redundant cir-

culation system in airports and restaurants, which he calls double tracking. Back corridors that are hidden from the public permit employees to move into and out of Goffman's back region without being seen.[76]

Proxemics, the study of interpersonal space, forms an important part of the behavioral literature. Its pioneer is Edward T. Hall, whose books *The Silent Language* and *The Hidden Dimension* have become classics. Hall is perhaps best known for his ideas about interpersonal distances. Although he readily admits that appropriate physical spaces between people vary by culture, for the United States he offers four classifications of distance: (1) intimate space, which is up to 18 inches from the body; (2) casual-personal distance, a separation of 18 to 48 inches between persons; (3) social-consultative distance, a leeway of 4 to 12 feet; and (4) public distance, which is separation from 12 feet to the maximum carrying distance of the human voice.[77]

In the casual-personal range, Hall points out, distances are short enough that slight differences in elevation can create status differentials. Within 4 feet, a person who is lower than another tends to look upward to the latter person by moving the head; farther away, the sightline differential diminishes to the point that it can be accommodated by eye movement rather than head movement. Four feet is also a crucial distance, according to Hall, because beyond it, physical domination by another is for all practical purposes impossible without a weapon (one is reminded of the sword lines in the House of Commons). If the public is placed well into public distance—that is, substantially beyond 12 feet—a formal, or even "frozen," speaking style is adopted, the manner of address assumed in speaking to strangers.

Hall also developed another typology that is useful for our purposes: space that is occupied by fixed features, such as perma-

nent walls, and space that is occupied by
semifixed features, such as furniture, railings, and moveable partitions. This distinction has implications for the adaptability
and malleability of the space. The space
consultant Fred Steele proposes a third category, which he calls pseudo-fixed features.
These are items such as small tables and
lamps, which could conceivably be moved
but are perceived and treated as fixed. As
for differing patterns of arranging semifixed-feature or pseudo-fixed features,
Humphrey Osmond has drawn a distinction
between sociopetal and sociofugal furniture.
The first encourages interaction between
people and is illustrated by circular groups
of inward-facing chairs; the second tends to
keep occupants apart, as in back-to-back
benches.[78]

Robert Sommer and others have conducted research on patterns of seating at
tables in public places, as in library reading
rooms and university seminar rooms, and
have found that those who expect to cooperate with each other tend to sit side by side,
while those who anticipate a competitive relationship sit across the table. In classroom
seminars, persons who take the head of the
table are perceived as leaders, while persons
on the leader's right hand are regarded as
being socially close to the leader.[79]

Environmental Design

Environmental-design research is, in a way,
more ambitious than are the experimental
studies of environmental psychology. The
aim is not merely to understand behavioral
responses to the physical setting but also to
alter that setting so that it will accommodate
and satisfy the needs of the occupants. Environmental designers, seeing themselves as
synthesizing the skills of architects, interior
designers, landscape architects, and planners, seek systematically and precisely to
bring the environment into equilibrium with

what they term human systems. This is attempted in architecture and urban planning,
just as the human-factors engineer tries to
design a cockpit or a control panel to fit the
human body. Raymond G. Studer and
David Stea describe the movement's early
aims thus: "The decision-making structure
in an environmental design problem involves the description of a system of human
requirements in a particular problem domain on all possible objective levels and
then the evolution, or invention, of an environment which precisely responds to
these."[80]

One product of the environmental-
design movement has been a series of recommended innovations in urban and school
architecture. At one stage it was urged that
public housing units be built with fewer stories and with entryways that provide defensible space. Mental hospitals were to have
more privacy and more recreational space. It
was recommended that city parks be made
smaller than in the past and that they be
filled more densely with benches and play
equipment. Schools were to have open
classrooms; office buildings were to have
more windows, and office landscaping was
to permit worker privacy and individualiza-
tion.[81]

A key tool of environmental-design research is a series of questionnaire and interview studies called POEs (postoccupancy
evaluations). These are seen as an objective
way to test whether the designed environment and its human occupants are, in fact,
in harmony. Unfortunately, the outcome of
the surveys is seldom clear-cut. The open
classroom was found to be flexible and conducive to interaction; but it was also noisy,
distracting, and hard on teachers. An open-
design, many-windowed federal building in
Ann Arbor, Michigan, was liked by citizens
but disliked by the people who worked
there, because of noise, glare, and lack of
privacy. One summary of research on

school design and on learning outcomes concluded that "the direct cause and effect relationship between most environmental factors and learning simply is not there except in extreme situations." Human behavior, the authors added, "is far more complex than implied by the conceptual framework underlying most of the research."[82]

With ambiguous results stemming from much environmental-design research and experimentation and with the expiration of such fads as the open classroom and the open office, the study of man-environment interrelationship has in recent years become more cautious and circumspect. It is now recognized that we cannot forthrightly redesign the physical setting to fit diagnosable human needs. Rather, we must accept the infinite complexity, subjectivity, and interactive character of the relationship between the setting and the occupant. The "architectural determinism" of the environmental-design movement, many in the field contend, led to simplistic, stimulus/response theorizing and to research designs that misapplied the methods of natural science and misread the nature of human behavior.[83]

Meanwhile, alternative approaches to environmental research have emerged which move beyond the confident assertions of the early environmental-design movement. Robert Gutman points out that while the architect's purpose in affecting a building's users can be deliberate and that although enclosed space certainly shapes its occupants, the space's capacity "to achieve the purpose intended depends on the presence of the right combination of other factors not architectural in character, but rather social, cultural, and psychological."[84] Along another tack, Jon Lang argues that a more reasonable position than architectural determinism is architectural "affordance." By this he means the ways and degrees to which the environment allows human occupants to act or affords them opportunities to do so.

Whether individuals then take advantage of such opportunities depends on their competence.[85] In a phenomenological vein, Lars Lerup suggests that nonenvironmental factors intervene in the relations between people and architecture by means of a two-step transaction. First, users do not accept buildings as initially conceived; instead, they "deposit" their own meanings on them. Second, these deposited meanings then influence the occupants' thoughts and actions. In this way, buildings are always "unfinished" and are continually being "built" with additional socially constructed meaning. The relationship between people and architecture is thus "volatile, dynamic, hard to capture and impossible to domesticate (if domestic means fully predictable)." Further, Lerup says, the deposited meaning "is not immediately visible in behavior, but is also contained in the way dwellers speak and think of their setting."[86]

David Canter argues that a place, such as a familiar room, is defined not only by physical attributes but also by the activities that occur there and the conceptions of it that are held by individuals who frequent it. Occupants of places create images, or schemata, of them, which they later remember as a reality. Different individuals who occupy the same place construct different schemata, depending on their social roles and, perhaps, their social class. Again, this relativism does not mean that the environment has no impact, says Canter. Rather, the impact is varied, interactive, and subtle. Sometimes the impact is essentially negative—for example, by excluding the influence of distracting stimuli such as noise and unpleasant weather conditions. These impacts can be easily ignored because of their very pervasiveness.[87]

In other comments applicable to interior space, Canter remarks that environmental influence in a place of prescribed activity can be self-reinforcing. Visitors observe certain conduct there, come to expect it, themselves conform to the pattern, and therefore help to perpetuate the pattern as a norm for others. Thus, for example, people tend to talk in hushed tones in a church, regardless of whether a worship service is being conducted. Canter further points out that when a room has a specified function, it may be possible for substantial agreement to emerge with respect to standards for its assessment, despite differing image schemata. This point is illustrated by comparing a space that houses generalized activity and thus can be manipulated according to personal taste, such as a living room, with one that is highly functional in character, such as a kitchen. We can, he says, agree more easily on what constitutes a good kitchen than we can on a good living room. Regardless of its assessability, space is instinctively understood as a "precious commodity," which means that its allocation will influence what happens there.[88]

Amos Rapoport, in many ways the dean of environmental studies, has contributed extensively to the mutual-interaction perspective on people and settings. He rejects, on the one hand, the early environmental designers' faith in deterministic effects and, on the other, the social scientists' downplaying of the physical setting as having only weak and secondary effects, which he terms possibilism. A sensible intermediate position is what Rapoport calls probabilism: it visualizes the environment as neither controlling nor receding into the background but as creating likely tendencies for thought and action.[89]

Although incapable of generating activities on its own, the environment may facilitate behavior by acting as a catalyst or by releasing latent tendencies, states Rapoport. Or conversely, it may inhibit behavior by transmitting cues or by constraining the range of possible interpretations. In the final analysis, the environment is a form of non-verbal communication, whose messages may or may not be heard and whose content is filtered by the motivations, judgments, and cultures of people. Yet messages are encoded by builders and then decoded by occupants, with powerful effects. "In its most general terms the environment can then be seen as a teaching medium. Once learned, it becomes a mnemonic device reminding one of appropriate behavior."[90]

Rapoport's views on research methodology stem from his theoretical position. He rejects out of hand the linguistic structuralism of semiotics. To him, nonverbal communication must be interpreted, not by the internal structure of the signs themselves, but by the meanings that they carry and by the behaviors that they are associated with (in linguistic terms, not syntactics, but semantics and pragmatics, respectively). As an alternative, Rapoport suggests, we should interpret the expressed meanings of the symbols of the environment. This has its own problems, he admits, including the differential meanings of symbols for various people and the fact that single symbols carry multiple meanings. Also, the extent to which symbols carry shared meanings in modern society is limited, as compared to the situation in ancient or primitive societies, or even the Middle Ages, as we have noted. Rapoport nonetheless regards some symbols as being probably pan-cultural, such as the superiority attached to height, centrality, and the right hand. Rather than deducing symbolic meaning from abstractions alone, Rapoport urges us to adopt a cognitive-anthropology orientation, by which we study on their own terms the meanings derived by present-day occupants of actual environments. This should be done first-hand, open-endedly, and extensively. Hence environments need to be observed and photographed directly, and their occupants need to be studied and consulted closely. Analysis should then proceed to make inferences based on thorough description and on comparisons of structurally and functionally equivalent units. This is precisely what we have attempted to do in studying civic space.[91]

RECAPITULATION AND SYNTHESIS

Let me now pull together the numerous ideas presented in this chapter into a form usable for our study.

Interpreting Social Meaning

As I pointed out in chapter I, by "social meaning" I refer to both the expressive and the influencing capabilities of architecture. The literatures that I reviewed clearly envision each. With respect to the expressive potentiality of the physical setting, Rapoport conceives of the environment as a form of nonverbal communication, a teaching medium, even a mnemonic device. Duncan, speaking from the dramatist's paradigm of sociology, regards the ceremonial setting as a scene for social staging, from which clues can be picked up as to hierarchical patterns in the community. Students of the ancient world, such as Ackerman and Lethaby, point out that at one time, public buildings reflected the builders' understanding of the cosmos, without affectation or apology. At the strictly political level, Holston argues that urban architecture constitutes a vivid inscription of the political order, while Milne sees public buildings as enshrining the legitimated code of law and order. At a more mundane level, Ameller (whom I mentioned in chapter I) avers that the physical layout of parliaments may reflect a political state of mind or outlook.

Raising the issue of what is expressed takes us to the Jungian notion of persona; if architecture is but an external mask to an inner reality, we must look to civic space for "official" statements, rather than for candid or personal confessions. If, on the other hand, Wilentz is right that the "clothing" of power may truly represent deeper realities, the settings of public rites become a key to the "master fictions" that uphold political orders.

As for the capacity of architecture to affect human behavior, Mead's symbolic interactionism anticipates that human beings will respond not only to inner drives but also to role, place, and territorial setting. Barker's ecological psychology expects that the physical setting and the group behavior within it will combine to create recurring, or "standing," patterns of action. Yet, as I noted, these patterns do not seem regular enough to be predictable in social-science experimentation, and the social-engineering dreams of the environmental-design movement have faded. Current opinion on the subject rejects a deterministic, directly causal model of environmental influence and pictures instead an indirect, residual, and interactive relationship between the physical setting, its occupants, and its culture. Still, even a theory of environmental influence as modest as Rapoport's probabilism model incorporates important facilitating and inhibiting effects. We cannot predict the influence of civic space on its occupants, but we can anticipate that effects will occur. When they do, they should be noted.

I now apply the ideas that I have reviewed to the question of how to conduct a study of civic space. As noted, my methodology coincides substantially with the recommendations of Rapoport. I employ firsthand, open-ended, extensive study of numerous examples of actual physical environments, comparing structurally and functionally equivalent units. As Rasmussen advises the student of architecture, I enter interior spaces, feel them close about, and attempt to become attuned to their meaning as a whole. In the striking metaphor suggested by Eisenman, I employ the comparative method across epochs to examine the "state of shear" between past and present civic spaces.

Rapoport and other authors are of course right in cautioning us to be circumspect in interpreting the meaning of the built environment. As Agrest and Gandelsonas have warned, architecture does not communicate efficiently and clearly, as the written word does. Medieval churches were "stone books," as Vidler points out, but today's city halls are not, at least for the most part.

In addition to the problem of obscure meaning is the problem of subjective meaning. As Lerup reminds us, we impose our individual meanings on the built environment. Furthermore, as Canter suggests, we even create our own personal schemata of settings and thereby impart to them reality. Sociologists and anthropologists remind us that the symbolism of physical spaces and objects is inherently difficult to interpret because of its vague, shadowy, and tentative nature.

The literatures that I have reviewed offer, nonetheless, substantial solace for the interpreter. Several commentators emphasize that both relativism and universalism prevail in architectural expression. This suggests the possibility of discovering conceptual anchors of stable meaning amidst the fluid sea of variable meaning. Sperber proposes that in symbolic expression, separate cultural systems interpret differently but from the same basic codes of meaning. Semioticians insist that signs possess meaning only by convention; they also refer to a deep structure of universal syntactical relationships. In the field of art history, Panofsky discerns not only infinite variety and cultural boundedness in works of art but also a Third Stratum of intrinsic meaning. Rapoport recognizes in study of the built environment the differentiated, nondiscursive nature of symbolic meaning, but he

also sees some symbols as pan-cultural. Jung builds his psychology on the notion that transcendent archetypes emanate from the collective subconscious, while Gestalt theorists contend that the human mind is dependent on imprinted structural forms, including the universal form of the human body.

The idea of some transcendent meaning in spatial relationships thus has wide acceptance. Various schools of thought and even contrasting paradigmatic positions share agreement on both the existence of certain cultural universals and their content. This opens up the possibility that as analysts we can fix our attention on certain conceptual lodestars that will place our interpretations on more solid ground than is possessed by personalistic or frivolous conjecture. Indeed, we find—repeatedly—from such disparate disciplines as anthropology, art history, psychology, sociology, and political science, specific ideas that can be applied as interpretive tools in different times and places. Let us compile an inventory of these ideas.

One set of lodestars consists of conceptual dichotomies. Examples are sacred versus profane (Durkheim, Eliade); closed versus open (Arnheim, Lasswell); solid versus void (Holston, Norberg-Schulz); and front versus back (Goffman, Heimsath; and body image theory). Others are the relationship of up and down, with height identified as the superior level; and the relationship of left and right, with the right hand identified as the preferred (Bevan, Hertz, Laponce, Schwartz, body-image theory). Another type of lodestar is common interpretations given to the meaning of certain geometric forms. This would include the square's association with mankind's earthbound existence; the aspiring character of the upright triangle; and the unifying implications of the circle (Raglan, Jung, Arnheim). Other powerful patterns of imagery are the mandala (Jung), the *axis mundi* (Eliade), and the cross (Wheatley, Marc). All three of these images impart a sense of cosmic wholeness, with the mandala embracing man and the universe, the *axis mundi* connecting heaven and earth, and the cross combining human upreach and outreach.

Then, too, interpretive guidance is received from the transcendent significance attached to specific architectural elements. These include the ceiling and the dome, with their celestial and protective implications (Raglan, Arnheim); the floor and the concave pit, with their terrestrial and niche implications (again, Raglan and Arnheim); the superiority identified with height in buildings and verticality in general (Bevan, Lasswell, de Superville); the ascendant, honor-bestowing nature of the staircase (Marc, Arnheim, Reinle); the threshold-crossing and value-imparting significance of the doorway (Wheatley, Eliade, Hammer); the impact of the window on the "closedness" of a room (Arnheim, Norberg-Schulz, Lasswell); and the baldachin's statement of reverence for persons positioned beneath it (Raglan, Reinle).

Categories for Analysis

Three categories of variables that are germane to civic space are investigated in this book. These are the composition of space, the design of semifixed features, and patterns of decoration and object display. This trio of subtopics forms the basis for organizing each of the three substantive chapters that follow. Let me complete my recapitulation and synthesis of the material reviewed to this point by noting ideas that are pertinent to each of these categories.

With respect to spatial composition, the prime idea is the notion of space itself. Preziosi's space cell is a formation of either mass or volume, and it is with the latter phenomenon that we are concerned here.

Civic space is what Norberg-Schulz would call an enclosure, as opposed to a mass center; he regards the enclosure as an inherently fitting locale for social ritual. While the idea of interior space did not become architecturally important until the Middle Ages, the Pantheon at Rome beautifully heralded what was to come.

Defining an enclosed space raises interesting issues, as we have seen. Thiel defines it in terms of clarity or explicitness, spatial volume, and the size of space-establishing semifixed features. Peterson contends that the relatively continuous, open, and flowing space preferred in Modern architecture violates the very idea of defined space and hence constitutes antispace. The degree to which enclosed space is punctured or perforated by "holes" versus "dematerialized walls" also affects its internal integrity, as Norberg-Schulz has pointed out. With respect to the symbolic significance of perforation, Arnheim and Lasswell contend that windowless spaces suggest a closed mind or a despotic political system.

As for ground plans, compact and squarish buildings characterized the Greek bouleuterion and the central-plan churches of the Renaissance. Oblong shapes were found in the Roman curia and in the Gothic cathedral. Rectangular plans create a directionality of attention along the major axis, which is not found in square buildings. Also they lend themselves to an oppositional use of space, as described by Doxtater. Perhaps rectangularity augments communication as well, a possibility suggested by Koehler's study of California council chambers. As for the proportions of rectangular space, the golden section, derived from the Fibonacci sequence, can be used as a standard of reference.

Curvilinear ground plans should also be mentioned. Round rooms were used in the earliest ancient temples, according to Raglan, for they symbolized the universe. This was especially true when the floor was also concave and the ceiling was a dome. This speculation receives support from Braidwood's discovery of round or ovoid ceremonial space in the remains of ancient buildings in Turkey. Also it coincides with Arnheim's notion of a comforting spherical hollow for the human occupant of space. Perhaps, too, the enclosing capability of curvilinearity provides prescriptive guidance to those who, like Moynihan, want public buildings to engender more intimacy and trust.

Lynch's "imaging" elements of paths and districts direct our attention to critical items for analysis in the composition of space. Although intended originally for application to urban design, his categories have been applied to child psychology and appear to have a wide relevance as conceptual tools. In the context of interior space, paths correspond to entry and circulation routes, while districts constitute floor regions, or zones. To illustrate the applicability of these ideas, we recall that path location was significantly different in the bouleuterion and in the curia. While the Gothic cathedral and the Bali temple are divided into numerous specialized and ordered sacred districts, Joiner found the business office to be divided into public and private zones, with an edge being formed by the skirt of the executive's desk.

I turn next to a second topical category: the design of semifixed features. This term of Hall's is used to refer to items such as platforms, railings, and furniture that are fastened to the floor. We include also Steele's pseudo-fixed features, that is, furniture that is moveable but is accepted as being permanently fixed. Applicable to the layout of semifixed features is Holston's discussion of solids versus voids. The issue that is raised is whether semifixed features are densely crowded into the floor space or are scattered out, with ample room between

them. In the first case—continuous solids with figurative voids—interstitial spaces such as aisles emerge as being visually dominant. In the second situation—figurative solids with continuous voids—attention can be deliberately directed to persons who are associated with isolated items of furniture. These considerations give concreteness to Canter's proposition that space is, in effect, a precious commodity whose manipulation possesses important implications for power. As Küller argues, extreme semifixed-feature crowdedness or emptiness in a space can create an especially intense sensation of enclosedness.

The physical distance between features can have other behavioral implications as well. When features place people close to each other, such as on benches or around tables, communication occurs within Hall's casual-personal distance or even within intimate space. Differences in elevation at that distance create sight-line angles that produce status differentials. Separation beyond 12 feet leads to an unauthentic, "frozen" style of speaking.

Lynch's imaging elements of node, landmark, and edge can be used to analyze semifixed features. A relatively isolated, unusual, and prominent feature can become either a node or a landmark, the distinction being that the first is occupied by people (e.g., a pulpit) and the second is unoccupied (e.g., a statue). As for the edge, this element corresponds to fences, barriers, low walls, platform edges, and, as mentioned, the front skirts of desks. Such edges can, obviously, demarcate floor zones. Koehler found in his empirical study that communication between the public and officials increased when edges such as railings and platform risers were downplayed.

The question of status is clearly germane to this book, and feature design can be used to express status or the lack thereof. This is done by the architectural devices of elevation (Caesar's raised platform), centrality (the Roman *suggestus*), distance (the curia, in comparison to the bouleuterion), the special backdrop (the Gothic chancel's reredos), ceremonial chairs (sedilia), and the throne-baldachin combination (as Raglan depicts in ancient palaces). Also, proxemics research suggests that right-handed placement can enhance status, just as the seminar students at the teacher's right seem to possess a special standing. As the study of iconography has warned us, however, we must be careful to determine whose right hand is operative.

Finally, ideas regarding collective seating arrangements are pertinent. The distaste shown in the Republican assemblies of Rome for providing any seating at all points up one extreme option. At the other extreme lies the amphitheater form of seating, which fascinated Goethe in terms of the possibility of a unified and animated public body. In Osmond's terminology, the first arrangement is sociofugal in nature; the second is sociopetal. Three intermediate patterns of seating are identified in the literature: parallel, oppositional, and circular. Parallel, or classroom, seating gives a commonality of purpose, according to Arnheim; yet the Stones find it inhibiting to communication; also, those "in front" are sharply differentiated from those in the rows. Oppositional seating is exemplified by arrangements in the Roman curia and in the House of Commons; it allegedly encourages conflict. Indeed, proxemics research finds that competitors tend to sit across the table from each other and that students dislike being across from the desk in a teacher's office. Semicircular seating is illustrated by the late bouleuterion and by most of the parliaments that Herman studied. The Stones contend that circular chair arrangements at meetings promote a sense of equality; also proxemics research concludes that individuals who expect to cooperate tend to sit side by side.

The third and last organizing category for analysis of civic space is patterns of decoration and object display. Room decoration and unfixed objects, perhaps more than spatial composition and semifixed features, establish the "place," or "domain," of which Moore and Allen speak. By the same token, surface decorations and portable objects form much of the phenomenological detail that Norberg-Schulz sees as creating the *genius loci*.

With respect to decoration, Edelman warns us that political stage settings tend to be massive, ornate, and formal because of the need to impress audiences, legitimize acts, and reinforce authority. Even more forbiddingly, Piñón raises the specter of attempts to infer a divine order within interior spaces where power is wielded. Possible methods for projecting an aura of power are the rhythmic repetition of classical ornament (suggested by Smeets) and symmetrical form (mentioned by Arnheim). Devices that architects use to introduce scale to a space could also affect its aura, such as decorative columns or pilasters, ceiling coffers, contrasts in ceiling height, and exposure of trusses or beams. Venturi's distinction between the "Heroic and Original" duck and the decorated shed is also germane in that it alerts us to the issue of whether decoration is conceived of as an integrated system or is ad hoc in nature. Jung's concept of persona invites us to look for ways in which decoration masks reality and presents contrived images. The rich decoration of a cathedral's East End suggests the possibility of more elaborate ornamentation in the immediate vicinity of the most powerful.

Other issues that are raised in the realm of decoration include the differing connotations of various building materials and surfaces. Do we encounter the permanence of stone, the coldness of steel, or the artificiality of plastic? Is the wood dark and formal or light and informal? Are the colors warm or cool? The decoration of doorways is also of special concern in view of Raglan's comment that entry thresholds are traditionally protected by sacred symbols. The *axis mundi* concept of Eliade and others invites us to look for evidence of a primal vertical thrust within spaces, conveyed by depressions in floors (as in the kiva) or oculi in ceilings (as in the Pantheon).

In regard to portable artifacts, we will inspect civic space for the presence of what Goffman would call stage props and Trexler would term the sacramentals of political power. Gusfield's distinction between cohesive and differentiating symbolic gestures can be used to categorize such displays. Examples of cohesive gestures are banners or emblems that represent the whole nation or community. Differentiating gestures are items that impart authority or privilege on certain individuals and withhold it from others. As Fleming prescribes for the study of cultural artifacts in general, I wish to analyze these objects in terms both of their own originating culture and of their meaning in the light of today's values.

III The Traditional Chamber: Imposed Authority

Let us turn now to the North American council chamber itself, the concrete example of civic space that I selected for detailed investigation and for the analysis of social meaning. In this chapter and in the two ensuing ones, I describe the three models of chamber that form the basis of our analysis. The three types emerged from the field data by themselves, so to speak. The study was not originally designed with these types in mind; in fact, it began with no concrete hypotheses, only my intuitive feeling that "something interesting" was bound up in these rooms.

As the study proceeded, various patterns and variations became more and more evident. In trying to make sense of these, I tentatively explored several independent variables: the type of urban place (large city, small town, suburban community, etc.); the geographical region of the country (Northeast, West Coast, Sun Belt, etc.); and the structure of the city government (strong-mayor form, weak-mayor form, council-manager form, and so on). None of these variables seemed to explain anything, however; that is, such classifications did not coincide with the patterns nor did they differ consistently from one another. The one variable that seemed to make sense was the era of construction. I noticed that the oldest rooms tended to fall into one category, rooms of intermediate age into another, and the newest spaces into a third. Out of respect to this overall pattern, and in effect testing it systematically, the seventy-five chambers that I subsequently examined in detail were grouped according to what seemed to be the cutting boundary years. These groups were then analyzed as separate categories of civic space.

Chambers built between 1865 and 1920 are called Traditional. Their design exudes a sense of the imposing nature of governmental power and the superiority of the governors over the governed and hence is said to express a concept of authority that is imposed. This chapter is devoted to this model. Rooms that were constructed between 1920 and 1960 suggest less sanctity on the part of authority and greater equality between the governors and the governed; they are termed Midcentury and are seen as expressing a confronted notion of authority. Chapter IV is concerned with these rooms. Finally, chambers that were built after 1960, which I call Contemporary, possess an all-enclosing, intimately embracing, subtly theatrical air; they are said to state a joined concept of authority.

Let us now examine the Traditional chamber and its imposed authority.

THE SOCIAL AND ARCHITECTURAL SETTING

The selection of 1865 as the beginning point for the study is suggested by the work of William Lebovich, an authority on the history of American city halls. He points out that although prior to the Civil War cities grew very fast, city government remained relatively weak, powerless, and cast in the colonial tradition. Numerous town halls were constructed during the eighteenth and the early nineteenth centuries, but this building activity was minor compared to what transpired during the Gilded Age after the war. In the last few decades of the nineteenth century, city government became a force to be reckoned with in U.S. politics. At this time, urban machines, with their pow-

Photo III.1. *Chamber of the Board of Estimate, New York City*

erful bosses, began to form. These urban bosses, with their personal egos, organizational pride, control of funds, and need for patronage jobs, possessed both the motivation and the means to produce the first flowering of American municipal architecture.[1]

The growing cities of an urbanizing America continued to build new municipal structures up to World War I. This was true in cities that were corrupted by machine government as well as in those that were affected by subsequent reformist zeal. Both bosses and reformers looked upon great palaces of city government as enduring monuments to their vanity or their idealism, whichever the case might be.

These buildings tended to be massive and overbuilt by today's standards, designed to last forever. Stylistically their inspiration was almost always from Europe, with Second Empire extravagance and classical or Renaissance revivalism being especially stylish. The "American" style of the

era, Richardsonian Romanesque, grew in popularity as well, and the Columbian Exposition of 1893 helped to make Beaux-Arts buildings fashionable.

Turning to the interiors of these pre-1920 city halls, an important point for the coverage of our study is that specialized space that was devoted to use by a city council did not generally exist prior to the Civil War, as I have indicated. In addition to a few simple offices, the interiors of town halls that were erected prior to 1865 consisted mainly of open, multifunctional space, with very few semifixed features. In the most important cities, such as Boston or New Orleans, the building might contain a public assembly room or a lyceum, but in smaller communities, not even this degree of specialized use obtained. Instead, simple, open, all-purpose space was the rule. This tendency is visible today in the Old Town Hall of Wilmington, Delaware, built in 1798–99 and now restored to its original condition. The second floor, on which the council convened, was

TABLE III.1
The Twenty-five Traditional Chambers Included in this Study (with date built)

Albany (N.Y.) City Hall: 1878–83[a]

Baltimore (Md.) City Hall: 1867–75

Bay City (Mich.) City Hall: 1894–97

Brockton (Mass.) City Hall: 1892–94

Cambridge (Mass.) City Hall: 1898

Charleston (S.C.) City Hall: 1882[b]

Cincinnati (Ohio) City Hall: 1888–93

Cleveland (Ohio) City Hall: 1911–16

La Salle (Ill.) City Hall: 1907

Louisville (Ky.) City Hall: 1870–73

Lowell (Mass.) City Hall: 1890–93

Milwaukee (Wis.) City Hall: 1893–95

New York City Hall: 1897[c]

Newark (N.J.) City Hall: 1902–6

Oakland (Calif.) City Hall: 1911–14

Peoria (Ill.) City Hall: 1897–99

Philadelphia (Pa.) City Hall: 1871–1901

Pittsburgh (Pa.) City County Building: 1915–17

Providence (R.I.) City Hall: 1875–78

Saint Louis (Mo.) City Hall: 1890–1904

San Francisco (Calif.) City Hall: 1913–15

Savannah (Ga.) City Hall: 1904–5

Springfield (Mass.) City Hall: 1910–13

Trenton (N.J.) Municipal Building: 1908–10

Worcester (Mass.) City Hall: 1898

[a]Remodeled 1919   [b]Building, 1801   [c]Building, 1803–11

used variously as a meeting room, a cultural center, a library, and a place for notables to lie in state.[2]

A few exceptions to this pattern of multipurpose municipal space exist, however. One is the Board of Estimate's Chamber in New York City. New York's City Hall, which was built between 1803 and 1811, is apparently the oldest city hall in the United States that has been continuously in use since its construction. The meeting room of the Board of Estimate—a kind of board of directors for the city, which is composed of eight ex-officio members—was restored to its original state in 1913. As such, it is the oldest representation of a specialized municipal chamber that we seem to have in this country. The room features churchlike pews; a vaulted ceiling; end-of-the-room semidomes supported by Ionic columns; a baldachin; a curved dais; and a protective railing that is 53 inches in height at its highest points (see photo III.1). Because of its pre-1865 origins, New York City's boardroom is regarded as Pre-Traditional for our purposes; later we shall encounter a cham-

ber constructed in the 1930s that revives many of this room's characteristics.

Twenty-five chambers of our sample of seventy-five were built during the period 1865 to 1919; they are listed in table III.1. Before moving on to a systematic analysis of these spaces as a group, I shall briefly introduce the chambers and the buildings that house them. One of the chambers is located only a few yards from New York City's boardroom. This is the New York City Council Chamber, situated in the opposite wing of New York's French Renaissance city hall. Originally converted from a courtroom, this chamber's decoration dates from 1897. The space has unfortunately been damaged by water in recent years and was undergoing repairs when I was writing this book (photo III.2).

In the Traditional group, another chamber that occupies a space that was originally meant for other purposes is housed in a Palladian-style structure located in the historic district of Charleston, South Carolina. What is today the Charleston City Hall was constructed in 1801 as a branch of the

Photo III.2. *Council chamber, New York City*

Photo III.3. *Council chamber, Charleston, South Carolina*

Photo III.4. *Council chamber, Baltimore, Maryland*

United States Bank. The bank building was converted to city purposes in 1818, and the upstairs council chamber was built essentially in its present form in 1882 (photo III.3).

Three of the Traditional rooms that I studied are in elaborate Second Empire city halls, which are distinguished by mansard roofs that have projecting dormer windows. One is the recently renovated domed structure in Baltimore, Maryland. The earlier character of much of the building's ceremonial space was retained in the renovation; the council chamber has been restored to its original condition except for audience seating and the foyer (photo III.4).[3] Another notable Second Empire city hall is in Philadelphia. This great landmark, which covers 4.5 acres and is reputed to be the tallest masonry-bearing building in the world, took thirty years to construct. Its council chamber is one of five restored ceremonial spaces in the edifice. Still another Second Empire example is the Providence, Rhode Island, City Hall, built in the 1870s. Like many New England city halls, it contained

chambers to accommodate a bicameral legislature; both the aldermen's room and the council room have been restored, with the latter still being in use.

Two other chambers that I studied are in French Renaissance Revival city halls located in the Midwest. The mammoth Saint Louis, Missouri, City Hall, which was built between 1890 and 1904, was inspired by the Hôtel de Ville in Paris. Its Board of Aldermen chamber remains in its original condition. A smaller but equally ornate city hall at Louisville, Kentucky, has been preserved with respect to exterior façades but has been substantially reconstructed inside. Its council chamber has been partially renovated yet retains much of its original furniture.

Five preserved or restored nineteenth-century chambers are found in Richardsonian Romanesque structures. The city hall at Albany was designed by Henry Hobson Richardson himself, although its chamber was remodeled by others in 1919. The building at Lowell, Massachusetts, contains a chamber that has been virtually untouched since the 1890s. The aldermen's chamber in an 1888 city hall in Cambridge, Massachusetts, has been recently restored. The council space in the 1893 city hall at Cincinnati, Ohio (see photo I.3), was altered in 1935 with respect to desks and layout but otherwise remains the same. A large Richardsonian building in the small town of Bay City, Michigan, has been largely restored to its original condition.[4]

Also included in the Traditional sample are some of the most notable examples of Beaux-Arts public architecture in the United States. These include the flat-domed Newark, New Jersey, City Hall, built between 1902 and 1906; the towered Oakland, California, City Hall, designed by the famous architect Henry Hornbostel; the San Francisco City Hall, a great Beaux-Arts masterpiece designed by the equally famous team of John Bakewell and Arthur Brown; and the smaller but grand Cleveland, Ohio, City Hall, constructed in a city park designed by Daniel Hudson Burnham, father of the City Beautiful Movement. In all four of these Beaux-Arts buildings the original council chamber is almost perfectly intact, as is the circulation space leading to it.[5]

The remaining Traditional chambers are in a variety of early public buildings, each distinctive in its own right. A great triangular structure resembling a German Rathaus is found in Milwaukee. Columned, Neoclassical temples exist in Springfield, Massachusetts, and Pittsburgh, Pennsylvania, the latter also by Hornbostel. Other revivalist or eclectic buildings are in Brockton and Worcester, Massachusetts; Savannah, Georgia; Trenton, New Jersey; and Peoria and LaSalle, Illinois. The chambers in Springfield, Pittsburgh, Worcester, Trenton, and LaSalle are essentially in their original condition, while those at Milwaukee, Brockton, Savannah, and Peoria have been partially modified.

THE COMPOSITION OF TRADITIONAL SPACE

Let us now make a detailed analysis of the social meaning of the Traditional city-council chamber, starting with spatial composition. In succession, I consider (1) the room's size and shape, (2) its principal zonal relationships, (3) the form of its surfaces, (4) its placement within the larger building, and (5) its perforation by windows and doors.

The Large Box

The twenty-five Traditional chambers range widely in size. The smallest, in Charleston, is a mere 25 by 45 feet in floor area, while the largest, in Milwaukee, is 76 by 104. Some of this difference can be accounted for by the different sizes of the cities that the buildings were to serve. Various measures of chamber size are given in table III.2, with the mean square footage of floor space and public gallery being calculated for communities under 100,000 population, 100,000 to 500,000, and over 500,000 (populations at the time the chambers were built). As can be seen in the table, while the mean of all samples is 2,906 square feet, the average area increases substantially for bigger communities, as one would expect. On a per capita basis, square footage drops precipitously, however, a pattern that generally prevails in public assembly rooms; smaller communities overbuild the norm so as to create spaces that are respectably large, and big cities underbuild to avoid unreasonable size.

The floor area of some Traditional chambers compares favorably in size with the parliamentary space built for national governments. Square footage in Cincinnati, Newark, and Oakland is in the 3,000 range, approximately the floor size of the deliberately intimate House of Commons (3,094 square feet). Philadelphia, New York, and San Francisco are each about a thousand

TABLE III.2
The Traditional Chamber: Measures of Size

	Small Cities (N=11)	Medium Cities (N=10)	Big Cities (N=4)	All Cities (N=25)
Mean area of floor and galleries, (sq. ft.)	2,032	3,214	4,539	2,906
Mean area per 1,000 population (sq. ft.)	34.0	13.6	3.5	6.1
Mean ceiling height (ft.)	26.5	34.2	30.5	30.2
Mean spatial volume (cu. ft.)	49,945	107,661	135,446	88,514
Mean audience seating capacity	106	170	197	146
Mean number of seats per 10,000 population	17.8	7.2	1.5	4.4

Note: City size is based on the approximate population at the time the chamber was built. Small is under 100,000; medium is 100,000 to 500,000; big is over 500,000.

square feet larger. The biggest chambers among the twenty-five are Cleveland's, at 5,445 square feet on the floor plus 2,295 in upstairs galleries; and Milwaukee's, at 7,925 on the floor alone (its galleries have been sealed off). As a standard of comparison, the floor of the United States Senate is 4,284 square feet (plus 5,064 in the gallery), and that of the House is 7,752 (plus 5,175).

The height of the ceiling in Traditional chambers is usually 25 feet or more, with the average about 30 (see table III.2). The highest ceilings are found in Bay City and Providence, both of which are 45 feet. In Baltimore, Cleveland, Newark, Oakland, and Worcester the ceiling is at least 40 feet, well above the height of the House and Senate chambers in Washington (36 feet).

The high ceilings of Traditional chambers, combined with their sizeable floor areas, means that their volume tends to be very substantial. As can be seen in the table, the average is over 88,500 cubic feet. Nine of the twenty-five Traditional chambers ex-

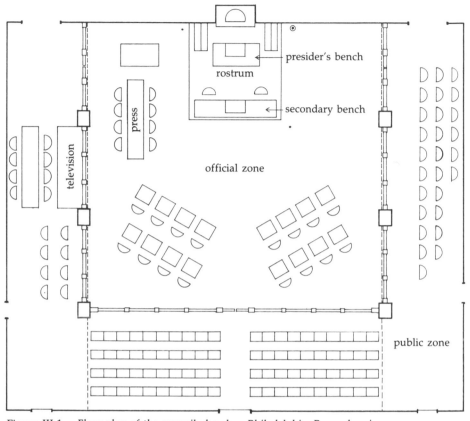

Figure III.1.   *Floor plan of the council chamber, Philadelphia, Pennsylvania*

ceed 100,000 cubic feet, with Cleveland and Milwaukee again being the largest—at 263,700 and 253,600 cubic feet, respectively. To use national parliamentary chambers for comparison once more, the volume of the House of Commons is 142,300 cubic feet, while that of the United States Senate is 245,400 and that of the House is 372,200 (including galleries). Hence we are talking about quite large spaces. The Traditional chamber is substantially larger than strict utilitarian functions or usual audience requirements would call for; it is seldom full of people. Yet the room's dimensions are not without their rationale. A generously big, enclosed space conveys importance to a place and imparts dignity to what occurs there. High ceilings permit degrees of verticality that can inspire awe. Also they ac-

commodate the upstairs public galleries and tall windows that were fashionable in pre-1920 public buildings. Ample horizontal dimensions likewise give officials an aura of importance by placing them far from the people, well into what Hall calls public distance. Furthermore, big spaces in big city halls convey a sense of community pride. We must remember that urban bosses did not have to account for every construction dollar and that they were delighted to "show off" themselves and their communities. Also, as a purely practical matter, high ceilings made the chambers cooler in the summer in an age without air conditioning. Because the buildings were constructed before the age of sophisticated heating systems, spatial volume was not directly equated with higher operating costs.

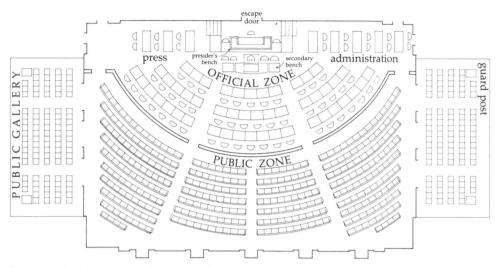

Figure III.2. *Floor plan of the council chamber, Cleveland, Ohio*

An important feature of the shape of these large civic spaces should be noted. They tend to possess chunky proportions—generally speaking length does not greatly exceed width. Two of the twenty-five—Baltimore and Lowell—are almost square; in ten others, length exceeds width by no more than 25 percent. In only six of the rooms does length exceed width by more than is called for by the standard of the golden section (about 62 percent). Moreover, in several of the oblong chambers the principal axis of the room from the standpoint of use is across the short dimension, not the long one; that is, the presiding officer faces from one side of the room to the other, not from one end of the room to the other. In short, the Traditional chamber tends not to be cathedral-like, in that there is no long nave and deep chancel. Instead, the space is more compact, on the order of the Renaissance central-plan church. Floor-plan proportions resemble the Greek bouleuterion, rather than the Roman curia.

The next feature to note with respect to spatial composition is how the space is zoned. The districts, or zonal territories, of a Traditional council chamber may not be as doctrinally critical as in cathedrals or in the Bali palace, but they are clearly demarcated nonetheless. Floor space that is essentially restricted to officials tends to be in the center of these squarish rooms. Often this "official zone," as I shall call it, abuts against one wall. The floor space that is accessible to visitors and to nonmembers of the council, which we shall term the "public zone," then surrounds the official zone on three sides. Illustrative is the floor plan at Philadelphia, shown in figure III.1. Another common pattern is one in which the perimeter of the official zone forms an arc, protruding outward into the public zone. Cleveland exemplifies this type, as seen in figure III.2. Typically this zonal boundary is very clearly articulated in Traditional chambers, in the form of either a fencelike rail, as in Philadelphia, or a balustrade, as in Cleveland.

Public galleries have been mentioned. These are found in fourteen of the twenty-five chambers today, and they originally existed in three more. Upstairs balconies, which were common in nineteenth-century English town halls, were also popular in early American council chambers as a way of accommodating the presence of citizens in the room without having the visitors on the floor itself. In fact, in some early cham-

Photo III.5. *Council chamber, Philadelphia, Pennsylvania*

bers, ordinary members of the public were not allowed at all on the floor as use of the room was originally conceived. This is the case in Baltimore, Cincinnati, and Saint Louis. The public galleries take two forms. In one, they are suspended in the larger space, usually at the sides or end of the room. This type is illustrated by the two side galleries at Philadelphia (photo III.5; designated by dotted lines in fig. III.1). The second form is where they face into the main space but are not suspended in it, as illustrated by Cambridge (photo III.6). In both types the public is located many feet above the floor, is given ingress and egress by means of an upper story of the building, and is segregated off (and protected from falling as well) by a retaining wall or a balustrade. Thus, those who occupy the galleries are inside the civic space but are not fully of it.

When one combines the three-sided or arc-shaped zonal patterns on the floor of the Traditional chamber with these suspended or onlooking forms of gallery, a picture emerges of peripheral treatment of the public. Whether allowed on the floor or restricted to galleries, citizens sit or stand at the sides or the back of the room, at the edge of power so to speak. They are placed as if they are outside spectators, witnessing an event rather than participating in it.

A further point of importance here is that despite the large volumetric size of the Traditional room, not many seats are provided for the public. As table III.2 indicates, the average seating capacity is 146. While chambers built for larger cities have greater capacity, seating on a per capita basis falls off quickly in the larger cities, as we saw with square footage. These civic spaces were not conceived by their builders as public auditoriums; rather, they were regarded as ceremonial sanctuaries to which a limited number of outsiders would be admitted and allowed to watch, from the sidelines and from upstairs.

Finally, it is important to note the form of the inner surfaces of the Traditional chamber. The walls are generally flat, vertical planes. The only exceptions are occasional

Photo III.6. *Council chamber, Cambridge, Massachusetts*

window bays and, at Bay City and Newark, a semicircular "apse" behind the rostrum (Newark's apse faces east, incidentally, but has no windows). Furthermore, the floors consist of flat horizontal planes. Built on the floor may be successive levels of platform superstructure, but all surfaces are still horizontal—including the rising tiers found in the galleries. In brief, the Traditional chamber is essentially a box, or a series of boxes, made up of cubic spaces, flat surfaces, and perpendicular angles. These volumes are clearly what Peterson would regard as static space, not flowing or dynamic antispace.

Yet, as we shall see later in this chapter, a grand ceiling often surmounts the box. Most Traditional chambers have ceilings that are coved, coffered, or vaulted in some way (see photos III.3, III.5 and III.6). In addition, these ceilings are often highly decorated and are sometimes hung with chandeliers. These figurative ceilings may be said to result from decorative practice rather than from spatial composition, however, in that

the design ethos of the ceiling contrasts sharply with the space's otherwise flat surfaces. No integrally conceived domed Pantheons here; only large boxes whose tops are high and fancy.

The Exalted Upper Room

Although in the Traditional chamber citizens are treated as spectators, this does not imply a lack of interest in the attitudes that they carry with them as they enter or leave the sanctuary. Far from being casual about the mind-set of onlookers, builders of early city halls in effect took steps to inculcate appropriate understandings in regard to the legitimacy of governmental authority. Certainly no attempt was made to overwhelm the visitor, as in the 725-foot walk to Hitler's office. But respect and even reverence for the deliberative process of government were sought by carefully fashioning the pedestrian route to the scene of power.

It should first be said that in most older city halls the council chamber is placed on

Photo III.7. *Rotunda stairs of the city hall, New York City*

an upper floor of the building. Often the chamber occupies the two uppermost floors, to allow sufficient ceiling height for galleries. This means that the citizen who comes to observe a council session must ascend to the chamber level. At the turn of the century, this often meant not riding up an elevator but climbing stairs. The circulation space that was provided by these stairs, plus associated lobbies, light courts, atria, rotundas, and connecting corridors, furnished an opportunity to impress on visitors, in advance of their arrival at the chamber, an image of the importance and the grandeur of the municipality and its governing bodies.

After being introduced to the circulation space via a vestibule or a foyer—itself often rich with architectural statement—the citizen is guided upwards via several flights of stairs. These often move through a large central space in the building, extending upward for several floors. In French Renaissance or American Georgian city halls the stairs bifurcate from the bottom and curve

around in circular form underneath the dome. A good example is in New York City (photo III.7). When the central court is rectilinear instead of round, as in Brockton, Providence, and Saint Louis, straight flights of stairs intersect at landings where civic tablets are displayed (for Brockton see photo III.8). In Richardsonian Romanesque edifices, such as those at Bay City and Lowell, the stairways move through immense structural support cages, whose ironwork itself expresses quality, strength, and solidity (for Bay City see photo III.9).

In Beaux-Arts buildings the staircases are curved, flowing escalations—dynamic in Arnheim's sense. In some instances a grand staircase flows upward in one grand sweep, while in others the stairs bifurcate midway at landings to achieve calculated effects. The landing itself becomes a splendid platform for viewing the surrounding space. Later in the ascension, at another landing or at the chamber entrance itself, the visitor arrives at subsequent viewing positions. This concept of processional or progressive spatial expo-

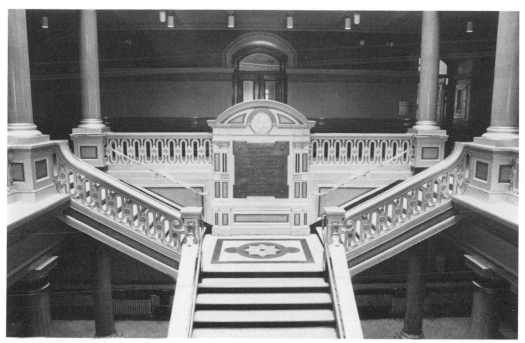

Photo III.8. *Central stairs of the city hall, Brockton, Massachusetts*

Photo III.9. *Ironwork stairs, Bay City, Michigan*

Photo III.10. *Central stairs of the city hall, Oakland, California*

sure is not accidental; it was explicitly taught at the École des Beaux-Arts in Paris.

The results are some marvelous interior vistas, beginning at the inside of the building's front door and ending at the portal of the council chamber. At Newark the visitor traverses 38 stairs to reach the chamber door, which is visible 123 feet away. In Oakland a grand staircase ascends 50 steps over three landings, with the visual angle to the chamber door 20 degrees above the horizontal (photo III.10, fig. III.3). In San Francisco's city hall, the supreme Beaux-Arts masterpiece of the group, the central staircase moves through a Great Rotunda, reaching 184 feet from floor to dome, a height that outdoes both the Pantheon in Rome and the Capitol Rotunda in Washington (photo III.11).

Another Beaux-Arts norm—in addition to progressive presentation—is symmetrical balance. Architects in this style, and in the Second Empire and Romanesque styles as well, designed buildings so that harmonious order would obtain with respect to the location of rooms on each floor. Ceremonial rooms such as council chambers were placed so that their importance was manifest in the floor-plan scheme itself. This was accomplished in a number of ways, depending on the circulation plan and practical requirements. In city halls where a continuous, ascending axis connects the building's front door and the entry to the council chamber, it is necessary to place the chamber in the center rear of the structure so that the axis will have enough reach. This is the case in Newark, San Francisco, and Oakland (fig. III.3). Where atrium stairs switch back and forth, instead of making a continuous run, it is possible to place the chamber in the front center of the building, as exemplified by Albany, Charleston, and Providence. This latter scheme has the advantage of permitting the windows of the chamber to penetrate the front façade of the building,

thus giving the room not only importance in terms of locational centrality and height but exterior visibility as well. In Albany and Providence, such frontal placement is especially effective, for each of these city halls faces a principal public square in the classical European manner.

In New England, architects faced the interesting problem of locating not just one chamber but two. This is because of the bicameral town government that was common in the region; cities were ruled both by a common council and by a board of aldermen. To preserve notions of balance, the two bodies would typically be placed in the opposite corners of an upper floor. This could be in the rear of the building, as in Lowell, or in the front, as in Springfield. In this way, neither body would possess a superior central location, and symmetry would be preserved. To facilitate communication between the two chambers, architects sometimes connected them by an impressive lobby, which adds to circulation grandeur, as in Springfield. In Lowell the architect dramatized the need for bicameral cooperation by providing a covered exterior bridge between them, in the manner of a tower-connecting overpass that one might find on a medieval castle (photo III.12). In this instance, architectural expression is directed not only to the importance of the public bodies concerned but also to the relationship between them, as was done at the colonial capitol in Williamsburg.

Generous Perforation

The final aspect of space composition that I will deal with is the extent to which Traditional chambers are perforated by doors and windows. As I discussed earlier, the degree of perforation contributes to the sense of openness versus enclosure and may affect as well Thiel's factor of "explicitness," or clarity of spatial definition. Lasswell, as we

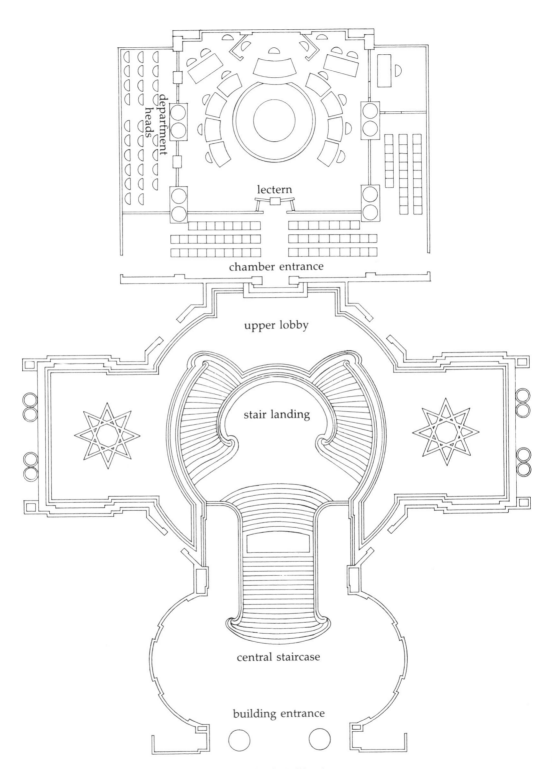

department
heads

lectern

chamber entrance

upper lobby

stair landing

central staircase

building entrance

Figure III.3. *Partial plan of the city hall, Oakland, California*

Photo III.11. *Rotunda of the city hall, San Francisco, California*

Photo III.12. *City hall, Lowell, Massachusetts*

Photo III.13. *Entrance to chamber, Oakland, California*

recall, proposed that democratic leaders are more favorably inclined to perforation than are despots. Arnheim associates windowless space with a "tightness of mind." Regardless of the validity of these generalizations, one can argue that the extent of transparent fenestration in a ceremonial room is an important indication of the degree to which activities that take place within are perceived as requiring secrecy or are presented as being accessible to public scrutiny.

Entryways to the Traditional chamber are both numerous and large. The typical room possesses one or two sets of doors meant for use by the public. These are invariably generous in size and lavish in decoration, as befits a notion of "threshold" to a place of dignity and importance. The openings are often 6 by 9 or even 8 by 10 feet in size and are frequently fitted with double swinging doors. The doors themselves are usually made of thick, heavy, and richly paneled wood. Furthermore, many public entryways are visually enlarged by transoms, architraves, fan lights, or other enhancing fea-

tures. The main entrance to the Oakland chamber, as a particularly dramatic example, consists of a 6-by-12-foot doorway, topped by a pediment and surrounded by a 30-by-40-foot arch, most of which is filled with transparent glass panes (photo III.13).

The Traditional chamber also has one or two smaller doors, meant for use by officials only. These private entrances often communicate to back lobbies or offices. Within the chamber their point of access is often in the public zone, rather than in the official one, a consequence of the fact that the public zone in many Traditional chambers surrounds the official zone on three sides. In any case, these private doorways are, by comparison to the public entrances, small and simple, measuring usually no more than 4 by 9 feet (note the contrast between the public and private doorways in Cambridge, photo III.6).

Two unusual cases of ingress/egress perforation should be mentioned because they foreshadow situations that we will encounter later. In Cleveland a set of escape doors

Photo III.14. *Rostrum backdrop, Cleveland, Ohio*

is built into the wood paneling of the backdrop, just behind what was originally the mayor's desk (photo III.14). These doors lead to a "double tracking" passageway in the Heimsath sense, in that it in turn communicates with back offices. Apparently Cleveland's Mayor Tom Johnson, who initiated the construction of the building but did not live to occupy it, wanted to be able to leave the room quickly if those who opposed his colorful progressivism became too turbulent. The other unusual perforation feature is a hall gateway leading to the Philadelphia council chamber (photo III.15). Philadelphia's cavernous city hall contains many such gates, whose doors can be pulled shut and locked. Though these are normally kept open today, they once served to remind the corridor-walking visitor that space of august importance was being approached, something in the manner of a cathedral's rood screen.

Turning to windows, fenestration in the Traditional chamber by no means "demate-rializes" the walls; but it is usually ample and sometimes awesome. In most rooms, several tall, clear windows perforate one or more walls of the space, bathing the chamber in natural light in the daytime and presenting an impressive exterior façade at night. Indeed, when the rooms are illuminated for evening meetings, the exterior image of the structure is dominated by tall panels of light shining from the uppermost floors of the building, in effect telling citizens in the street below that something important is going on inside. In several instances the row of windows is principally along one side wall. At San Francisco three 10-by-22-foot openings face out to the west façade of this great Beaux-Arts palace. At Pittsburgh, five 9-by-30-foot windows reach from floor to ceiling, looking onto the Neoclassical portico that protrudes from the front of the building. Also, rows of windows are sometimes found at the rear of the room (e.g., Cleveland, Philadelphia, Saint Louis) or in front, behind the rostrum (e.g.,

Photo III.15. *Corridor gate of the city hall, Philadelphia, Pennsylvania*

Albany, Bay City, Providence). In still other chambers, fenestration perforates two or even three walls, creating a particularly cheerful and open atmosphere (e.g., Brockton, Cincinnati, Worcester).

Traditional windows are not always colossal openings, as in San Francisco and Pittsburgh, yet their dimensions usually range in the vicinity of 4 to 5 feet wide and 10 to 12 feet high. Except for peripheral stained decoration, these windows are fitted with transparent lights and are sometimes curtained. The average number of windows in a Traditional room is eight; the mean fenestration area per room is 675 square feet. The most perforated room of the group is Milwaukee, whose walls contain sixty windows. Although Norbert-Schultz would no doubt consider these windows to be mere "wall holes," there are certainly plenty of them. Only Louisville has no windows whatsoever, though it probably did have some originally.

TRADITIONAL SEMIFIXED FEATURES

The composition of space in the Traditional chamber is, then, characterized by large spatial volume, high ceilings, chunky proportions, circumscribed zoning, boxlike form, elevated and conscious building placement, awesome circulation, big doors, and generous fenestration. We now consider the design and placement of heavy furniture and anchored dividers in the Traditional room—that is, its semifixed features.

The Traditional Rostrum

The centerpiece of the Traditional council chamber is the rostrum. This term, which by strict definition means the beaklike prow of a ship, is being used here to refer to the total assembly of several individual components: (1) a podium or elevated platform on which the entire assembly is mounted; (2) the desk or bench behind which the presiding officer sits, for example, the mayor or the president of the council; (3) other secondary benches for lesser officials; (4) an especially elaborate chair meant for the presiding officer (throne); (5) other specialized chairs reserved for dignitaries (sedilia); (6) an overhead canopy if one exists (baldachin); and (7) backdrop panels positioned on the wall behind to give added visual emphasis via a framing effect. In some cases such framing is accomplished by a separate backdrop screen (reredos).

In Lynch's city-imaging terminology, such a complex of furniture would be considered a "node," that is a prominent, visually obvious element that is occupied by human beings. In the Traditional chamber this node is, beyond doubt, the central object of focus. In Gusfield's language, it is the supreme differentiating symbolic gesture contained within the room. Emphatically and unmistakably, the rostrum singles out and confers honor on certain individuals and on the ceremonial roles that they perform.

Several architectural devices are employed to achieve such a focus. For example, almost without exception, the rostrum of the Traditional chamber is spatially centered. Its vertical axis typically coincides with the vertical centerline of one wall of the room. Furthermore, the visual focal point within the rostrum, which is the upper torso of the presiding officer, is almost always horizontally centered within the rostrum complex itself. The only exceptions that I encountered are at Albany and Brockton, where an even number of platform sedilia allows for no central throne for the presiding officer.

In addition to centrality, the device of elevation directs attention and honor to the presiding officer. In all Traditional chambers that I examined, this dignitary stands or sits noticeably above floor level. Such elevation increases this person's vision and visibility; it also symbolizes his or her superior authority. The height of the podium ranges from 6 to 48 inches, with an average of 21. The height of most of these platforms is roughly in multiples of six—for example, 12, 18, 24, and 30 inches—reflecting a common building practice of constructing platform steps with six-inch risers (a little higher in the earliest rooms). It would not do, of course, for distinguished personages to stumble on irregular or unexpectedly high steps while ascending to their elevated perches before the onlooking public.

The effectiveness of this elevation in conveying authority depends on a number of factors, including the upward sight-line angle of those who are seated on the floor below as they look toward the presiding officer. That angle depends not only on the height of the podium but also on the horizontal distance from it. For the Traditional chambers as a group, the average upward sight-line angle is about 4 degrees, as measured from the front row of floor-level audience seating (the mean distance from the rostrum being 28 feet). In individual rooms, relationships differ. At Philadelphia the podium on which the president of the council sits is 4 feet high, but because the closest audience is 40 feet away, the sight-line angle is only 5 degrees (see photo III.5). In the more intimate LaSalle chamber the mayor's podium is half that height, but the spectators are only 25 feet away from him and hence must look upward at an angle of 10 degrees.

The principal item of furniture in the rostrum assembly is the desk or bench behind which the presiding officer sits. This is typically a heavy, dark-stained wooden piece of furniture. It is from 4 to 32 feet long, with an average length of about 11 feet. Usually only the mayor or the council president sits behind this piece of furniture, although sometimes he or she is flanked by nonelected officials (e.g., the city clerk or the city attorney). Frequently the middle position is accentuated by a raised reading sur-

Photo III.16. *Rostrum bench, Pittsburgh, Pennsylvania*

face in the center of the bench or by a distinctive panel protruding from the front skirt of the bench.

Overall, the frontal face, or skirt, of Traditional rostrum desks is from 30 to 64 inches high, with a mean of 46 inches. This vertical face sometimes incorporates the height of the podium as well, when the front of the desk is positioned precisely at the podium's leading edge. Almost always the rostrum skirt is richly decorated, either by carving or by paneling or by both. The one at Pittsburgh is intricately carved and inlaid (photo III.16). The huge Worcester bench, over 15 feet long, is executed in carved oak and provides the mayor with a raised reading surface (photo III.17). The top edge of the skirt usually extends 3 to 6 inches above the full length of the bench's writing surface, providing the person sitting at it a "parapet" of visual protection from the front. This raised edge means that the audience cannot see what is on the surface of the

desk, particularly from the floor below. Also, if high enough, the parapet hides the hands of the presider and even a significant part of the upper torso.

This central piece of furniture is, then, massive, ornate, formal, and protective. Its size and its character suggest that persons who occupy it are important—in fact, the most important persons in the room. No other visible piece or ensemble of furniture rivals this semifixed feature in elevation or weight. Furthermore, no other desks or benches afford as much psychological protection; not only do other pieces of furniture lack the mass and the concealing qualities, they are usually located closer to the middle of the room. Only the occupants of the rostrum in a Traditional room are, as a rule, backed against a wall and thus afforded protection from the rear as well as the front.

In about half the Traditional sample, additional protection is given by placing a secondary bench in front of the presiding

Photo III.17. *Rostrum bench, Worcester, Massachusetts*

position. This is situated between the presider's bench and the council and the audience (note figs. III.1 and III.2). Typically this secondary bench is occupied by the city clerk, recording secretaries, or comparable officials. Because these officers are inferior to the mayor or to the council president in status, their bench is invariably lower in physical elevation. This differential is attained either by a lower frontal skirt or by a lower podium, or the two in combination. Frequently the secondary bench is also a smaller piece of furniture overall, as illustrated by Lowell (photo III.18). Sometimes, however, it is considerably longer, as illustrated in Baltimore (photo III.19). In the latter case a 12-foot-wide secondary bench, occupied by four clerks and council staff, presents a formidable outer defense perimeter for the rostrum assembly. A similar pattern obtains in New York (photo III.2) and Philadelphia (photo III.5).

Chairs that are reserved for use by officials alone are an integral part of the rostrum complex. The fact that such seats are meant only for designated occupants confers a sense of importance on those individuals. Then, too, the sedilia themselves become physical symbols of the authority that their occupants possess. Rostrum chairs in Traditional chambers are invariably ceremonial as well as instrumental in design, provided the original furniture is still in use. There are generally two ceremonial indicators: (1) rich decoration and handsome materials—that is, intricate carving and fine woods or leathers; and (2) a high back. Recall that Hazard found both of these characteristics in chairs used by judges. The backs of chairs used by presiding officers in the Traditional chamber are usually at least 5 feet high; often they are 6 or even 7 feet high. Normally, no other chair in the room has such a high back, thus making the presider's seat stand out visually even when it is not occupied. When such a chair is occu-

Photo III.18. *Rostrum ensemble, Lowell, Massachusetts*

Photo III.19. *Rostrum ensemble, Baltimore, Maryland*

pied, the persona of the seated person is given a decided vertical thrust.

Ceremonial chairs for presiders are visible in several of the photographs previously seen. The throne at Baltimore is 62 inches high (photo III.4); and the one at Philadelphia is 72 (photo III.5); Cleveland's is 67 inches (photo III.14); and Lowell's is 72 (photo III.18). A particularly splendid array of churchlike sedilia is found at Brockton, ranging in height from 70 to 76 inches (photo III.20). Most are seldom used, but they lend a silent dignity to the room.

Finally, the position of the presiding officer within the rostrum may be accentuated and magnified by backdrop framing. The best example of such framing is found in the council chamber in New York City. It includes a wooden hood that immediately surrounds the council president's carved French Empire chair (photo III.21). Above this republican throne, supported by Corinthian columns and surmounted by a carved shield of the city, is an elegant baldachin

(visible in photo III.2). This framing ensemble reminds one of Trexler's Florentine sacramentals of power.

The Milwaukee chamber possesses what is perhaps the best example of a secular reredos in the United States (photo III.22). It is a massive wooden façade, 30 feet long and 17 feet high, standing along the back wall but positioned 30 inches out from it. Composed of numerous Renaissance-style architectural elements, it sets off the rostrum with pilasters, columns, arched panels, and a nascent portico, topped by an open pediment and an ornate clock.

A Neoclassical example of a backdrop is found in San Francisco (photo III.23). Here, modified Doric columns, adjoining pilasters, and flags enclose a 12-by-20-foot panel of Manchurian oak, with a decorative clock and floral carving. This composition deftly draws the eye to the council's president and gives the presider's position an exalted status. A precisely identical decorative framing (minus the clock) occurs at the opposite end

Photo III.20. *Ceremonial sedilia, Brockton, Massachusetts*

of the chamber, where a small visitors' gallery replaces the rostrum. In this manner the San Francisco chamber perfectly illustrates the Beaux-Arts penchant for symmetry, plus the principles of centrality and elevation that govern Traditional rostra.

The Aldermanic Desk

With the rostrum as the semifixed-feature centerpiece of the Traditional chamber, the aldermanic desk is the node of next order of importance. It is the furniture "home" of the individual member of the elected body: the alderman, councilor, or supervisor. In the context of representative government, this desk is literally the seat of an elected delegate, in effect promising representation to that official's constituency. In the context of the legislative process, the aldermanic desk symbolizes the equal legal standing of each legislator in writing the laws.

Although the aldermanic node is not the target of central visual focus, as the rostrum

is, it is given substantial prominence in the Traditional chamber. This is not done by centrality or elevation, however, for aldermanic desks are multiple in locus and rest on the floor of the room or on a very low platform. Instead, these pieces of furniture gain attention by their dignified design and by being placed in an open part of the chamber that is surrounded by a barrier. The pattern of this placement is also important symbolically, because the council is a collegial body and hence several desks or seating positions must be provided, creating the question of how they interrelate spatially.

Usually the aldermanic desk is a separate piece of furniture, together with an accompanying chair. In twenty of the twenty-five Traditional chambers the desks are freestanding. In about half of these cases the desks are spaced physically apart, from 5 inches to about 3 feet. The pattern is hence ambassadorial in terms of Goodman's discussion of the United States Senate. This

Photo III.21. *"Throne" of the president of the council, New York City*

Photo III.22. *Rostrum ensemble, Milwaukee, Wisconsin*

Photo III.23. *Rostrum ensemble, San Francisco, California*

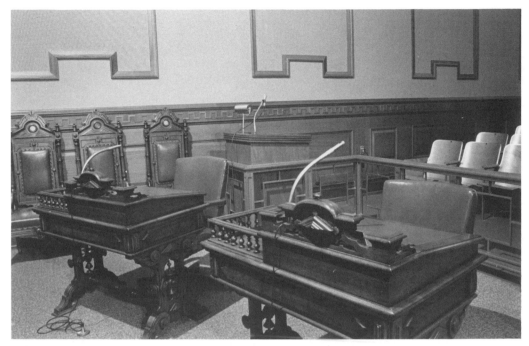

Photo III.24. *Aldermanic desks, Louisville, Kentucky*

separation is clearly visible in photographs that we have seen of Philadelphia, Cambridge, and Milwaukee (photos III.5, III.6, and III.22). Another example is Louisville, where ornate aldermanic desks are the prize antiques of the chamber (photo III.24).

A second pattern of desk arrangement is where individual desks immediately adjoin one another. This situation is nicely illustrated at Charleston (photo III.3), where individuality is maintained but is compromised somewhat by a competing theme of corporate unity. Also composite or integrated benches are used; that is, seating space is provided to several councilors at one structure. Individuality is still maintained, however, by moldings between desk surfaces or by separate segments in the skirt paneling.

An unusual situation at Pittsburgh illustrates the behavioral importance of these spatial relationships. There, as in several parliaments of the British Commonwealth, the legislators' desks accommodate two persons, sitting side by side. As we have noted, proxemics research tells us that collaborators tend to sit next to each other; thus it should not surprise us that the Pittsburgh council is informally composed of two-person dyads, congruent with these double desks. One of these dual positions is known as the "Irish bench," for example, while others are called the "Jewish" and "Serbo-Croatian" benches.

As for patterns of placement of the aldermanic desks in the official zone, the most common configuration is the crescent, or arc, form. Desks are circled around the front of the rostrum, facing it. This pattern depicts the councilors, together with their presiding officer and those seated at the secondary bench, as constituting a distinct ruling group, or circle. Governing is presented as a private internal affair of those who are formally in charge of the affairs of the community. This image does not admit of a need to face outward, toward the citizenry; the purpose of the audience is to watch from

Photo III.25. *Council chamber, La Salle, Illinois*

above and from afar. Cleveland illustrates this arc form perfectly, as shown in figure III.2. In Philadelphia the aldermanic desks are set at an angle, but the same effect is achieved (fig. III.1). A three-sided rectilinear version of this grouping is found at Charleston (photo III.3). At LaSalle the desks are in a straight row, facing the rostrum (photo III.25), while at Worcester they are in opposing rows, facing each other (photo III.26). The latter case reminds us of the opposing benches of Commons.

The full symbolic import of this inward-facing group configuration will become apparent later. In post-1920 chambers, we will see that councilor seating eventually reverses in direction, with officials facing the citizens, rather than each other. Although in the latter-day remodeling of a few Traditional chambers the councilors were turned around, original plans and early photographs indicate that in no room of the sample did a citizen-facing arrangement exist originally.

In Oakland we see what might be thought of as an aldermanic turnabout in process. The original configuration was a round grouping of rostrum and eight aldermanic desks, circled about a city seal that is woven into the carpet. In later years, however, councilors have complained that this arrangement suggests that the people's representatives are "circling the wagons," western style, against the "enemy" of the citizenry. To counter this notion they partially rotated the desks outward in the manner shown, anticipating perfectly what was in store for later eras (see photo III.27 and also fig. III.3).

When multiple aldermanic desks exist, their sequential order of placement can be important. Several systems are used: a left-to-right ordering by ward number (from the presider's perspective); a left-to-right alphabetical series by surname of councilor (again, presider's perspective); and placement by seniority, by the personal preference of senior members, by lot, or by politi-

Photo III.26. *Council chamber, Worcester, Massachusetts*

cal party. A left-to-right ideological spectrum is rare; only Cincinnati approaches this Continental practice. The aldermanic desks at Cincinnati, which once had been separated in arcs, were grouped in an open rectangle in 1935 (photo III.28). The Charterites—leftovers of a progressive reform movement of the 1920s—occupy the two desks at the presider's left. Three Republican councilors sit at the extreme right, and between them are the Democrats. True to Cincinnati's reform tradition, the city manager is given a symbolically neutral position; his desk is located in the exact center of this spread.[6]

Features of Segregation and Subordination

With the citizenry cast in the role of outsiders to the governing process, it is not inconsistent to segregate it from officialdom. Indeed, as has already been pointed out,

much of the public seating space in Traditional rooms is in upstairs galleries. Segregation is also clearly in evidence on the floor of the chamber. This is accomplished most obviously by an upright fence or barrier, located along the border between the official zone and the public zone, which makes the two zones wholly separate and distinct. The Traditional barrier is typically a balustrade, constructed of dark-stained wooden balusters and a horizontal beam. Other forms are the wooden or brass rail, a metal fence, and a rope or chain, strung along vertical standards. The height of the barrier ranges from 29 to 43 inches, with the average being 36. Usually the barrier is continuous—that is, it runs from one side of the room to the other, interrupted only by swinging gates or suspended ropes. In some instances the gates are equipped with heavy latches, as in Oakland, or are even locked, as in San Francisco.

The altar-rail analogy comes to mind

Photo III.27. *Council chamber, Oakland, California*

Photo III.28. *Council chamber, Cincinnati, Ohio*

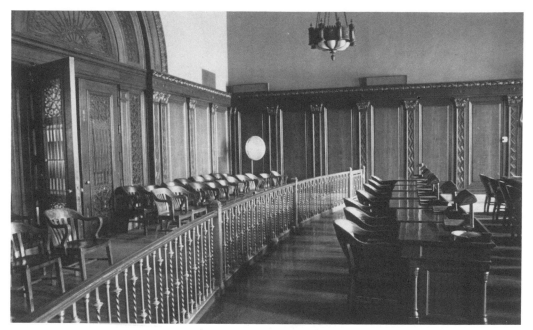

Photo III.29. *Chamber of the Common Council, Albany, New York*

when one notes specific examples of these barriers. In Albany a striking brass balustrade seals off most of the room, with gates located at the far ends (photo III.29). In Providence an extremely heavy balustrade is opened at the center by wooden swinging gates (photo III.30). A rail is seen in Philadelphia (photo III.5), a wall in Oakland (photo III.13), a decorated fence in Louisville (photo III.24), simple fences in LaSalle and Worcester (photos III.25 and III.26), and a chain in Cincinnati (photo III.28).

The Traditional chamber not only segregates but also discriminates against the citizenry. Spectators are furnished with very plain and simple seating, nothing like the opulent thrones and ornate sedilia provided to the officials. Traditional public seating is almost never padded or given more than the bare minimum of expenditure or attention. The most common form is plain wooden benches, as in New York, Worcester, and Providence (photos III.1, III.26, and III.30). Bench seating tends to subordinate individ-

uality; each person is given, not a separate place, but only linear distance on a "shelf." Another possibility is plain wooden chairs, as in Philadelphia, Cincinnati, and Albany (photos III.5, III.28, and III.29). Whether bench or chair, Traditional seating is invariably in straight-row classroom-style formation.

In a more subtle way, semifixed features also discriminate against the citizenry. Whereas the downstairs official zone is largely composed of empty floor space that is occupied here and there by a rostrum or other items, the public-zone galleries upstairs are crowded with benches.[7] In Holston's terminology, the official zone is composed of figurative solids (such as rostra) on continuous voids of floor space. The public zone, by contrast, consists of continuous blocks of audience seating and figurative voids of aisles. The visual impact of this differentiation is powerful: the rostrum and the aldermanic desks are clearly visible to all and thus are objects of prominent visual in-

Photo III.30. *Council chamber, Providence, Rhode Island*

terest in the room. The public, meanwhile, is confined to an undifferentiated and uninteresting composite that is organized in gridlike "city blocks" of seating and "streets," or aisles. In other words, while officials occupy grand nodes, citizens are afforded mass treatment.

Another semifixed-feature indicator of the role that is visualized for the citizenry in the Traditional room is the provision made for the public to speak before the council. In several big-city chambers, no equipment whatsoever is provided for this, which is logical when one realizes that citizens are rarely permitted to address these councils. When members of the public can speak, it is usually done at a simple standing microphone. (This was not the case, obviously, before public-address systems were invented.) The microphone is usually located in the official zone, with the result that the citizen must enter "alien" territory in order to use it, as in Baltimore (photo III.19, visible on far right). Furthermore the thin, upright shaft of a standing microphone provides no concealment or psychological support. Recognizing this point, the mayor of Bay City urged her city manager to provide a lectern for use by the public, but he declined to do so on the grounds that it would only encourage too much public comment at council meetings.[8] Instead, citizens who speak at Bay City are given only a low typing table, which holds the speaker-registration book (photo III.31). When signing the book on this low table, speakers are forced to "bow" toward council.

Sometimes the citizen addresses the council while he or she is seated at a witness table, as in Cambridge (photo III.6, far left). This gives the protection of a substantial piece of furniture, but the table is normally used by nonelected officials as well and is located deep inside the official zone. In a few Traditional chambers, intermediate levels of protection and neutrality are provided, such as an angled reading surface mounted on the zonal barrier, as in Oakland

Photo III.31. *Public microphone, Bay City, Michigan*

Photo III.32. *Gallery guard post, Cleveland, Ohio*

(photo III.13), or a pedestal-style lectern placed just inside the barrier, as in Worcester (photo III.26). Only rarely is a box-style lectern provided, and if so, it is not original equipment, as in Louisville (background of photo III.24).

Citizens were not only unwelcome as speakers during the Traditional era, they were looked upon as if they were dangerous rabble in some instances. In the enormous chamber at Cleveland, one finds four brass-fenced guard posts, located at the far corners of each public gallery (photo III.32 and fig. III.2). Unused today, their original purpose was presumably to provide watch stations for uniformed officers. The gallery at Worcester also contains a small walled landing that could have served as an observation post (visible in photo III.26).

The Traditional chamber subordinates lesser officials as well as members of the public. I have already noted that many Traditional rostra contain a secondary bench. Usually occupied by the city clerk, this is always lower than the presider's bench and is always nearer to the audience. Hence, on the counts of both height and distance, the clerk's position is inferior.

In strong-mayor cities the mayor usually presides, and in the role of presiding officer, he or she is accorded the highest possible status in regard to furniture. In several big cities of the Traditional sample in which the separation-of-powers governmental structure leaves the mayor weak, this officer is typically subordinated from the standpoint of chamber furniture, even to the point of humiliation. In several rooms, no special position or even chair is provided for the mayor: he or she is an artificial nonperson within the confines of legislative space.

The city-manager movement was introduced to U.S. local government during the Traditional era. The manager is usually afforded substantial respect with regard to furniture, definitely more than a nonpresiding mayor. In accordance with the doc-

trine that the manager serves at the pleasure of council, the desk or table that is provided to him or her is typically located apart from the rostrum and is given no elevation. I have already mentioned the city manager's desk in Cincinnati; other illustrative manager positions are at Lowell (secondary bench, photo III.18), Oakland (upper center of photo III.27), and Bay City (far left of photo III.31).

Lower-level administrators, such as departmental heads and lesser staff, are given even less recognition in the Traditional chamber. Typically these bureaucrats have a simple wooden table with a few functional chairs drawn around it. The Administration Table, as it is sometimes called, is always in the official zone and is not elevated (for Milwaukee, see right background of photo III.22). Sometimes the treatment of bureaucrats is even more modest; they may be given a few plain chairs or the two front rows of public seating. Some exceptions exist to this rule. At Cleveland, several desks are reserved for departmental heads and executive assistants (fig. III.2), and at San Francisco a special area for administrators is elegantly set off by a balustrade. Oakland's bureaucratic zone is fitted with comfortable fixed chairs, each labeled with a position title. These are, however, located outside of the official zone (background of photo III.27).

The press is treated, with regard to seating, much as the bureaucrats are. Typically, reporters are given a simple table with chairs, placed inside the official zone. Examples are visible at the far left of photographs of Philadelphia (III.5) and Milwaukee (III.22). Although these tables are usually located at the periphery of the zone or at one of its sides or ends, a second pattern is to place them in the exact center of things, as if to highlight the importance of the fourth estate to democratic governance. Illustrations are at Cambridge (photo III.6, far right), Worcester (photo III.26, center), and

Cincinnati (photo III.28, far left). At San Francisco a balustraded press gallery matches the administrators' gallery and is across from it.

We conclude this discussion of patterns of subordination by examining two across-the-board indicators of status. One of these is the height of chair backs. As we recall, the presiding officer in the Traditional chamber is often furnished with a high-backed ceremonial throne. Almost without exception, lesser officers have chairs with lower backs. The difference between the presiding officer and the next-ranking official (usually the clerk) ranges from 3 to 39 inches, the average being 14. The drop from this second echelon to a third (usually a councilor) is another 2 to 31 inches, with a mean difference of 13 inches. In short, differences in chair height can be quite substantial in Traditional rooms. In absolute terms, average measured heights are: presiding officers, 56 inches; city clerks, 42; city managers, 39; councilors, 38; administrative staff, 36; and the press, 33. The only exceptions to a hierarchical chair pattern are at Charleston, where the mayor's chair is modestly six inches lower than those of the councilors; and LaSalle, where strict equality prevails (photo III.25).

The second across-the-board indicator has to do with directionality. The notion of the superiority of the right hand, when applied to seating patterns and floor placement, is upheld more often than not, if we assume that it is the presiding officer's perspective, not the audience's, that we are using in order to determine direction. That it is indeed the presider's orientation that counts seems warranted by virtue of the fact that when aldermanic desks are ordered numerically or alphabetically, the natural reading sequence of left to right is almost always from the presider's viewpoint, not from that of spectators who face in the opposite direction.

Right-hand superiority predominates in several relationships. In six of seven cases when two subordinates flank the presider at the rostrum, the more important of the two is on the presider's right (e.g., the clerk, rather than the deputy clerk). In all instances in which two or more officials sit side by side at other benches or tables, the right-seated individual outranks the left-seated. In six of eight cases in which the desks or the chairs of council officials are located off-center in the room, they are placed on the right side, rather than on the left. Similarly, when bureaucrats are not symmetrically placed, they are usually at the right side of the room, with the press usually at the left.

TRADITIONAL DECORATION AND DISPLAY

Spatial composition and the design of semifixed features are the first two categories by which I organize my analysis. The third and final category is patterns of surface decoration and the display of portable objects.

Classic Decor and Ornamentation

Norberg-Schulz would probably characterize the Traditional chamber as possessing a classical *genius loci*. Its decorative features are clearly articulated. The design is a conscious composition that is complete unto itself—a Heroic and Original "duck" in the terminology of Venturi, not a "shed" which has been absent-mindedly put together. Furthermore, the chambers tend very much to be classical (or Neoclassical), in the sense of reusing well-developed decorative formulae of the past. In their detailing they recall the worlds of ancient Greece and Rome, as well as that of the Renaissance. This was a standard practice in American and European architecture prior to the Modernist revolution. As a consequence, the chambers share the enduring qualities found in public buildings of the West over the centuries: solidity, permanence, and, in some instances, monumentalism. Overall, the ornamentation tends to duplicate the classical orders, or at least to suggest them. The rooms are marked by decorative repetition, symmetrical balance, strong verticality, and the prolific use of dark-stained wood, which is intricately carved and paneled. These rooms present themselves, not as informal gathering places or utilitarian workshops, but as elaborate political stage settings in the Edelman sense, a locus for the presentation and exercise of power.

Let us discuss the details of decoration and ornamentation from the top down. The ceilings of Traditional chambers are, as I mentioned earlier, frequently high and richly figured. They are often elegant works of craftsmanship and, in some instances, even art. When sitting in these rooms, one feels not merely covered over but as if one were beneath an artistic achievement. The direction "up" takes on the significance of looking to the most beautiful part of the room.

Several styles and techniques of ceiling embellishment are used. Charleston's century-old ceiling, which has borne up through many a hurricane, is manufactured of toleware panels (photo III.3). At Lowell, heavy wood beams form a powerful visual grid. At Philadelphia, transverse ceiling beams enclose decorated coffers (partly visible in photo III.5). The ceiling at Cambridge is gently coved above a Neoclassical cornice (photo III.6). New York's water-damaged ceiling is also coved, and at its center there is a great horizontal oil entitled "New York City Receiving the Tribute of the Nation" (partly visible in photo III.2). One of the most elaborate ceilings is in San Francisco: it is executed in Italian Renaissance style, with eight chandeliers hanging from the coffers by corded chain. Other coffered ceilings are at Albany, Milwaukee, Springfield, and Cleveland (photo III.33). Painted ceilings

are found at Brockton, Pittsburgh, Saint Louis, and Providence (photo III.34). At Peoria a barrel-vaulted ceiling is unfortunately hidden by a dropped ceiling; by contrast, the great barrel vault at Oakland is visible, resting on Doric columns.

Walls, too, are enhanced. Three themes are intertwined in Traditional wall decoration. The first is the use of wooden wainscoting and paneling. Quite simple dark-stained wainscoting is found at New York, Cambridge, and Worcester (photos III.2, III.6, and III.26), while intricately inlaid or carved wainscoting decorates Louisville (photo III.24), and Albany (photo III.29). Panels of Cuban mahogany rise to a height of 13 feet in Springfield, giving the room not only a dignified appearance but also a distinguished odor (photo III.35). At San Francisco, Manchurian-oak woodwork in Neoclassical style rises to the ceiling (photo III.36). The walls at Charleston are fitted top to bottom with butternut siding, whose vertical grooves accentuate the height of the room (photo III.3). Thus, as we can see, wood, that ancient building material which is considered to be warm, pliable, organic, and yet fit for the dwellings of kings, is exceedingly prominent in the Traditional chamber.

The second theme in wall decoration is the elaborate use of Neoclassical architectural details, such as pilasters, columns, cornices, friezes, entablatures, architraves, and pediments. These are generally executed in molded plaster, but sometimes in a dearer medium, such as scagliola, as at Baltimore (photo III.4), or gold or silver leaf, employed in Oakland (photo III.27). Also, the surfaces are often painted in light pastels, with detailing done in darker coloring, as at Philadelphia and Providence.

The third decorative theme is mural art. Peoria's apse bears the images of Education, Columbia, and Agriculture, executed by an itinerant painter. Above the podium at Cleveland is the large mural "Where Men

Photo III.33. *Coffered ceiling, Cleveland, Ohio*

Photo III.34. *Painted ceiling, Providence, Rhode Island*

Photo III.35. *Council chamber, Springfield, Massachusetts*

Photo III.36. *Chamber of the Board of Supervisors, San Francisco, California*

Photo III.37. *Council chamber, Trenton, New Jersey*

and Minerals Meet," which was moved there from a bank in 1951. A mural that dominates the backdrop at Trenton is by Ashcan School painter Everett Shinn; it depicts early industrial activity in the area (photo III.37). Newark's chamber is a combination of classical decoration and mural art; a great arch with accompanying archivolt frames the backdrop apse, while four thematic frescoes decorate each side wall (photo III.38).

Ornamentation extends to other features as well. The public door at Oakland bears a Neoclassical pediment (photo III.13), and the entryway at Albany is topped by an ornate fanlight (photo III.29). The tall windows in New York are surmounted by intricately carved pediments (photo III.2), and those at Trenton are flanked by white-marble pilasters (photo III.37). Floor barriers can be perfectly utilitarian and yet add aesthetically to the room, as illustrated by the brass gates at Philadelphia and the oak balusters

at Springfield and San Francisco (photos III.35 and III.36). The same is true with artificial lighting: chandeliers hang in many Traditional chambers, with San Francisco's already having been mentioned (photo III.36). The rostrum is graced by triple brass girandoles at Lowell (photo III.18) and by eight-foot lamp stands at Baltimore (photo III.19). Still other examples of ornamentation are the brass grillwork at Cleveland (photo III.32) and wall clocks at San Francisco and Springfield (photos III.23 and III.35). Everywhere one looks in these rooms one finds evidence of a desire to project sufficiency if not opulence, dignity if not taste.

Objects of Ceremony and History

A great many unfixed or moveable objects are also found in council chambers, but a few stand out as prominent. One such class of objects is flags. City, county, state, and

Photo III.38. *Wall frescoes, Newark, New Jersey*

national banners are found in all chambers, and in some they are particularly obvious. At Pittsburgh, two United States flags flank a golden eagle, while city, county, state, and bicentennial banners stand at the sides. At Newark, no fewer than six American flags are on view, plus one municipal banner. At LaSalle a single large American flag hangs above the mayor, the place to which all solemnly look as they make the pledge of allegiance at the commencement of each council session (photo III.25). From the standpoint of right-hand superiority, in all rooms where the American flag is displayed along with other banners, the national emblem is always at the presider's right, as called for by the Flag Code.

A flag is what Gusfield would call a "cohesive" symbolic gesture, aimed at unifying all those present under a common value system. Other physical symbols also tie people together by virtue of common references. At Baltimore and Milwaukee, copies of historic documents are displayed, such as city charters and copies of the Declaration of Independence. At Cincinnati, one finds a framed "Prayer for a City," by Walter Rauschenbusch of Social Gospel fame (seen on back wall in photo III.28). Paintings or photographs of past mayors are displayed in several chambers, ranging from the prairie town of LaSalle (photo III.25) to historic Newark, America's third oldest city (photo III.38, lower right part of picture). In addition, busts of famous community leaders are sometimes displayed, as in Savannah and Trenton (photo III.37). At Cincinnati a small statue of Cincinnatus gazes upon the proceedings from the middle of the chamber floor (photo III.39).

In addition to documents and pictures, one finds a fascinating assortment of miscellaneous physical objects that may also be thought of as cohesive in their symbolic impact. Often they are historical or simply old looking. Exhibited at Savannah are models

Photo III.39. *Statue of Cincinnatus, Cincinnati, Ohio*

of a steamship and a cruiser named after the city. At New York a colonial flag dating from 1625 is framed beneath the baldachin (photo III.2). Standing in one corner at Milwaukee is a ceremonial chopping block, which is used in destroying matured municipal bonds (photo III.40). On the steps of the rostrum in Philadelphia rests an 18-inch block of black granite; cut from the rock of Devil's Den at Gettysburg, it serves as a memento of that great Civil War battle (photo III.41). Charleston's chamber, the most extreme by far in terms of the objects that are displayed, exhibits a fireman's speaking

Photo III.40. *Chopping block, Milwaukee, Wisconsin*

trumpet dating from 1841, the sword of General P. G. T. Beauregard, four statuary busts ensconced in wall niches, and twenty-nine valuable oil paintings, including one of John Trumbull's portraits of George Washington (photo III.3).

In addition to cohesive symbols, Gusfield's differentiating gestures are also displayed. These perform the function of distinguishing those who possess authority from those who do not. For example, fresh flowers (one of Hitler's symbolic tools) are placed beside the rostrum at San Francisco and on the desks of councilors at Oakland, but not elsewhere in the room. Old spittoons are located adjacent to aldermanic desks in Baltimore, Charleston, and Saint Louis. A pair of wooden voting pans are on hand in Worcester, the kind in which marbles were once placed to blackball somebody. On top of the presider's benches of many rostra are found gavels and accompanying striking plates. These plates are often carved from marble or granite and function

themselves as visible symbols of authority, as illustrated at Cleveland (photo III.14) and Louisville (photo III.42).

That ancient symbol of authority the mace is brought to the chamber when council is in session in at least three cities, all of which are old and eastern. These artifacts differ greatly, however. Philadelphia's mace is like what we picture from the House of Commons or the House of Representatives—a heavy club with a ball and an eagle at the top. The one in Cambridge is a 5-foot white shaft with an eagle at the end, while Baltimore's mace—at the opposite extreme—is a simple wooden dowel, 12 inches long, mounted on the rostrum's secondary bench (visible in the center of photo III.19).

THE AURA OF TRADITION

Let us summarize the Traditional model by describing the elements that create its overall aura. Post–Civil War machine bosses and the urban reformers that followed them

Photo III.41. *Granite block, Philadelphia, Pennsylvania*

built large council chambers, the biggest of which are on the scale of national parliamentary houses. Access to these rooms is by awesome circulation routes leading to the upper floors of city hall, recalling what Greenberg noted in older courthouses. Large windows and doors suggest a sense of openness and project images of power. Within rather chunky proportions of floor space, officials are given great prominence by means of elevated rostrum ensembles and inwardly facing aldermanic desks. The governors, in this setting, confer with themselves, facing each other; the governed, for their part, are treated as spectators, set beyond a 3-foot balustrade or fence and confined to upstairs galleries. There, citizens sit on benches or simple chairs as an undifferentiated mass in contrast to the high-backed chairs and protected positions that officials occupy in the open floor space below. Administrative subordinates and members of the press corps, meanwhile, are admitted to the official zone but are relegated to inferior furniture. As a final touch, this scene of hi-

erarchy and discrimination is dignified by an ornate ceiling overhead and wood paneling along the walls. These surfaces are decorated by a proliferation of Neoclassical architectural details; also visible are objects that invoke the past, celebrate a common heritage, and identify those with power.

In short, the Traditional chamber expresses values of superior, wise, and unquestioned governmental authority, exercised unilaterally on a pliant people with the blessings of past precedent. While this aura is not, of course, seen in its full meaning by all who enter the Traditional chamber, aspects of it do not escape the sensitive observer. Persons whom I casually interviewed about these spaces volunteered such comments as: "Visitors are awed by the dignity of this place" (Springfield); "The room's formality makes people behave" (Bay City); "You feel the past and present come together in this place" (Bay City); "Speaking to the council in this chamber is very intimidating" (Oakland); "Loud activist groups always quiet down when they come into this

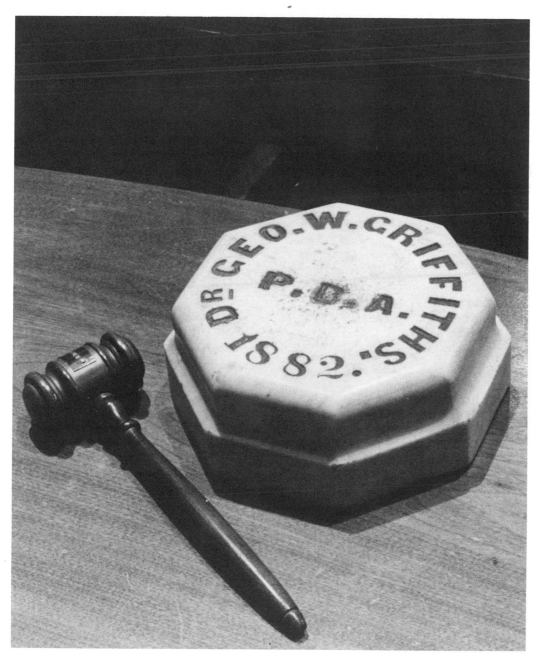

Photo III.42. *Gavel and striking plate, Louisville, Kentucky*

chamber" (Milwaukee); and "The old painting and sculpture add an air of decorum to the discussion" (Charleston). Even though the Traditional chamber is the outmoded record of what is now a long-ago past in American architecture and governance, it still exerts an attitudinal impact on contemporary users—and one that may not be too different from what was felt originally.

IV The Midcentury Chamber: Confronted Authority

What I am calling the Midcentury city-council chamber was built during the four decades after World War I, more specifically between 1920 and 1960. Compared to the Traditional chamber, it is simpler, more modest, less hierarchical, more corporate, and less segregationist. Rather than presenting the relationship between governors and governed as one of superiors imposing their authority on inferiors, it suggests a relationship of bilateral interaction between officials and citizens. Authority is not merely imposed; it also confronts and is confronted by those over whom it is exercised.

THE SOCIAL AND ARCHITECTURAL SETTING

The year 1920 is pivotal for our subject. In his review of the history of city halls in the United States, Lebovich points out that the 1920 census was the first one to show that a majority of Americans were living in cities.[1] This shift signaled a momentous transition in the nature of American society and in the role of cities in subnational governance. In an urbanized population the municipality is not merely one of several units of local government; it is also the crucial enforcer of public order, the provider of public service, and the symbol of community life.

In municipal architecture, as Lebovich points out, the 1920s mark the beginnings of a break from classic European traditions. Although Neoclassical, revivalist, and Beaux-Arts city halls did not suddenly go out of style, an increasing number of public buildings exhibited New World themes. These include the celebration of the colonial past, as in American Georgian revivalism;

the assertion of an exuberant anticlassicism, as in art-deco decor; and the recognition of ethnic and regional traditions, as in Spanish colonial architecture.

The depression deeply affected American public architecture. Despite diminished municipal revenues, much public construction continued in order to create jobs. The emergence of New Deal programs such as the Works Progress Administration (WPA) and the Public Works Administration (PWA) made the federal government an important factor in the funding of local public-building projects. Some new city halls were particularly monumental, reflecting in a way the larger role of government in society that was contemplated by the New Deal. Skyscraper-height municipal buildings began to appear on American cityscapes for the first time, a point that the late Harold Lasswell would certainly have wanted to note as part of the New Deal's "signature of power."

During World War II, the construction of city halls ceased, for all practical purposes. In the postwar period, contrary to the fears of many, the country was not reimmersed in a depression but instead experienced unprecedented economic growth and prosperity. The cities prospered too, but in ways that did not lead to an immediate resurgence in the construction of downtown city halls. Because of federal subsidies to middle-class housing and highway construction, suburbanization replaced urbanization as the principal manifestation of municipal growth. This meant that city centers declined in relative importance, while suburban ring communities developed and incorporated, eventually needing new city halls of their own. Meanwhile, no incentive existed to replace older municipal buildings.

It is not surprising, then, that the older city halls became cramped for space as the responsibilities and programs of urban government expanded during the postwar era. Contributing also to space shortages was the growth in the bureaucracy that was traceable to civil-service professionalization and the city-manager movement. As a consequence, bureaucratic administration now competed with civic ceremony as a user of valuable city-hall space. A frequent result was remodeling: quite commonly, council space was carved up to acquire more office space. The historic-preservation movement had not yet come on the scene to counter this tendency, and many older surfaces and appointments were modernized in a pedestrian manner. Our twenty-two Midcentury chambers therefore are classified as such not only if they were originally built between 1920 and 1960 but also if they were extensively remodeled during that era.

A list of the twenty-two chambers is given in table IV.1. The Midcentury room with the earliest origins is that of Maryland's capital in Annapolis. Exterior portions of the building that presently house the chamber date from 1767–68. The original structure was a municipal ballroom which witnessed, among other events, sessions of the colonial legislature, the entertainment of General Washington by the Continental Congress, and occupation by Union troops in the Civil War. In 1867 the structure was raised to two stories, and in 1934 a council chamber was built within, the decoration of which is reminiscent of an eighteenth-century ballroom. In 1983, limited redecoration occurred, without violating the original ambience (see photo IV.1).

Another chamber that has relatively early origins is in Alexandria, Virginia. The oldest parts of Alexandria's city hall date from the period 1871–73; the chamber as

seen today was constructed in 1945. Visually dominating the Alexandria space is a 10-by-13-foot sepia-tint lithograph of the city as it appeared in 1863, which gives the room a nineteenth-century atmosphere (photo IV.2).

Many Midcentury chambers are in city halls whose exteriors are styled in classic European architectural traditions. Of these, some are in old buildings that antedate 1920. San Antonio's city hall is an ornate Italian Renaissance structure that was constructed on the city's venerable Plaza de Armas between 1888 and 1891. Its chamber was built in 1927 and was remodeled during the 1950s. The Berkeley, California, chamber is housed in the "old" Berkeley city hall, a Beaux-Arts structure designed by Bakewell and Brown, the team that was responsible for San Francisco's city hall. The present configuration of this room dates from the 1950s, although a 10-by-16-foot mural was added in 1973, which gives the space a conflictive air (photo IV.3). Two other Beaux-Arts city halls, both completed in 1911, are found at Sacramento, California, and Des Moines, Iowa (for an exterior view of the latter building see photo I.4). The Sacramento chamber was remodeled in 1939 and again in 1959. The one in Des Moines was remodeled in 1950, after the form of municipal government was converted from the "Des Moines Plan" of city commission to the city-manager form.

As for classical buildings constructed after 1920, the massive City and County Building in Denver possesses a curved semicircular façade that features a centered Georgian Revival portico. Behind this portico is the council chamber, unchanged in decor since 1932 but importantly altered with respect to furniture placement in 1970. A full-blown Georgian Revival city hall is found in Schenectady, New York. Designed by McKim, Mead, and White, this building possesses an early-American air, and its

TABLE IV.1
The Twenty-two Midcentury Chambers Included in this Study

CHAMBER	DATE BUILT
Alexandria (Va.) City Hall	1945 (building, 1871–73)
Annapolis (Md.) Municipal Building	1934 (exterior, 1767–68)
Berkeley (Calif.) Old City Hall	1950s (building, 1908–9)
Buffalo (N.Y.) City Hall	1929–31
Charleston (W. Va.) City Hall	1921–22
Charlotte (N.C.) City Hall	1924 (repeatedly modified)
Chicago (Ill.) City Hall	1958 (building, 1906–11)
College Park (Md.) City Hall	1959
Denver (Colo.) City and County Building	1929–32 (rearranged in 1970)
Des Moines (Iowa) City Hall	1950 (building, 1910–11)
Duluth (Minn.) City Hall	1927–28
Honolulu (Hawaii) City Hall	1929 (remodeled in 1960)
Houston (Tex.) City Hall	1938/39
Kansas City (Mo.) City Hall	1935–37
Los Angeles (Calif.) City Hall	1926–28
Madison (N.J.) Hartley Dodge Memorial	1935
Minneapolis (Minn.) City Hall–Courthouse	1950s (building, 1889–1905)
Pasadena (Calif.) City. Hall	1926–27
Sacramento (Calif.) City Hall	1939, 1959 (building, 1909–11)
Saint Paul (Minn.) City Hall and Ramsey County Courthouse	1930–32
San Antonio (Tex.) City Hall	1927, 1950s (building, 1888–91)
Schenectady (N.Y.) City Hall	1930–31

chamber reminds one of the meeting room of the New York Board of Estimate (photo IV.4)

Other classically styled city halls are in Italian Renaissance buildings in Charleston, West Virginia, and Duluth, Minnesota; a Beaux-Arts edifice in Charlotte, North Carolina; and a Greek-revivalist temple in Madison, New Jersey. Duluth's city hall is notable in that it is positioned in a City Beautiful–style cluster of public buildings designed by Daniel Burnham, although Burnham's design for the municipal build-ing itself was rejected in favor of the plans of a local architect. The construction of Madison's elegantly crafted granite-and-marble edifice, which was completed in 1935, provided income for many unemployed laborers and craftsmen. The finished building was presented to the borough of Madison by Geraldine Rockefeller Dodge in honor of her deceased son; hence it is officially known as the Hartley Dodge Memorial.

Capturing the spirit of America's Spanish-colonial past is the city hall at

Photo IV.1. *Council chamber, Annapolis, Maryland*

Photo IV.2. *Council chamber, Alexandria, Virginia*

Photo IV.3. *Council chamber, Berkeley, California*

Photo IV.4. *Council chamber, Schenectady, New York*

Pasadena, California, also designed by Bakewell and Brown. The building surrounds an open courtyard, and its council chamber exudes a Mediterranean flavor.[2] Another Spanish-style building in the sample is the city-county building in Honolulu, which is affectionately called the Hale ("home" in Hawaiian). It incorporates an Italian Renaissance court and is faced with art stone made from Hawaiian sand.

Four Midcentury chambers are in buildings that reflect an art-deco influence. These were built during the 1930s and have been untouched by remodeling or rearrangement. The chamber in Buffalo, a masterpiece of art-deco decoration, is interwoven by Indian motifs and is furnished with amphitheater-style seating. The Saint Paul City Hall and Ramsey County Courthouse in Minnesota features an elaborately decorated interior that was described as Zigzag Moderne at the time of construction in 1932.[3] Houston's city hall, which was half-financed by PWA funds, possesses a round-cornered chamber paneled with blond walnut and detailed in light metals.[4] The Kansas City, Missouri, City Hall is basically Beaux-Arts but is replete with art-deco touches; built during the twilight years of the Pendergast machine, it was taken over shortly after its completion by civic reformers who made Kansas City one of the best-known homes of the city-manager form of government.[5]

As I have mentioned, 1930s-era city halls were often tall. At Buffalo, a twenty-eight story tower soars upward from a massive base with successive setbacks. From Saint Paul's stereobate rises a nineteen-story shaft; the tower at Houston reaches ten floors, and the one at Kansas City, thirty floors. An even higher, as well as more massive, municipal building is found in Los Angeles, where the city hall's 452-foot tower extends from a white granite base that is 476 feet long and 250 feet wide. A sizeable council chamber at the front of the base

features vaguely Romanesque and Spanish-colonial styling, not the art-deco influences that mark the chambers of other municipal skyscrapers.[6]

In two cases from our Midcentury sample we encounter an interesting paradox: the presence of avant-garde chambers buried by remodeling within particularly old buildings. The city hall–courthouse in Minneapolis is a block-sized Richardsonian Romanesque structure built between 1889 and 1905. Its original council chamber was renovated during the 1920s by the installation of false ceilings and inset walls within the original shell. Then, in the 1950s, still another chamber-within-a-chamber was created when a second layer of ceiling and walls was inserted, making the space even smaller. A similar but less drastic reduction took place at the combined city hall–county courthouse in Chicago, a Beaux-Arts edifice constructed from 1906 to 1911. After the original chamber was gutted by fire in 1957, Mayor Richard J. Daley's administration had it rebuilt with angled and curved surfaces set out from the old boxlike walls.[7] Thus, in their design properties, the Minneapolis and Chicago chambers must be said to date from the 1950s. Moreover, they prefigure what was to come even later.

SPACE COMPOSITION AT MIDCENTURY

The space of the Midcentury chamber is, in comparison to its Traditional predecessor, smaller, lower, and longer. It is also laid out in a radically different way.

The Long Box

The largest Midcentury room is the 54-by-104-foot chamber in Los Angeles, whose floor area is 5,616 square feet; the smallest is Charlotte's 24-by-40 space, with 960 square feet. As table IV.2 shows, the mean floor area for all twenty-two chambers in the Midcentury sample is 2,406 square feet. For the Traditional rooms, the comparable figure was 2,906 square feet. Thus, the average square footage declined between the two eras by exactly 500 square feet, a drop of 17 percent. By comparing the data in tables III.2 and IV.2, one can see that this smaller size, as measured in absolute terms, obtains for cities in all three classes of size. Such reduction in size is not consistently true when one measures floor area on a per capita basis, however. A comparison of the two tables indicates that the two eras are, amazingly, identical in square footage per 10,000 population on an aggregate basis—namely, 6.1. Yet when city size is considered, the equivalence ends. Probably as a consequence of suburbanization, small cities provide considerably more floor space per capita in the Midcentury period, while medium and big cities do not have as much. Indeed, the four big Midcentury cities of Buffalo, Chicago, Los Angeles, and Minneapolis provide only 2.6 square feet per 1,000 residents, or approximately one-fourth less than their Traditional counterparts. It is important to point out that the Midcentury sample contains no truly big chambers. No room in the sample comes close, for example, to a Milwaukee-sized chamber, which is as big as the House of Representatives in Washington. The two largest, Los Angeles and Chicago, are more on the scale of the United States Senate. The third-largest Midcentury room, at Honolulu, is in the range of the House of Commons and is the only one in that category.

Further comparison of tables III.2 and IV.2 shows that ceilings have dropped substantially. The height of Midcentury rooms averages 21.4 feet. This compares to 30.2 in the Traditional sample, a reduction of 29 percent. This reduction pertains for all sizes of city, and as a consequence, the total spatial volume drops significantly—from

around 88,500 cubic feet during the Traditional period to about 57,000 in the Midcentury one, a decline of 36 percent. Only three chambers, those of Buffalo, Kansas City, and Los Angeles, possess ceilings that rise above the United States Congress's height of 36 feet, and only the volume of Los Angeles is on a parliamentary scale; at 204,000 cubic feet it is midway between the House of Commons and the United States Senate.

Let us conjecture as to reasons for this significant decrease in chamber size. At least three factors seem to be involved. First, the upstairs public gallery is for all practical purposes eliminated from the Midcentury chamber. Without a gallery, 10 to 20 feet can be lopped off the top of a civic space with no loss in the square footage of floor area. Only Chicago and Kansas City have any kind of upstairs seating; even there, Chicago's gallery is closed off by glass and hence is not really integral to the room, and in Kansas City the upper space is more in the form of a theater balcony than an old-fashioned gallery. Even without galleries, the average public-seating capacity remains about the same between the two eras, just under 150.

A likely second factor in the decrease of size is the previously mentioned demand for more office space in municipal bureaucracies. Lowering the ceiling height from 30 to 20 feet can itself create thousands more feet of office space, by having the chamber occupy one or two stories, rather than two or three. The third factor is also practical in nature. As I have mentioned, many Midcentury chambers were originally built during the Traditional period and were later remodeled. In such reconstruction, it was common to install false ceilings so as to accommodate new airducts and wiring. These were typically made of ordinary acoustical tile, flush-fitted with fluorescent lamps. In Charlotte and San Antonio, the hung ceiling

TABLE IV.2
The Midcentury Chamber: Measures of Size

	Small Cities (N=9)	Medium Cities (N=9)	Big Cities (N=4)	All Cities (N=22)
Mean floor area (sq. ft.)	2,021	2,130	3,892	2,406
Mean floor area per 1,000 population (sq. ft.)	44.5	8.1	2.6	6.1
Mean ceiling height (ft.)	17.6	21.8	29.2	21.4
Mean spatial volume (cu. ft.)	37,486	49,345	118,193	57,011
Mean audience seating capacity	94	142	269	145
Mean number of seats per 10,000 population	20.6	5.4	1.8	3.7

Note: City size is based on the approximate population at the time the chamber was built. Small is under 100,000; medium is 100,000 to 500,000; big is over 500,000.

is a mere 10 feet off the floor, creating an almost claustrophobic atmosphere.

As for shape, the Midcentury chamber in general retains the boxlike, static composition of the Traditional room. Floors are usually flat horizontal surfaces. Walls are flat vertical surfaces, set perpendicularly to each other. Ceilings tend to be flat in remodeled rooms; this also is the case in many original spaces, with a few exceptions such as a semigabled roof in Honolulu and a shallow barrel vault in Schenectady.

Three of the Midcentury rooms are definitely not boxlike, however. Buffalo, Chicago, and Minneapolis stand out, not so much as exceptions to Midcentury practice, but as forerunners of an era to come. As I

have mentioned, the art-deco chamber in Buffalo possesses amphitheater seating, which recalls the later bouleuterion of Athens and antedates the Contemporary model (photo IV.5). The room is roughly semicircular in shape, with banked, concave rows of seating that face a well below. The rooms in Chicago and Minneapolis, which consist of remodeled inner shells, are also rounded. In Chicago a series of flowing surfaces is set within the old static box of the original chamber (photo IV.6). The walls in Minneapolis are canted inward at 10 degrees; also a domed artificial skylight overhangs the official zone, creating a sense of drama and intimacy (photo IV.7).

Apart from these atypical rooms, how-

Photo IV.5. *Council chamber, Buffalo, New York*

Photo IV.6. *Council chamber, Chicago, Illinois*

Photo IV.7. *Council chamber, Minneapolis, Minnesota*

ever, the Midcentury civic space is again boxlike. The Midcentury box is shaped differently from the Traditional box, however. Rather than being squarelike or chunky, it tends to be long and narrow. Rectangularity is a hallmark of Midcentury floor plans. All are much longer than they are wide, with the exception of Charleston, which was built just after the Midcentury era began. The length of the major axis is at least double that of the minor axis in thirteen of these twenty-two rooms, for all practical purposes. None of the spaces, except in Charleston, is materially below the golden-section criterion of proportionality.

Two of these long boxes bear special mention. The Los Angeles chamber appears even longer and narrower than its outside dimensions would suggest, because of a colonnade on each side (photo IV.8). The result is a churchlike clerestory effect, with side aisles and a middle nave 84 feet long and 38 feet wide. A civic activist who has addressed the Los Angeles council on numerous occa-

sions has confided that walking down that long aisle to speak before the council is a highly intimidating experience.[8] The room in Saint Paul also seems to be particularly extruded. Its overall dimensions are 36 by 75 feet, but a sense of narrowness is accentuated by side-wall insets at the two ends of the room and by four columns in between (photo IV.9). These elements narrow the space to 25 feet, creating the impression of a 3:1 ratio of length to width. An added distinctive feature of the Saint Paul chamber is the location of the official zone. It is in the center of the room, between two public zones, thus causing it to become a kind of isolated island surrounded by a sea of audience.

The more typical zoning pattern in Midcentury chambers is to locate the official zone at one end of the long rectangle. The public zone then consists of the remainder of the floor area. The zonal boundary is usually a straight line that crosses the space at a 90-degree angle from one side wall to the

Photo IV.8. *Chamber of the city council, Los Angeles, California*

Photo IV.9. *Council chamber, Saint Paul, Minnesota*

other. Thus the two zones directly abut each other, approximately in the middle of the room, making the spatial division between the two an obvious and central aspect of the room. The result is a pattern of bisected segregation between the governors and the governed that gives approximately equal terms to each side. Moreover, since the governors are turned around in the Midcentury room so that they face the audience, this segregation lays the basis for direct confrontation between the people and the officials.

In short, the spatial composition of the Midcentury chamber does not place the public at the periphery or upstairs, as in the Traditional room, but on the same horizontal plane as officials and on an equal footing with them. The governors are located at one end of a rectangular space; the governed at the other. An oppositional spatial relationship is created, in the manner outlined by Doxtater.

Just Another Room

How is the Midcentury chamber placed in city hall? We recall that in Traditional municipal buildings the chamber is deliberately located so as to endow the room with heightened importance. It is positioned at the top floors of the building, often in a location that corresponds with the principal features of the building's external façade. Circulatory access to the chamber is typically up a grand staircase through a rotunda or court. Although in a few Midcentury city halls we encounter these same features, in general a very different pattern of placement and access obtains. First of all, the council chamber is usually located, not at the top of the building, but somewhere in its middle. In Charlotte, Des Moines, Pasadena, and Schenectady, the chamber is on the second floor of a three-story structure. In the four-story city halls at Charleston, Duluth, Honolulu, and San Antonio, the

chamber is on the second or third floor. In the five-story Minneapolis building, the twice-remodeled chamber is reached by a newly created mezzanine, which has been inserted between the old third and fourth floors. As for the remodeled Chicago chamber, it occupies the second and third floors of an eleven-story building; the prefabricated girders that support the eight stories above the chamber's ceiling each weigh forty-four tons and were considered an engineering marvel of their time.

The newer skyscrapers, without exception, do not give the uppermost floor of honor over to the council. In Houston, the council chamber is on the second of ten floors; in Saint Paul, on the third of eighteen; and in Los Angeles, the third of twenty-three. At Buffalo the chamber is exactly halfway to the top, on the thirteenth and fourteenth floors of a twenty-eight-story structure. In the highest city hall that I studied, Kansas City's thirty-story tower, the chamber is on the twenty-sixth and twenty-seventh floors. Above it were, when the building was new, the city attorney (twenty-eighth floor), the mayor and the city manager (twenty-ninth), and the observation deck (thirtieth).

With the council chamber now demoted from top-floor status, it is also less often in a conspicuous or central part of the floor plan. Typically the room merely occupies one side, wing, or corner of the building, as if possessing no special importance. In Pasadena, for example, the chamber occupies the southeastern corner of the second floor; in Alexandria, the southwestern corner of the second floor; in Des Moines, the southern end of the middle floor. In Annapolis, College Park, and Charlotte, the chamber is located at the back of the building, on the second floor. Although in Houston the chamber's windows face out to Hermann Square, the importance of the inside space is not discernible from the square. A similar situation obtains in Berkeley and Saint Paul. As for the huge city halls in Buffalo, Chicago, Kansas City, Minneapolis, and Los Angeles, as well as lesser buildings in Charleston, Duluth, Honolulu, Sacramento, and San Antonio, the location of the council chamber can in no way be deduced externally or rationalized internally. It is simply tucked away somewhere inside the structure's mass and is locatable only by consulting a room directory or by making inquiries. The only exceptions to this practice are Denver, Madison, and Schenectady, where the chamber is behind a Neoclassical portico that is centered on the outside of the building.

With respect to stairs, the principle in these Midcentury city halls—both large and small—is reliance on basic, utilitarian flights that extend upward through closed stairwells. While it is true that enclosed, plain stairs are cheaper to build and safer from the standpoint of fire, they do not prepare the ascender for what to expect above. All that is encountered when one arrives at the chamber's floor is a plain corridor, since the room's main entrance is usually not at the head of the stairs. To find it, one must advance left or right down a nondescript hallway. When the portal is located, it is usually not highlighted architecturally, although Madison and Schenectady are again exceptions. More typical are the simple entrances in Kansas City (photo IV.10) and Chicago (photo IV.11). On council-meeting days, Chicago's entrance is "enhanced" by an airport-type metal detector, which is brought in for security reasons.

In the taller Midcentury city halls, access to the council chamber is intended to be by elevator. The absolute height of ascension to these civic spaces is much greater than in Traditional city halls, but the medium of a closed elevator cab creates an experience of efficient transportation, not reverential inspiration. This means that the elevator

lobby below becomes important as circulation space, and it is here that self-conscious civic displays tend to be concentrated. In lobby space at Buffalo, Houston, Kansas City, and Saint Paul, we are treated to carvings, statuary, walls in various hues of marble, terrazzo floors, allegorical murals, historical paintings, civic slogans, and gigantic city seals executed in metal. Frequently the elevator doors in the lobby, now the funnel for most building traffic, are also decorated, as historical motifs in Saint Paul exemplify (photo IV.12).

In some cases, circulation space on the main floor takes on truly monumental proportions. In Saint Paul the vast War Memorial Hall connects to the elevator lobby. The space is 85 feet long and rises to a height of three stories, is executed in black marble with a gold-leaf ceiling, and is dominated at one end by a tall floodlit onyx statue of the "Indian God of Peace." In the Des Moines municipal building a giant "counting room" traverses the main axis of the ground floor; its open character was intended to symbolize the climate of open government established by the Des Moines Commission plan, which was instituted at the same time the building was designed. The Los Angeles City Hall, probably the most flamboyant of the period, boasts a large main portal, which is entered from an extensive forecourt. Above its decorated bronze doors is the inscription "Righteousness Exalteth a People's Solomon." Just inside is a shrine dedicated to the Declaration of Independence and the Constitution (photo IV.13).

Reduced Perforation

I have mentioned that the Midcentury chamber's main door, as viewed from outside the room, is typically nondescript. As seen from the inside, it is not much more impressive. Whereas in the Traditional chamber, public entrances are decorated

Photo IV.10. *Entrance to chamber, Kansas City, Missouri*

Photo IV.11. *Entrance to chamber, Chicago, Illinois*

Photo IV.12. *Elevator door, Saint Paul, Minnesota*

Photo IV.13. *Lobby shrine, Los Angeles, California*

and are 9 to 10 feet high, Midcentury doorways are 7 or 8 feet tall and are considerably
more plain. Those that are decorated tend to
be modestly so, such as Charleston's Neoclassical walnut doorway and Houston's
public entrance, which is enhanced by
nickel tablets and a civic slogan overhead
(photos IV.14 and IV.15).

Modifications that have been made in the
Honolulu chamber over time illustrate these
utilitarian tendencies vividly. When built in
1929, it had no less than five frontal entrances facing a balcony. Each was bordered
by columns and surmounted by a semicircular fanlight. All arched openings, as well as
the doors themselves, were fitted with clear
glass. When the chamber was remodeled in
1960, four of the doorways were permanently closed, and their glass was heavily

draped. All public traffic now enters
through a single secure door. The once light,
airy, and accessible Honolulu chamber is
now a confined and secure inner room.

An interesting change occurs between
eras with respect to the private door used by
officials. As we recall, the private doors of
the Traditional room usually communicate
to the halls outside from the public zone. In
Midcentury spaces they do so from the official zone. One explanation of this shift
would be that once the public had been
brought downstairs, a more controlled escape path for officials was necessary. Indeed, I discovered a nicely hidden private
door in Madison (photo IV.16). On other occasions the private door is quite obvious: at
Des Moines it is exceedingly prominent because of its central placement in the back-

Photo IV.14. *Public doorway, Charleston, West Virginia*

Photo IV.15. *Public doorway, Houston, Texas*

drop, just behind the mayor (fig. IV.1). Another explanation, less conspiratorial, is that since the zonal barrier now bisects the chamber, it does not isolate the officials near the middle of the room; it is convenient to allow them ingress and egress at their own end of the floor (note doors in the background at Berkeley, photo IV.3).

The great, tall windows that were common during the Traditional period are all but gone in the Midcentury chamber. Only Los Angeles, with thirteen 10-foot windows, and to a lesser degree Houston, with three 20-foot ones, compare to the Traditional room's capacity to be bathed in natural light. Except for these cases, the number of windows is restricted in both number and size. On an all-sample basis, the average number of windows in Midcentury chambers is 4.7, just over half the Traditional mean of 8.0. Mean fenestration area per room drops from the Traditional sample's 675 square feet to 269, a decline of 60 percent. Even those Midcentury chambers that

look out on a square or under a portico do so with puny openings compared to what was found in the fenestrated façades of the past. Norberg-Schulz's depiction of some windows as mere holes begins to ring true.

Furthermore, most Midcentury windows are translucently or opaquely covered, reducing or even entirely eliminating their ability to admit light and thus be visually open. The coverings used include venetian blinds (see Annapolis and Schenectady, in photos IV.1 and IV.4), grillwork or translucent glass (Buffalo, photo IV.5), and translucent curtains (Los Angeles, photo IV.8). Fully opaque drapes cover all or most window areas in Charlotte, Denver, Des Moines, Pasadena, San Antonio, and Saint Paul (photo IV.9). The three remodeled rooms in Chicago, Minneapolis, and Sacramento have no windows whatsoever, unless one counts light-shaft openings in the back of Chicago's closed gallery (visible in photo IV.6).

Photo IV.16. *Concealed doorway, Madison, Wisconsin*

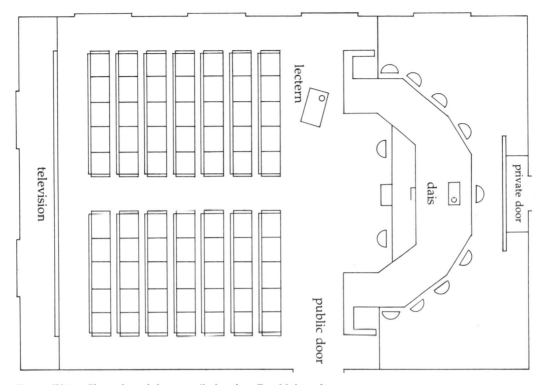

Figure IV.1. *Floor plan of the council chamber, Des Moines, Iowa*

SEMIFIXED FEATURES IN MIDCENTURY CHAMBERS

Let us now examine the design and the arrangement of the semifixed features in the Midcentury chamber. Traditional rooms include a dominating rostrum assembly, separated aldermanic desks, and various devices for segregation and subordination. How do Midcentury chambers differ?

Emergence of the Dais

The most important and most obvious change in feature composition that takes place around 1920 is the emergence of the dais. The word *dais* here means a common table at which all elected officials sit together, including both the members of the council and the presiding officer, whether mayor or council president. In its "pure"

form—attained to the fullest degree in the Contemporary chamber, but definitely emergent in the Midcentury room—we find the following combination of features: (1) the seating of the entire council at one table, the dais, which is roughly concave in form; (2) the placement of all officials on the exterior perimeter of this dais; (3) the central placement of this dais at one end of a rectangular room, with the concave opening facing the seated public at the opposite end; (4) the use around the dais of utilitarian, nonceremonial chairs, each of which is equivalent in design; (5) the placement of the table and the chairs on a low platform; and (6) the incorporation of backdrops that direct attention to the council as a whole, rather than to the presiding officer alone. The arrangement at Houston is a classic example (fig. IV.2).

In Traditional chambers the dais concept

was never installed originally, although it was adopted later in a few instances. In the Midcentury era, by contrast, we find its deployment in a majority of instances. Eight of the twenty-two Midcentury rooms use the dais system in its pure form, with six others doing so in almost pure form. Four additional chambers depart from the dais system significantly but do not follow the Traditional pattern. The four remaining chambers are cast in the earlier Traditional mold. The eight pure examples are Alexandria (photo IV.2), Berkeley (photo IV.3), Charlotte, College Park, Houston, Des Moines, Pasadena, and San Antonio. The six nearly pure illustrations are Annapolis (photo IV.1), Minneapolis (photo IV.7), Saint Paul (photo IV.9), Denver, Duluth, and Sacramento. The principal imperfections in these six latter systems are: (1) the side-by-side abutment of separate councilor desks, rather than the use of an integrated table (Annapolis, Denver, Minneapolis); and (2) giving the presider a slightly higher desk surface than the rest of council (Denver, Duluth, Sacramento).

All of these dais systems are placed on an elevated platform, or podium, the height of which (i.e., the level on which councilors' chairs rest) varies from 5 to 24 inches, with a mean of about 11 inches. In half the cases the platform is comparable to one step, and in the other half it is the equivalent of two steps. The only platform that is higher than 15 inches is at San Antonio, where four steps must be climbed to reach a 2-foot-high podium. For purposes of comparison, the podium height for Traditional rostra was 6 to 48 inches, with an average of 21. While the average upward sight-line angle in Traditional rooms was about 4 degrees, in this group of rooms it is about 2 degrees.

These platforms usually cover only the floor area directly behind the dais. This means that the front skirt of the dais drops all the way to floor level. The layouts at Des Moines and Houston illustrate this (figs.

IV.1 and IV.2). This point is significant, because it means that by incorporating the height of the platform, the skirt of the dais displays a greater vertical height than is required by the internal height of the table's writing surface (usually 29–30 inches). Adding further to the skirt's height is its top parapet, or vertically extended edge, which rises above the writing surface. As a consequence of these combined factors, dais skirts range from 29 to 44 inches in height, averaging 39. Comparable figures for the Traditional rostrum bench were in a range of 30 to 64 inches and a mean of 46. Hence, despite these augmenting factors, the Midcentury dais tends to be lower than the traditional rostrum.

With respect to other dimensions, the concave dais is usually 20–25 feet long by chord, or straight-line, measurement, thus presenting a considerably broader visual image than did the Traditional rostrum bench (whose mean length was 11 feet). Still, the running length of the perimeter of the outside curve where the councilors sit may be as much as 50 feet or more. The straight-line depth of the dais ranges from 5 to 15 feet, depending on how radical the curve is. The writing surfaces of daises are typically 24 to 32 inches deep, allowing enough room to accommodate the users' forearms and normal tabletop activities.

The precise ways in which these daises describe a concave arc differ widely. The gently rounded table at Berkeley illustrates the simple curvilinear approach (photo IV.3). A nonuniform but symmetrical arc is found in Sacramento (fig. IV.3); a much deeper U-shaped form occurs in Saint Paul and Houston (fig. IV.2); and various rectilinear versions of the U are located in Des Moines (fig. IV.1), Minneapolis (photo IV.7), Charlotte (photo IV.17), and Pasadena (photo IV.18). Despite their differences, all of these dais forms are symmetrical, with a clear midpoint. That midpoint is not unduly

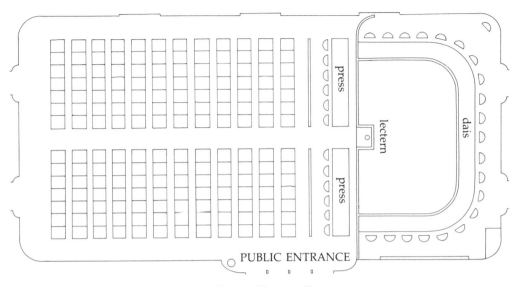

Figure IV.2.   *Floor plan of the city-council room, Houston, Texas*

prominent because of the rounded form, except in an occasional V-shaped table, such as in San Antonio. This means that when the presider is seated at the midpoint—which is almost always the case—his or her person is focused upon but is not unduly accentuated.

Indeed, the dais as a semifixed feature of the Midcentury chamber symbolizes the corporate nature of council governance. The mayor or the president of the council is portrayed as the leader of a body of which he or she is a full member. Gone is the segregated republican monarch, reigning from an isolated throne, as in Traditional rostra. Furthermore, all members of the body sit together, grouped about a common, unifying piece of furniture that connects them in a consistent way. This is true whether the councilors are elected by district or at large. The sociofugal character of segregated aldermanic desks is, in short, abandoned in favor of a more sociopetal arrangement, which bonds the elected officials together as a single legislative forum. In proxemic terms, the councilors are separated from their immediate neighbors by inches rather

than feet; as Hall would say, they are now able to communicate within the confines of intimate space, or at least casual-personal distance. By contrast, Traditional aldermanic desks were separated by social-consultative or even public distance.

The notion of corporateness is expressed as well in the councilors' chairs. Usually the presiding officer is furnished a chair that in pretentiousness and height is identical to those given to all other members of the council (exceptions are Annapolis, Denver, Duluth, Minneapolis, and San Antonio). Moreover, this standard chair is hardly ever a ceremonial sedile or throne; instead, it is a solid and perfectly utilitarian seat. It normally swivels and is handsomely but not ostentatiously covered in fabric or leather (visible in photos IV.2, IV.3, IV.6, IV.7, IV.9, IV.17, and IV.18).

Because council meetings often go on for hours and even late into the night, bodily comfort is very important in council chairs. This factor motivates cities to purchase equipment that seems expensive to the ordinary householder. Such a matter makes good press gossip, and at Houston two

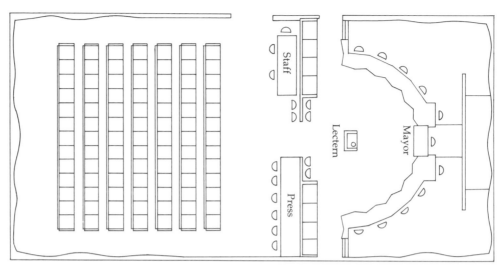

Figure IV.3.   *Floor plan of the council chamber, Sacramento, California*

councilors, for political reasons, steadfastly refuse to use their new $1,500 chairs (photo IV.19, left of photo).

From seven to nineteen people sit at the dais, with the most common numbers being nine and eleven. The number is usually odd, allowing for a middle seat and, hence, centrality for the mayor or the council's president. When councilors represent individual districts or wards, the seating order usually counts from right to left, from the presiding officer's perspective, thus making the order left to right from the public's vantage point. Traditional aldermanic desks, we recall, were usually ordered in the opposite direction. Because the natural way for westerners to read is from left to right, it would appear that this itself is evidence of a shift to a more audience-oriented mentality. In Minneapolis, with its tradition of partisan politics, the Continental practice of ideological left-to-right seating is followed—the Democratic Farmer-Labor members are seated at the left bank of desks (presider's perspective), while the Republican and independent members are at the right (photo IV.7).

Behind these daises we find backdrops that symbolize the corporate identity of the community in some way. Backdrops do not sanctify the presiding officer, as in Traditional rostra, and the reredos has disappeared. We have already taken note of the early lithograph at Alexandria and the abstract mural at Berkeley, both of which try to capture an overall sense of community (photos IV.2 and IV.3). City seals are another popular feature; they are found in Annapolis (photo IV.1), Minneapolis (photo IV.7), Charlotte (photo IV.17), College Park, and San Antonio. Blandly utilitarian backdrops are used as well—for example, an electric vote-tallying board at Des Moines, a projection screen at Pasadena (photo IV.18), and an electoral map at Sacramento (photo IV.20). Such items focus attention on the overall task of governance, not on the person of the mayor or council president.

In the pure dais form, the concave opening of the table faces the public. This arrangement occurs in all dais systems except Saint Paul's, where the table faces sideways on its island (photo IV.9). In short, members of the council have been "turned around"; the process of rotation that we saw beginning at Oakland is now complete. The social meaning of this new face-to-face relation-

Photo IV.17. *Dais system, Charlotte, North Carolina*

Photo IV.18. *Dais system, Pasadena, California*

Photo IV.19. *Dais system, Houston, Texas*

Photo IV.20. *Dais system, Sacramento, California*

ship is that the governors are depicted as being engaged with the governed, instead of with each other. The officials are no longer members of a private parliamentary club whose rituals are being observed by outsiders; instead, they are members of an accountable organ of government that is performing under the gaze of assembled citizens. From a behavioral standpoint, the officials and the citizens have each other within their field of vision constantly; this invites oral interaction, mutual relationships, and bilateral confrontation. Such bilateralism comports with and is reinforced by the Midcentury spatial composition of rectangularity: the visual confrontation between the governors and the governed is conducted down the length of a kind of corridor of power.

True, the dais system and its accompanying spatial opposition do not obtain in all Midcentury chambers, although it is the most common pattern. Denver is an instructive variant on this pattern (photo IV.21). Here the room is decidedly rectangular (37 by 72 feet), but the dais runs the length of the room rather than its width. This means that the governors and the governed face each other along the minor axis of the space, not its major one. Prior to 1970 a Traditional aldermanic-desk type of grouping was located at one end of the room. The council's staff director perceived the arrangement as being too closed, however; and therefore he decided to turn the desks around so as to symbolize the councilors' accountability to the public. At the same time the council expanded in size, which would have made a lengthwise oppositional pattern impossible. So instead, the desks were moved to the side of the chamber, abutted against each other, and turned in a gentle, continuous arc facing the audience. The rationale, in the staff director's words, was that "members of council should face the people—those they are responsible to."[9]

I conclude this section with a few words about the semifixed features of those Midcentury rooms where dais systems are used only partially or not at all. In Honolulu and in Kansas City, aldermanic desks face the presiding officer in the Traditional mode, although true rostra are not found. At Madison a kind of rostrum exists, but the councilors sit at a common table placed below it. In Schenectady there is a curved dais, very similar to the one seen in the Pre-Traditional New York Board of Estimate; the councilors do not sit at it, however, but at separate desks grouped back to back in the official zone.

Charleston, Los Angeles, and Buffalo employ orthodox combinations of rostra and aldermanic desks, with Buffalo's Traditionalist semifixed features being in sharp contrast to its avant-garde spatial composition (photo IV.5). As for Chicago, the feature layout is strictly Traditionalist, but the rostrum that Mayor Daley had built for himself is set off against giant black-and-white marble slabs that bring to mind the United Nations General Assembly chamber (photo IV.22). Although this analogy was brought to my attention by city-hall informants, repeated inquiries among Chicago's political observers have not confirmed that a "miniature UN" is what Daley had in mind. The floor in front of this rostrum slopes 5 degrees; this feature, combined with the curved aldermanic benches, makes Chicago join Buffalo in foreshadowing the amphitheater form, which we encounter in the Contemporary room.

Diminishment of the Barrier

As we recall, the Traditional room strictly segregates the governors and the governed. The former are protected behind a fence, and the latter are put upstairs in galleries. In the Midcentury chamber the overtness of this segregation is reduced in several ways, although it is not eliminated.

One important change is to bring the citi-

Photo IV.21. *Dais system, Denver, Colorado*

Photo IV.22. *Rostrum and benches, Chicago, Illinois*

zenry downstairs. In the Midcentury sample, only Kansas City has an upstairs seating area that is integral to the chamber space itself. This means that the governors and the governed are now on basically the same horizontal plane, itself an equalizer of sorts. Furthermore, as already indicated, Midcentury floors tend to be flat, the only exceptions being the inclines at Buffalo and Chicago. We have also found that daises and podiums in Midcentury chambers are lower than their rostrum predecessors. In short, differentials in elevation generally are reduced in Midcentury chambers, thus lessening the degree to which this factor contributes to physical segregation.

Overt barriers on the chamber floor itself also diminish in importance. In the first place, a "fence," in the usual sense of that word, is often omitted. No midfloor barrier whatsoever is found at Annapolis or at Charlotte, for example (photos IV.1 and IV.17); in these spaces, only empty floor space stands between the governors and the governed. Elsewhere, barriers may exist but are relatively nonsegregating. At Alexandria and Sacramento they are obscured by the presence of tables (photos IV.2 and IV.20 and fig. IV.3). At Buffalo a semicircular wall at the base of the amphitheater seating appears less like a barrier than like a retaining wall to keep the audience from falling into the well (photo IV.5). At San Antonio, Minneapolis, and Saint Paul the barricade constitutes not a solid obstacle, but a spindly fence mounted at the edge of the dais platform (photos IV.7 and IV.9). The situation with regard to floor barriers in the Midcentury style remains mixed, however; for example, Traditionalist 3-foot balustrades or fences are seen in Schenectady, Chicago, Pasadena, and Denver (photos IV.4, IV.6, IV.18, and IV.21).

This trend toward the decreased frequency of overt segregation leads to interesting subtleties in dividing the governors

and the governed. One technique is to have blockage performed by features whose primary function has nothing to do with interdiction. At Berkeley, two 3-by-8-foot staff tables are positioned end to end across the zonal boundary, creating an effective demarcation between the officials and the citizens. At Charlotte, the skirt of the dais acts as an effective barrier because its 40-inch height runs from one side of the room to the other; this creates a nonfence barrier of sorts, in that it is not located midfloor and hence is not very noticeable (photo IV.17). A similar arrangement is found at Des Moines, although the skirt does not quite connect with the side walls of the room (photo IV.23 and fig. IV.1).

Front audience benches can be used as disguised barriers. At Los Angeles a rope that hangs across the aisle between the two front benches stops citizen passage, thus in effect placing the seating capacity of these benches within the official zone (photo IV.24). At Duluth the front benches extend to the side walls of the room and their backs drop to the floor, unlike the remaining benches behind them (photo IV.25). This makes the foremost benches seem "off limits" to the casual visitor, giving them a subtle protective role.

The impression that one gets of segregation or its absence derives from combinations of factors, not from the presence or absence of just one feature. At San Antonio the barrier is low and spindly and is appended by press tables, but the combination of an oppressive 10-foot ceiling, an unusually high dais skirt (43 inches), and a sharp V-shaped dais creates an intimidating scene (photo IV.26). San Antonio's dais system is made even more frightening by tall, gooseneck microphones, stern lectern warnings, and the seating of clerks at the "crotch" of the V with their backs turned contemptuously to the speaker (photo IV.27). By contrast, Houston's chamber appears to have all

Photo IV.23. *Council chamber, Des Moines, Iowa*

Photo IV.24. *Official zone, Los Angeles, California*

Photo IV.25. *Audience benches, Duluth, Minnesota*

of the technical ingredients of segregation but nonetheless seems more open. Two barrier walls, not just one, separate the council and the citizens, plus a set of press tables located between the two walls (photo IV.19 and fig. IV.2). Yet the combination of a 25-foot ceiling, upbeat civic slogans on the blond walnut walls, and a 40-inch central aisle that leads straight toward the mayor does much to undo the sense of a protected fortress that might otherwise prevail (photo IV.28).

Speaking of the placement of aisles, we recall from the discussion of Holston's distinction in the previous chapter that the public zone consists of continuous solids, as compared to the official zone's continuous voids. The figurative voids of the public zone are essentially the aisles, hence they take on particular clarity as spatial statements. Moreover, it is in the long and narrow space of the Midcentury chamber that

these pathways acquire potential significance as access routes into a "deep chancel." When aisles penetrate only a few peripheral rows of benches—which is often the case in Traditional rooms—their placement is much less significant.

The layout of aisles is mixed in the Midcentury model. In somewhat over half the rooms, aisles do, in fact, infer accessibility. They vary in width from 30 to 91 inches, averaging 46. They aim in the direction of the presiding officer and hence offer themselves visually as a direct route to power. This is generally achieved by their central placement along the major axis of the space, not merely as exemplified by Houston but also Schenectady, Minneapolis, Los Angeles, Des Moines, and several other cases (photos IV.4, IV.7, IV.8, IV.23, and fig. IV.1). In the semicircular floor plans at Buffalo and Chicago, the aisles are not axial; nonetheless they aim at the presider by

Photo IV.26. *Oblique view of dais system, San Antonio, Texas*

Photo IV.27. *Direct view of dais system, San Antonio, Texas*

Photo IV.28. *Council chamber, Houston, Texas*

constituting approximate radii (photos IV.5 and IV.6). In the remaining Midcentury chambers, aisle placement does not suggest access. At Alexandria, Annapolis, College Park, and Denver, double aisles trisect the audience seating block. These aisles are certainly adequate physically as access routes, but they aim only generally toward the front and not at the presiding officer. In San Antonio, Saint Paul, Charlotte, and Sacramento, no aisles at all cut through the block of seats, thus forcing forward passage to occur along the side walls only (photos IV.9 and IV.17 and fig. IV.3). In this latter group of chambers the continuous solid of seating is not cut by voids except at the margins, ironically making the mass audience itself a subtle barrier to its own participation in governance.

Diminishment of Subordination

We have seen, then, somewhat less segregation in the Midcentury room in comparison to the Traditional one. A parallel trend of diminishment is found in the extent to which citizens and others are portrayed as being subordinate to the members of the council. This is achieved in part by an upgrading of the treatment of citizens in terms of semifixed features. We see this in audience seating, for example. In Traditional chambers, plain wooden benches are the rule; although they are still occasionally to be seen (note photos IV.4, IV.7, IV.8, IV.25, and IV.28), the most common form of Midcentury seating is theater style. Chairs are individual, linked, fixed to the floor, equipped with armrests, and sometimes padded. The seating at Chicago, Charleston, and Des Moines is illustrative (photos IV.6, IV.14, and IV.23). The individualism of separate, unanchored chairs is occasionally permitted as well; this is exemplified by Charlotte (photo IV.17). With the exception of Buffalo's and Chicago's semicircular rows of seats, the seating for audiences in all Midcentury chambers is in straight rows, classroom style.

Enhancement of the citizen's status is also achieved in the Midcentury room by furnishing a more substantial and dignified place from which to address council. The provision of a public lectern of any consequence was comparatively rare in Traditional space. By contrast, Midcentury rooms are equipped with substantial lecterns in almost all cases. At Alexandria and Minneapolis the lectern consists of a tilted reading surface, which is mounted on the barrier (photos IV.2 and IV.7). At Charlotte, Pasadena, Des Moines, and Los Angeles the reading surface is mounted on a freestanding pedestal (photos IV.17, IV.18, IV.23, and IV.24). Solid box-style lecterns are found in Sacramento, Denver, and San Antonio (photos IV.20, IV.21, and IV.26). At Houston a box-style lectern is built into the barrier itself (photo IV.19 and fig. IV.2). At Saint Paul we find the most splendid of Midcentury lecterns, a 28-by-128-inch witness table made of Madagascar ebony and golden padouk wood, inlaid in peanut-grained Hungarian ash (photo IV.29).

Aspects of these lecterns other than their own design features can confer status on the public. Microphones are always furnished, either mounted on the lectern itself or standing nearby. Lecterns may be located in the public zone instead of the official zone, which means that they are in friendly, rather than alien, territory (fig. IV.1). Some are positioned centrally in the room (fig. IV.3); when this is not the case, the audience's right is preferred by a ratio of two to one.

Similarly, the subordination that is imposed on noncouncilor officials, which we saw in the Traditional era, is on the wane in Midcentury chambers. While the few chambers that are still equipped with rostra continue to place clerks at secondary benches, such officials are now likely to sit at the dais itself. This puts them on a par with members of the council. The city clerk or the equivalent sits at the dais in Annapolis, Houston, Minneapolis, Pasadena, Sacramento, and Saint Paul; the city manager does so at Des Moines, Pasadena, and Sacramento. The city attorney or equivalent has a dais position in all of these places save Sacramento.

In several rooms, nonelected officials are given substantial prominence in other ways than a seat at the dais. In Berkeley, College Park, Duluth, and Los Angeles, they sit at large desks or tables that are placed prominently in the official zone. These pieces of furniture are often along the sight lines between the council and the public, suggesting a critical and perhaps mediating role (photos IV.3 and IV.24). In Alexandria, nonelected officials occupy a table that abuts the front of the dais but is six inches lower, indicating substantial status yet a measure of subordination (photo IV.2). This pattern parallels what Rubin found in the Midwest. In Saint Paul, two 26-by-60-inch ebony-and-padouk desks, equivalent in design to the public witness table, are provided for departmental heads; when the room was originally built, a city-commission form of government was in use, and the commissioners wanted their administrative experts nearby (photo IV.29, at right). In Kansas City, where the city-manager movement has been strong since the demise of the Pendergast machine, the manager is dignified by an aldermanic desk all his own (photo IV.30, desk with gooseneck microphone nearest the presiding mayor's right side). In chapter III we saw a similar status accorded to the manager in Cincinnati, another community famous for its use of the city-manager system.

Elsewhere, the clear and overwhelming subordination of nonelected officials re-

Photo IV.29. *Public witness table, Saint Paul, Minnesota*

Photo IV.30. *Council chamber, Kansas City, Missouri*

mains well intact. Simple tables for the staff, set well out of the way of normal sight lines, are provided in Charleston, Denver, Honolulu, and Pasadena. At Buffalo the departmental heads occupy the front row of amphitheater seating (photo IV.5). At Chicago they are confined to a restricted area—or pen, as it is locally known—on the mayor's extreme right (background of photo IV.22). At San Antonio the city manager and the city attorney sit at a table in a corner of the official zone, which cannot be seen by the audience because of pillars and the high dais; when these officials are called upon to speak into their microphones, their voices seem to emanate in ghostly fashion from nowhere.

The press, meanwhile, remains at roughly the same level of prestige that it possessed earlier. Reporters are likely to be assigned to tables located at the back or on the side of the official zone. Sometimes they are placed just in front of the dais, as in Duluth (photo IV.31). In Buffalo, reporters are offered seats up front at the secondary bench (photo IV.5), and in Kansas City they are given a recessed press loge at the mayor's extreme left, plus additional tables at his extreme right (photo IV.30). In a pattern that completely departs from Traditional practice, journalists are seated just outside the official zone in Alexandria, Minneapolis, Houston, San Antonio, and Sacramento (photos IV.2, IV.7, IV.19, and IV.26 and figs. IV.2 and IV.3).

In the last chapter we analyzed the heights of backs of chairs as an across-the-board indicator of comparative status. In Midcentury rooms a similar gradation obtains, albeit to a lesser degree. Of the fourteen pure or nearly pure dais systems, five show gradations between the presider, the councilors, and others (means of 45, 35, and 34 inches respectively); five show differences between the council as a whole and others (means of 41 and 34 inches); and four have identical chairs for everyone—namely

Berkeley, Saint Paul, Charlotte, and Des Moines (photos IV.3, IV.9, IV.17, and IV.23).

With respect to right-hand placement as a general indicator of status, mayors pro tem and vice-presidents are usually seated on the right side of the presider. City managers are seated at the presider's right in seven of eleven cases of noncentrality; other senior officials are so positioned in five of nine instances. The press is still on the left hand in a majority of instances of noncentral location; in more than one way, then, the subordination of the fourth estate remains relatively undiminished in Midcentury rooms.

MIDCENTURY DECORATION AND DISPLAY

Having examined spatial composition and semifixed-feature design in chambers built from 1920 to 1960, we look now at their decoration and objects.

Eclectic Decoration

It would be intellectually elegant, after finding the decoration of Traditional rooms to possess what Norberg-Schulz calls a classical *genius loci*, to discover that Midcentury chambers reflect his Romantic spirit—that is, are irrational, mysterious, and idyllic. That is not the case. Not only does this characterization fail to fit; no single characterization of any kind fits. The decoration of these chambers does not follow any single consistent pattern: four quite distinct approaches can be identified. This variety is interesting in itself; it also designates the period as a transitional one in the decorative aspect of chamber evolution.

The first of the four patterns conforms largely to what was found in Traditional rooms. That is, the decoration is intricate, repetitive, symmetrical, and duplicative of classical or Renaissance forms. Prolific use is made of molded plaster, stone, and dark-

Photo IV.31. *Dais and press table, Duluth, Minnesota*

stained woods. The rooms are formal, look to the past, present embellished and elaborate imagery, and express values of solidity and permanence. Nearly half of our Midcentury sample falls into this category: the essentially Neoclassical Revivalist spaces in Annapolis, Charleston, Denver, and Madison; the less high-style rooms in Alexandria, Duluth, and Honolulu; the monumental Romanesque basilica in Los Angeles; the rich Mediterranean chamber in Pasadena; and the Georgian reproduction in Schenectady.

As would be expected, the ceilings in these chambers are coffered or vaulted or both (photos IV.1, IV.4, and IV.21). Cornices, executed in classical designs, outline their perimeters. Nonclassical ceiling elaborations include frescoed Hawaiian scenes at Honolulu, painted zodiacal signs at Los Angeles, and elaborately stenciled beam work at Pasadena (photo IV.18). Chandeliers or otherwise ornamented lamps hang from ceilings, as at Schenectady (photo IV.4). Other surfaces of these rooms emulate Tra-

ditionalist decoration: fluted pilasters, as at Madison and Schenectady; arched window architraves, as at Alexandria and Denver; and wood wainscoting and paneling, as at Charleston and Duluth (photos IV.14 and IV.25). At Los Angeles the clerestory arcades, twelve supporting columns (each made of a different marble), and a backdrop canopy that incorporates a faience tile panel suggest an Eastern mosque or temple (photo IV.24).

The second pattern of Midcentury decoration is equally studied but exhibits the cleaner lines, softer curves, and lighter tones associated with art-deco or Modern styling. The four rooms in this category—Buffalo, Houston, Kansas City, and Saint Paul—are characterized by vertical thrust, pictorial decoration, verbal inscriptions, and the use of light metals along with wood. Dominating the amphitheater at Buffalo are seven half-round columns at the backdrop, which carry the eye upward to a giant sunburst skylight made of prismatic glass. Its shape and location are practically identical to what is found in the ceiling of the French Chamber of Deputies (photo I.1). Other decorative details at Buffalo include bronze filigree in the backdrop windows; the faces of twelve councilor virtues, peering from the tops of rear pillars; a symbolically ornamented public doorway; and walls and ceiling patterns in Indian motifs (photo IV.5). Houston, with its round-cornered walls covered in book-matched panels of blond walnut, features art-deco chandeliers, nickel door tablets, and several civic inscriptions (photo IV.28). These wall slogans might be thought of as modern-day parallels to the medieval cathedral's "word in stone." In Kansas City there is a more verbose example of a wall inscription (photo IV.32). Permanently attached to the chamber's backdrop, its wording reveals how the Pendergast machine wished to present itself to the public. At Saint Paul, perhaps the most outstanding example of an art-deco chamber in the nation, we discover English pollard-oak paneling that reaches to the ceiling; tall inset murals that depict the city's history; 30-inch columns, encased in extruded bronze; and a bronze and nickel-silver barrier mounted in a black and gold marble base (photo IV.9).

A third decorative pattern is very different from the first two. Instead of constituting a unified concept or style of design, it is a pragmatic assemblage of ideas. Considerations are overwhelmingly utilitarian and economic, not aesthetic or even manipulative. Like Venturi's "decorated shed," the rooms are unthinking accumulations of individually desirable features. Berkeley, Charlotte, College Park, Des Moines, Sacramento, and San Antonio fall into this category. All were built or renovated after World War II. They tend to have ceilings that are fitted with acoustical tile; recessed or hanging fluorescent lights; painted or acoustically treated walls (usually in white or tan); plain doors and windows; the wide-spread use of wall or window drapes, mass-manufactured paneling, and floors covered with cork tile or neutral-hued carpeting (photos IV.17, IV.20, IV.23, and IV.26). These rooms bear traces of molded plaster here and there as evidences of a more glorious past (e.g., Berkeley, photo IV.3) but today constitute hodgepodge, prosaic space.

The fourth decorative pattern is again very different. Like the first two, it presents an integrated concept; but unlike them, it looks to the future rather than to the past. Chicago and Minneapolis fall into this category. Here we find that verticality, formalism, and elaboration are eschewed in favor of more seductive ploys. The rooms neither intimidate nor charm; instead, they lure the visitor into a kind of personal identification with the process of government. This is accomplished by shapes and surfaces, rather than by explicit decoration and ornamentation. At Chicago the walls are rounded and uncluttered, with only the glassed-off gallery and ceiling spots looking down from above (photo IV.6). At Minneapolis the combination of a coved artificial skylight and inward canted walls creates a theatrical scene that is both comforting and manipulative (photo IV.7). The only articulated ornamentation in both spaces is a backdrop city seal, itself fascinating in the contrasting use to which it is put in each chamber. Mayor Daley's 16-inch plate at Chicago confers authority on "Hizzoner" without detracting attention away from him (photo IV.22). The 5-foot specimen at Minneapolis seems to try to compensate for the lack of strong leadership found in that city's weak-mayor form of government.

Objects of Culture and Communication

Let us lastly comment on portable objects of presentational importance. We recall that objects in Traditional chambers stressed ceremonial ritual and the community's histori-

Photo IV.32. *Backdrop inscription, Kansas City, Missouri*

cal past. In Midcentury rooms we find these kinds of objects, plus a new type—objects and devices whose purpose is the augmenting and structuring of communication between the governors and the governed.

Flags are again ubiquitous. National banners, as well as state and/or municipal ones, are found in all Midcentury spaces. They are usually fixed in an upright standard along the backdrop wall, although some variations do occur. At Charlotte, small American flags fly at each dais position (photo IV.17). In College Park and Los Angeles, reproductions of flags flown in colonial times are displayed (photo IV.24). United Nations flags are found in Saint Paul and Houston, and an All America City emblem hangs in Des Moines (photo IV.23). The flag is a cohesive symbolic gesture. Other ceremonial objects that act as differentiating symbolic gestures, a number of which were found in Traditional rooms, seem less common in Midcentury chambers. No maces were in evidence, for example. Gavels or striking plates were noted in a few chambers, but they are not visible from the audience area.

Some historical and cultural materials are displayed. Paintings hang on the walls in Alexandria, Houston, Sacramento, and San Antonio; and we have already mentioned the murals in Berkeley and Saint Paul. A tapestry is mounted in Kansas City (visible at the right in photo IV.30), and a display case of historical artifacts is found in Los Angeles. In Madison, Geraldine Rockefeller Dodge provided the wherewithal to furnish the Hartley Dodge Memorial's council chamber with a small museum of cultural objects, similar to what we noted earlier in Charleston, South Carolina. The room features portraits of George and Martha Washington by Rembrandt Peale, of John Quincy Adams by George Healy, and of Abraham Lincoln by Willem Travers, as well as a bust of Napoleon by Auguste Rodin. On one wall hang two Gobelin tapestries, reminding us of the Hotel Majestic ballroom in

Paris. In one corner of the room is the desk that Lincoln used in the United States House; also displayed is a bust of Lincoln and a chair that was presented to him, forming a small shrine of Lincolniana (partially visible in photo IV.16).

The new and emerging theme of public communication that is sounded by Midcentury objects departs significantly from such historical culturalism. In the first place, the objects themselves are present to be used and not merely seen. Secondly, they facilitate the activity stressed by the rectangular, oppositional, confrontational room that is the Midcentury chamber: namely, the interaction between the governors and the governed. Some of these objects assist communication by the governors to the governed and are thus cohesive symbolic gestures in at least a unilateral sense. Others underscore the distinction between the two sides and hence may be thought of as differentiating in character.

One category of communication objects on the cohesive side consists of devices for visual display. Blackboards and bulletin boards are found in several cities, such as Houston, Des Moines, and Duluth (photos IV.19, IV.23, and IV.25). Maps and calendars are visible in Buffalo and Sacramento (photos IV.5 and IV.20), while projection screens are readily apparent in Berkeley, Pasadena, and Houston (photos IV.3, IV.18, and IV.28). A vote-tallying board is mounted at the top of the rear private door in Des Moines (photo IV.23); straddling the backdrop canopy in Los Angeles are display boards, for member voting on one side and committee scheduling on the other (photo IV.24). At Alexandria, clashing somewhat with its genteel nineteenth-century atmosphere, is an electronic numerator, indicating which agenda item is currently under consideration.

Technical equipment is another communication-facilitating item. While modern tape-recording, public address, broadcasting, and televising equipment is available for contemporary use in all chambers regardless of age, the degree to which such equipment is publicly displayed varies surprisingly. In Traditional rooms it is seldom seen: about the only examples are antiquated broadcasting booths in Brockton and the New York boardroom. Elsewhere such equipment is either not used or is hidden away in cabinets and equipment lockers. In Midcentury rooms we begin to see a more overt presence of the technology of modern communications, although such display is nothing compared to what emerges later on.

One example of highly visible communications equipment occurs in Des Moines, where a cabinet containing a tape recorder is placed on the floor between the chairs of clerks who are seated at the crotch of the dais (photo IV.23). In this location it is just below the central sight line of the room and hence is very obvious to onlookers. In Charleston a tape recorder and a microphone control panel are prominent at one end of the secondary bench (photo IV.33). Gargantuan loudspeakers hang from each side of the Minneapolis chamber; they are all the more obvious because of the generally bare walls (photo IV.34). In several chambers, television cameras stand in the official zone as silent eyes that observe the proceedings on behalf of the outside world.

Communicative signs constitute another important group of objects in Midcentury rooms. Identifying nameplates are almost always displayed at the seating positions of the dais. This is done at Traditional aldermanic desks only about half the time. The most common type of display utilizes nameplate holders that rest on the surface of the daises—visible, for example, in photos IV.2 and IV.18. Another approach is to affix the nameplate to the dais skirt or to the chairs of the councilors (see photos IV.1 and IV.3). Sometimes the name of the individual only is given, a practice that suggests accountability for one's official actions; in other cases

a title also is attached, making the nameplate perform as a differentiating gesture as well. Often, nameplates are also used for nonelected officials, such as city manager, usually with the differentiating title included.

Signs that state behavioral requirements for the audience may also be thought of as differentiating communicative gestures. Since these directive signs are obviously aimed at visitors to the chamber, they can be thought of as transmitting orders from those who are in authority to those who are under it. We have already noted the warning sign on the lectern in San Antonio (photo IV.27). Lectern warnings are also found in Los Angeles and Saint Paul, asking witnesses to state their names and addresses; this request seeks a kind of accountability for the citizen side of the confrontational relationship (visible in photos IV.24 and IV.29). No Smoking signs can be seen in some chambers, as illustrated by Saint Paul (photo IV.9). Other directive signs reserve seats for aides and reporters (Alexandria), stop people from sitting on top of tables (Denver), and ask visitors to Please Be Quiet (Buffalo). A particularly prominent sign, just inside the public entrance at Los Angeles, requests advance registration of those who wish to address the council (photo IV.35).

THE MIDCENTURY AURA

For the most part, the Midcentury council chamber, built for an urbanizing America in the context of architectural diversity, economic change, and governmental growth, is smaller, lower, and longer than its Traditional counterpart. Power is administered, not from a majesterial rostrum, but from a corporate dais. The public is not removed from the circle of governance by galleries and balustrades; instead, it is confronted face to face in an oppositionally organized space. At one end of this space is a concave

Photo IV.33. *Communications equipment, Charleston, West Virginia*

Photo IV.34. *Public-address speaker, Minneapolis, Minnesota*

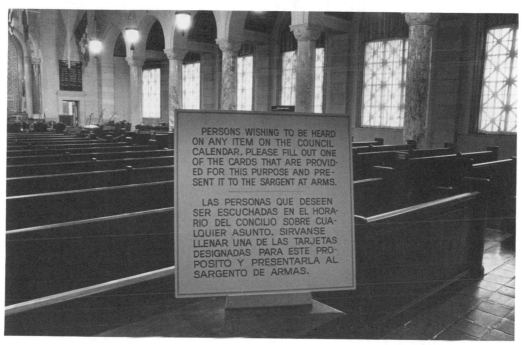

Photo IV.35. *Registration sign, Los Angeles, California*

dais, with its hollow side facing the public and with the council seated along the outside rim; at the other end is the public, seated in theater-style seats arranged in straight rows. Furthermore, the space is bisected from a zonal standpoint; floor-space barriers are downplayed; elevations at each end are roughly equivalent; and a public lectern is provided to complement the official dais. The result is not equivalency or union but is a direct engagement of the governors and the governed. Citizens no longer observe governmental authority imposed from afar; instead, they confront it head-on and at close range.

At the same time, the authority of government is secularized. The council chamber is now reached via elevator and corridor, not grand staircase. Ornamented lobbies now serve the whole building, not just the access route to the chamber. Moreover, the chamber is now midway in the building, not at its top; and from a floor-plan standpoint, it is just another room, not a spatial center-

piece. Windows are smaller and less transparent, no longer looking down on the streets below with lit majesty at night. Public entrances are smaller and simpler, room decoration is less likely to be elaborate and formal, and the display of objects is more likely to perform communicative rather than merely ceremonial tasks. In short, duly constituted authority does not govern by the mystique of distant superiority but through immediate, frontal, bilateral engagement. Rule is no longer by bench, throne, and mace, but by dais, lectern, and microphone.

In addition to presenting its own concept of political authority, the Midcentury model portends the future. Just as the partly rotated desks in Oakland foresaw Midcentury bilateralism, the sculpted planes of Buffalo, Chicago, and Minneapolis look ahead to the Contemporary period. It is to the post-1960s council chamber that we now turn, the civic space in which confronted authority becomes something quite different.

V The Contemporary Chamber: Joined Authority

Unlike the Traditional chamber, whose authority concept is one of unilateral, almost sacred superiority, and unlike the Midcentury chamber, whose notion of authority is that of a bilateral and more secular confrontation, the Contemporary chamber reveals a conception of authority whose effects are subtle and ambiguous. Neither overwhelming the citizens nor confronting them, the Contemporary civic space embraces them as part of a unitary whole. The very distinction between the governors and the governed becomes clouded. Authority is "joined."

THE SOCIAL AND ARCHITECTURAL SETTING

By 1960, when the Contemporary era of our study opens, the United States had become a society of big cities. Two dozen metropolitan areas possessed a million or more inhabitants each. Seventy percent of Americans lived in an urban area. During the subsequent decade, metropolitan areas were the locale of the great events of a turbulent time: the Northern phase of the civil-rights movement, street demonstrations against the Vietnam War, rising indignation over a polluted environment, and concerted demands to act against poverty.

The social turbulence of the 1960s had many effects on city governments. Programs of the Great Society greatly expanded municipal activities in areas of public housing, community development, affirmative action, and antipoverty effort. City bureaucracies grew rapidly, financed in part by new infusions of federal grant money. Minorities and women were elected to city councils in unprecedented numbers, ending the traditional white-male grip on elective office. A new ethos of citizen participation in government emerged, stressing citizen boards, the prompt consideration of taxpayer complaints, minority employment in the bureaucracy, and an active citizen voice at public hearings and in city-council meetings.

The quarter-century after 1960 saw a boom in the construction of city halls. Although the Vietnam War was the longest war in American history, it did not cause a diversion of resources from civilian construction, as had been the case in World Wars I and II. The period was marked by several recessions, but these did not slow down the construction of public buildings. In the northeastern-midwestern Frost Belt, a new city hall was often a part of an urban revitalization program; meanwhile the southern-western Sun Belt experienced extraordinary urban growth and economic prosperity, stimulating a surge of governmental building activity. At the same time, the process of suburbanization in all sections of the country went on unabated, encouraged by the postwar baby boom and by the construction of interstate highways. Thousands of new city halls were built, in central cities as well as in the suburbs.

From a design standpoint, post-1960 city halls were different from their predecessors. New trends in systems engineering led to additional interest in cost effectiveness. Long-term maintenance and energy consumption were now of major concern. Rising crime rates and an atmosphere of social unrest made designers more aware of problems in regard to deterring vandalism and protecting the security of city personnel.

In architectural style, Modernism was finally in, even with conservative municipal

TABLE V.1
The Twenty-seven Contemporary Chambers Included in this Study (with date built)

Arlington (Tex.) City Hall: 1981

Austin (Tex.) Municipal Building Annex: 1975

Boston (Mass.) City Hall: 1962–69

Brea (Calif.) Civic Cultural Center: 1980

Dallas (Tex.) City Hall: 1972–77

Fairfield (Calif.) Civic Center: 1969–71

Fort Worth (Tex.) Municipal Office Building: 1969–71

Fremont (Calif.) City Government Building: 1966–69

Greensboro (N.C.) Municipal Building: 1968–73

Kettering (Ohio) Governmental Center: 1968–70

Long Beach (Calif.) City Hall: 1973–74

Lynchburg (Va.) City Hall: 1982[a]

Mesa (Ariz.) Council Chambers Building: 1979

Miamisburg (Ohio) Civic Center: 1974

Paradise Valley (Ariz.) Town Hall: 1973–74

Phoenix (Ariz.) Muncipal Building: 1961

Raleigh (N.C.) Municipal Building: 1984

Rockville (Md.) City Hall: 1963

San Bernardino (Calif.) City Hall: 1970–72

Santa Rosa (Calif.) Civic Center: 1970

Scarborough (Ont.,Can.) Civic Centre: 1969–73

Scottsdale (Ariz.) City Hall: 1967–68

Tempe (Ariz.) Municipal Building: 1969–71

Toronto (Ont., Can.) City Hall: 1961–65

Tucson (Ariz.) City Hall: 1966–67

Walnut Creek (Calif.) Civic Center: 1979–80

Wilmington (Del.) City-County Building: 1975–77

[a]Building, 1933

governments. As we recall from chapter I, the public sector was several decades late in adopting the ideas of International Style architecture that emigrated to this country during the 1920s. In fact, a leading sociocultural history of American architecture regards the year 1960 as marking the beginning of full U.S. acceptance of the architectural revolution wrought by Frank Lloyd Wright, Walter Gropius, Le Corbusier, and Ludwig Mies Van Der Rohe.[1]

It would be a mistake to characterize Modernist architecture too rigidly, for one of its assumptions is that each architect is privileged to express his or her individual creative genius, unimpeded by clients or conventions. Yet several themes recur continuously in International Style buildings: interest in aesthetic form as an end in itself; the treatment of spatial volume as an inherently important element; a disregarding of earlier preoccupations with symmetry and balance; an antihistorical bias in general with regard to classical form; a new interest in materials, including white stucco, glass, steel, and unfinished concrete; a replacement of ornamentation by characteristics of clarity, sparseness, and austerity; a worship of sun and light; and concern (at least in some quarters) for making architecture "socially responsible."[2]

Twenty-seven city halls that were built after 1960 are incorporated into this study (see table V.1). Of these, three are internationally famous buildings. The Toronto City Hall, designed by the Finnish architect Viljo Revell (who did not live to see it completed), consists of two curved towers which cup a circular council-chamber building between them. This assembly is mounted on a two-story base, which in turn faces an extensive civic square (photo V.1).[3] In contrast

Photo V.1. *City hall, Toronto, Ontario, Canada*

to Toronto's grace, Boston's new city hall is a massive monument of brick and concrete with a hooded frieze surrounding the top perimeter. Designed by Gerhard M. Kallmann, Noel M. McKinnell, and Edward F. Knowles, the building rests on a plaza planned by I. M. Pei.[4] The third famous example is Pei's own Dallas City Hall. It too is monumental but daring because of its elongated trapezoidal form. The 560-foot northern façade of the building, cantielivered outward at a 34-degree angle, is visually (but not structurally) supported by three vertical stair towers (see photo I.5).[5]

Three more of these Contemporary buildings are equally innovative but less famous. The new Phoenix Municipal Building, designed by Edward L. Varney and Ralph Haver, consists of an administrative office tower and a separate council building, sited 50 feet from the main building (photo V.2). The Government Center in Kettering, Ohio, whose architect was Eugene W. Betz, consists of a low, white tetrahedron that

seems to hover effortlessly just above the ground on an eight-acre wooded site. Inverting this idea in a sense is the Municipal Building at Tempe, Arizona. Designed by Michael and Kemper Goodwin, the structure is an upside-down glass pyramid whose point rests in the center of an underground square base (photo V.3).

Eight of the post-1960 structures that I examined are part of comprehensive civic centers. These are complexes of several public buildings, such as a community center, a convention center, a public library, a public-safety building, and a city hall. The complex is typically tied together by a plaza, a square, or a park whose land has been cleared through urban redevelopment. Frequently it is situated near a mall or commercial area and is seen as a means of promoting economic development as well as providing public space. Reflecting pools, pylons, statuary, parking lots, and even artificial lakes may surround the buildings, creating a commercialized equivalent of what

Photo V.2. *Council-chamber building, Phoenix, Arizona*

Photo V.3. *Municipal building, Tempe, Arizona*

Photo V.4. *Kiva in city hall, Scottsdale, Arizona*

was contemplated by the City Beautiful movement.

The earliest and probably most creative building in this group is the Scottsdale City Hall. Located outside of Phoenix and designed by Bennie M. Gonzales, the structure suggests a combination of Indian, Mexican, and contemporary themes. It possesses an almost entirely open interior, with a sunken council chamber, or kiva, as the central focus (photo V.4).[6] Five other civic-center city halls that I studied are in California: Fremont, by Robert Mittelstadt; Santa Rosa, by Jacques DeBrer and Richard Heglund; Fairfield, by Robert W. Hawley; San Bernardino, by Cesar Pelli; and the Los Angeles suburb of Brea, by John Carl Warnecke and Dan Dworsky. Among these city halls, Fairfield's is of particular interest because it provides, like those of Phoenix and Toronto, a separate building for the city council. Pelli's hall in San Bernardino, the most architecturally striking structure of the five, is sheathed in six stories of bronze-tinted mirrored glass.[7] Other versions of the civic-center idea include a municipal building and a county courthouse in Greensboro, North Carolina, built adjacent to the old Guildford Courthouse to form a governmental center. At Scarborough, Ontario, which is part of metropolitan Toronto, Raymond Moriyama has designed the Civic Centre, which houses not only borough offices but the boards of education and health as well. The interior is dominated by a gigantic open atrium that is five stories high (photo V.5).

The remaining post-1960 city halls vary in character. At Paradise Valley in Arizona, there is an unusual village lodge, featuring an open homelike interior (photo V.6). The skyline of Long Beach, California, includes a fourteen-story city hall whose council chamber is half-buried at the base of the tower. The new city-county building at Wilmington, Delaware, which is shared with New Castle County, contains a chamber located in a separate wing that is attached to an administrative tower. A connected council wing is also found in Arlington, Texas, and in Tucson, Arizona. In

Photo V.5. *Atrium of Civic Centre, Scarborough, Ontario, Canada*

Photo V.6. *Reception area of town hall, Paradise Valley, Arizona*

TABLE V.2

The Contemporary Chamber: Measures of Size

	Small Cities (N=12)	Medium Cities (N=11)	Big Cities (N=4)	All Cities (N=27)
Mean floor area (sq. ft.)	2,042	3,325	4,920	2,991
Mean floor area per 1,000 population (sq. ft.)	44.4	13.1	2.8	7.7
Mean ceiling height (ft.)	16.8	18.9	29.4	19.5
Mean spatial volume (cu. ft.)	33,036	61,857	135,773	59,998
Mean audience seating capacity	108	210	224	167
Mean number of seats per 10,000 population	23.5	8.3	1.3	4.3

Note: City size is based on the approximate population at the time the chamber was built. Small is under 100,000; medium is 100,000 to 500,000; big is over 500,000.

the Arizona city of Mesa a separate chamber building is located several hundred feet from the city hall's office building, the most distant such separation that I encountered. Other city halls in the sample include ones in Fort Worth, Texas, by Edward Durrell Stone; Miamisburg, Ohio; Raleigh, North Carolina; Rockville, Maryland; Tucson, Arizona; and Walnut Creek, California. Somewhat unusual structural situations obtain at Austin, Texas, and at Lynchburg, Virginia: the Austin chamber was built within a 40-foot opening between two buildings, and the Lynchburg room was newly constructed inside a 1933 Neoclassical post office and courthouse.

THE COMPOSITION OF CONTEMPORARY SPACE

A Sculpted Enclosure

William L. Lebovich states that the large, elaborate council chambers of the nineteenth century "have been replaced in the 1960s and 1970s city halls by smaller, much simpler, more functional council rooms."[8] As we shall see, Contemporary chambers are simpler and more functional in some ways, but they are not necessarily smaller.

Table V.2 gives the same kind of data on measures of chamber size that were provided earlier on Traditional and Midcentury rooms. In this table we see the now-familiar pattern of greater absolute size in larger cit-

TABLE V.3
All Chambers: Measures of Size

	Traditional (N=25)	Midcentury (N=22)	Contemporary (N=27)
Mean floor area (sq. ft.)	2,906	2,406	2,991
Mean floor area per 1,000 population (sq. ft.)	6.1	6.1	7.7
Mean ceiling height (ft.)	30.2	21.4	19.5
Mean spatial volume (cu. ft.)	88,514	57,011	59,998
Mean audience seating capacity	146	145	167
Mean number of seats per 10,000 population	4.4	3.7	4.3

Note: The chamber of the New York Board of Estimate, completed in 1811, has been considered Pretraditional and has been omitted from this table. For the record, its floor area is 2,952 square feet, its ceiling height approximately 12 feet, its volume is about 35,400 cubic feet, and its seating capacity about 134.

ies yet smaller proportionate size on a per capita basis. The smallest Contemporary chamber is an intimate space at Kettering that covers only about 1,200 square feet. The largest is at Toronto, where approximately two-thirds of a 124-foot-diameter circular room is given over to council meeting space; while not the biggest chamber of the seventy-five that were studied in terms of audience capacity, it possesses the most square footage if one counts all seating and circulation space (8,000). Other large chambers are at Dallas (5,400 square feet) and Scarborough (5,037). In short, big civic spaces have not disappeared in new city halls.

Table V.3 summarizes all measures of size for all three eras. We note that the Contemporary chamber's mean floor area of 2,991 square feet and per capita floor area of 7.7 square feet exceed those of both the Traditional and the Midcentury rooms. In other words, the trend of floor-area diminishment that began in the 1920s seems to have been reversed in the 1960s. This is somewhat true of spatial volume as well, although because ceiling height continues to drop, the resurgence of volumetric size is restricted to substantially less than the Traditional standards. Contemporary chambers average about twenty more audience seats than before, but because of population growth, per capita seating capacity does not quite reach the Traditional level. To summarize: except for a 2-foot drop in ceiling height, the Contemporary chamber is substantially bigger than its Midcentury counterpart, and it exceeds even its Traditional predecessor in square footage and number of seats.

While in terms of gross size the Contemporary chamber is in a sense reminiscent of an earlier time, that cannot be said of its shape. Spatial composition in Contemporary chambers departs radically from the

Photo V.7. *Council chambers, Austin, Texas*

Photo V.8. *Council chamber, Greensboro, North Carolina*

past. This shift is one of the most important to occur in the symbolism of civic space; it is central to the essence of the Contemporary model.

For the first time, except for avant-garde rooms such as those in Chicago and Minneapolis, space itself is being freely molded as a key design variable. The primary use of flat planes is abandoned in favor of the extensive incorporation of curved surfaces. Varied angles, rather than perpendicular intersections, are used to join surfaces. Curved surfaces, formerly encountered only in ceilings, are now found in walls and floors as well. In other words, space no longer merely encloses air in the manner of a boxlike container; it is sculpted, in the manner of a block of ice. In Rudolf Arnheim's words, space becomes dynamic, not static; in Steven Peterson's pejorative terminology, the rooms comprise, not space, but anti-space. No longer is the *genius loci*, as Christian Norberg-Schulz would call it, established primarily by mass objects or surface decoration; it is conveyed, in large part, by the volumetric space between these elements. What is culturally expressed by the Modernist Contemporary chamber derives from that which *surrounds* what the occupant sees, not merely the objects of perception themselves. This makes that expression less tangible and hence more subtle as a symbolic index.

It is not as if the rectangular floor plan has disappeared. One-third of our sample of twenty-seven Contemporary chambers possess essentially such a configuration. But several characteristics of this floor plan set it apart from its predecessors. First, the long and narrow Midcentury room, wherein officials are situated at one end of the major axis and the citizens at the other, is no longer in vogue. The ratio of length to width in rectangular Contemporary rooms is such that the space is again fairly compact, reminiscent of Traditional rather than Midcen-

tury space. With one exception (Austin), in no Contemporary space that I studied did length exceed width by substantially more than 25 percent. Furthermore, when officials and audience are axis-centered, the two natural contenders usually face each other across the width, rather than the length, of the room. This arrangement creates less distance between the governors and the governed than otherwise would be the case.

In Austin, the only truly narrow room in the group, which was required because of the plot of ground that was available for its construction, the dais faces the citizenry in the manner of Denver's—that is, across the 31-foot width, rather than along the 84-foot length. The resulting sense of chamber intimacy was deliberately planned this way by city officials (see photo V.7). Their thinking on the subject is recounted this way: "The plan, as built, was done in this manner to put the audience closer to the Council, both for sight and sound reasons. This arrangement offers a rather intimacy [*sic*] between Council and audience; the other arrangement would have created a 'theatre' effect, with an attendant 'polar' effect."[9]

A second feature of the rectangular Contemporary room is that officials and citizenry alike are often removed entirely from symmetrical placement along either axis. Examples are off-center arrangements in Tucson and Greensboro (photo V.8) and diagonally aligned ones in Lynchburg and Walnut Creek (photo V.9). Asymmetrical arrangements break up the formality of the space and lessen a one-on-one confrontational relationship between officials and citizens. Moreover, with the dais in a corner, as in Walnut Creek, the two intersecting walls set the dais off with subtle drama, focusing attention on the officials by means of the background itself rather than the semifixed features or overhead decoration.

A third departure from the orthodox spa-

Photo V.9. *Council chambers, Walnut Creek, California*

tial box is to sculpt the floor. In previous eras, floors were generally horizontal planes, except for low platforms and stepped galleries. By contrast, in almost all Contemporary rooms—rectangular as well as otherwise—inclined audience areas are found. The incline is 5 degrees in Mesa and Tempe, a common degree of slope. At Dallas the angle is 20 degrees, which creates a rather precipitous bank of seating (photo V.10). Sometimes, floor construction is more sophisticated than inclined planes; as we shall see, complex bowl raking, as in a theater, is not uncommon.

Finally, the rectangular Contemporary chamber departs from its predecessors in ceiling design. Instead of being symmetrically coved or vaulted in classical architectural fashion or, for that matter, flattened to a utilitarian plane of fluorescent lighting, the ceiling is treated as a surface to be molded. The purposes of these ceiling shapes may be primarily the improvement

of acoustics and the hiding of ductwork and lights; nonetheless, Contemporary ceilings take on a design interest in and of themselves. Their forms and surfaces visually impose an order on the occupants below, just as do the vaults, coffers, and skylights of old.

The ceiling at Arlington is illustrative. A curved soffit above the dais accommodates an air duct, but it also highlights the dais by curving in unison with it (photo V.11). It serves, in other words, as a kind of canopy to accentuate the importance of the officials by drawing attention to them and scaling them up to look bigger. Also noteworthy at Arlington is the ceiling indentation, created just in front of this element by a second curve that opposes it (photo V.12). The resultant football-shaped recess is used to mount spots, but at the same time it accentuates the importance of the well of the chamber immediately below. Those who

Photo V.10. *Council chamber, Dallas, Texas*

Photo V.11. *Council chamber, Arlington, Texas*

Photo V.12. *Ceiling of chamber, Arlington, Texas*

Photo V.13. *Council chamber, Boston, Massachusetts*

Photo V.14. *Council chamber, Fairfield, California*

regularly address the Arlington council from the well are fully aware of the indentation: they refer to it as "the eye."[10]

The Kallmann-Knowles Boston chamber also illustrates how ceilings can impose order. This architecturally reactionary room features aldermanic desks, side galleries, and boxlike space (photo V.13). Dominating the entire scene is the ceiling. Only about 15 feet high, it appears even lower because of the much higher cavities above the public galleries. Massive concrete gridwork, accentuated by light fixtures, transforms the ceiling into a metaphor for suppressive social control.

Rectangularity only begins to describe the variety of spatial forms found in Contemporary chambers. One category of variation is to cut pieces out of essentially boxlike spaces, thus forming an angled but still rectilinear composition. In Mesa and Rockville, for example, corners are severed and sides are shaved to create polygonal floor plans

that direct attention forward to the dais and funnel sound acoustically backward to the audience. Even more drastic spatial surgery was performed by the architects at Fairfield and Miamisburg. In Fairfield, angled partitions point up the significance of the dais, while a sharply inclined ceiling creates a lofty and chapel-like ascendancy overhead (photo V.14). In Miamisburg, one corner of a square is cut off for public ingress, while the opposite corner is extended to receive the dais (photo V.15).

Still more radical are the chambers in Fremont, Scottsdale, Tempe, and Kettering, whose floor plans are so irregular that they no longer constitute doctored squares or rectangles: they are creative shapes in their own right. The multiple-sided planes and the three banks of inclined seating at Fremont foster an unusual degree of intimacy (photo V.16). Scottsdale's kiva, sunk in the city hall's atrium, is open rather than intimate, exactly as architect Gonzales intended. He

Photo V.15. *Council chamber, Miamisburg, Ohio*

Photo V.16. *Council chamber, Fremont, California*

Photo V.17. *Seating in kiva, Scottsdale, Arizona*

envisioned that at council meetings, casual visitors and city staff would stand around the atrium's periphery to observe the meetings from above, and his expectation has been realized (photo V.17).[11]

The floor plan at Tempe is shaped like a lopsided coffin (fig. V.1). The fact that this space is underground at the point of a buried pyramid makes the likeness of a sarcophagus seem particularly apt. The room's official zone is, in fact, configured like the head of an Egyptian mummy case. Designs that are common in Egyptian funerary sculpture are, moreover, repeated in the space's sculpted ceiling and its illumination system. A 3-foot orb with twelve radiating arms, centered directly above the public lectern, quite literally puts the citizen who is addressing the council on the spot (photo V.18).

The Kettering chamber is like a cubic megaphone lying on its side, with the mouthpiece at the rear of the audience area (photo V.19). Sloping downward from this elevated point are the audience seating tiers, angled at 10 degrees below the horizontal. Sloping upward at 10 degrees from the horizontal is the ceiling, formed by the underside of the building's tetrahedron roof. On each side, angled outward at 30 degrees, are retaining walls that form the chamber's walls. An additional compositional feature at Kettering is a massive ceiling crevice that runs from the rear "mouthpiece" forward to a window, decorated with the symbol of the city, that perforates the outer roof (photo V.20). Below, at the wide end of the space and beneath the window, stands the dais. The chamber's shape seems to symbolize a kind of trumpet, to amplify the people's voice for the benefit of the council and the community outside, although architect Betz denies having had this in mind.[12]

The floor plans of Contemporary chambers, in addition to being modified rectangles or otherwise rectilinear, are also curvilinear. Indeed, curved lines and rounded surfaces characterize the essence of spatial

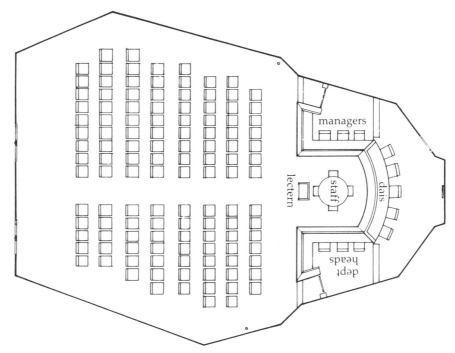

Figure V.1. *Floor plan of the council chamber, Tempe, Arizona*

composition in many recent chambers. In Traditional rooms, curvilinearity was the exception and thus stood out, as in apses, coving, and vaulted ceilings. In Midcentury spaces, it was generally absent, except for rounded art-deco forms. In Contemporary chambers, by contrast, curvilinearity and rounded shapes are commonplace, almost to the exclusion of straight lines and flat planes. This aspect can be variously interpreted. Some may regard Contemporary chambers as softer or more feminine than their predecessors.[13] Others, such as Norberg-Schulz, may consider them romantic or even womblike. Also, as we have seen, students of ancient temples often portray the circle as representing the cosmos, while Jungians regard it as an archetypal symbol of wholeness and perfection. In the behavioral realm, Arnheim contends that round rooms give the occupant the feeling of being the focal point of the space; and

when vertical-axis sculpting is added, as in a domed ceiling and concave floor, a hollow is created, into which the individual psychologically fits.

My own view is that the principal significance of curvilinearity and rounded surfaces for council chambers is that they help to create the impression that the occupants are bound together. This is especially so when roundness is complete, as in the circular room. One is hard-pressed to think of a spatial shape that is better able to express a concept of integrated governmental authority than is perfect circularity. When human beings are arranged in the sociopetal form of a circle, they become joined, equalized, and—if facing each other at close range—intimate.

In illustrating this contention, let us begin with Tucson, an instance where curvilinearity is prominent even though the room is not circular. The floor plan at Tuc-

Photo V.18. *Council chamber, Tempe, Arizona*

Photo V.19. *Rear of council chamber, Kettering, Ohio*

Photo V.20. *Front of council chamber, Kettering, Ohio*

son, though it is based on a right angle between two walls, is complex beyond this aspect (fig. V.2). Audience seating areas are backed against arcs that radiate from a point behind the dais (top of diagram). Aisles between the areas radiate also from that point, transmitting visual foci straight to the dais. The dais, the administration table, and the lectern are curved essentially in the opposite direction. On the ceiling, curved soffits encircle the room, with the concave public lectern positioned at the approximate midpoint of this encirclement. This spatial composition, together with the semifixed features that I have mentioned, highlight both the officials and the public witness. Moreover, all of the room's occupants are drawn together by a substantially common focus and a uniting circumference.

Another curvilinear example is at Brea. There, the concept of the Greek amphitheater or late bouleuterion is almost perfectly

replicated (photo V.21). A downward-sloping semicircle of stepped seating faces onto and partially encapsulates a well below. The furniture in the well is grouped in a circle; the public lectern is included along with dais and administration tables. A round domed opening heightens the ceiling space above, whose edge is concentric to an encircling wall below. The result is an integrated spatial composition. In Arnheim's imagery, the room's occupants are nested together in a concave hollow that surrounds vertically as well as horizontally.

Several fully circular chambers demonstrate this line of argument further. Six rooms in the Contemporary sample are perfectly round, namely Long Beach, Phoenix, Raleigh, Scarborough, Toronto, and Wilmington. In all of these cases, the audience seating is curved back against an outer circumference, raked downward toward the well from 5 to 30 degrees, and placed oppo-

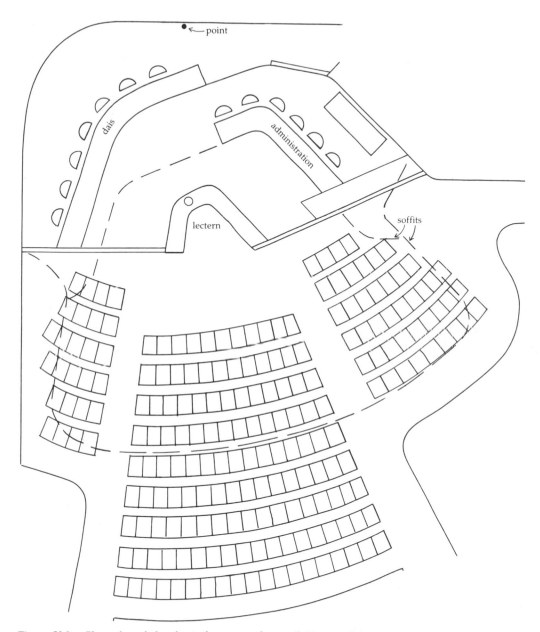

Figure V.2. *Floor plan of chambers of mayor and council, Tucson, Arizona*

Photo V.21. *Council chamber, Brea, California*

site to curved daises or other official furniture. Floor aisles usually point toward this furniture as radii. The floor plan of Long Beach, a typical arrangement, is shown in figure V.3. In all of these round rooms the ceiling is sculpted or configured in some way. At Long Beach it is decorated by a cross-shaped set of wooden strips, intersecting at the circle's center point. Phoenix's ceiling is embossed by converging scallops, in the manner of the roof of a circus tent. At Toronto the ceiling is a giant concave dome, formed by the underside of the council building's roof (visible in photo V.1).

The Wilmington chamber is particularly noteworthy as a round space. The circular sides of the room slope inward 8 degrees, thus defining the enclosure as a truncated cone. The ceiling is dramatically sculpted in the form of a giant spoked wheel or gear with a black hub at the center (photo V.22). When questioned about this centrum, the architects had no idea why it had been included.[14] One of Mircea Eliade's readers might view it as symbolization of a vertical *axis mundi* reaching to the sky, while a student of the Pantheon might think of it as a closed oculus, or perhaps one seen at nighttime. All that can be objectively said on the matter is that if one stands directly below this feature, at the precise center of the room, a distinct echo effect is experienced, a fact known by everyone who is familiar with the chamber. This centerpoint is, incidentally, directly forward of the zonal barrier gates, just inside the official area.

As I noted in chapter II, symbolists place particular importance on the mandala as a geometric form. In its preferred version, the mandala is a circle centered within a square. As it happens, the circular Wilmington chamber, with its centered oculus, is itself also centered in a square formed by the exterior building that encases it. The room's narrow windows are located only at the four points where the circle is tangent to the

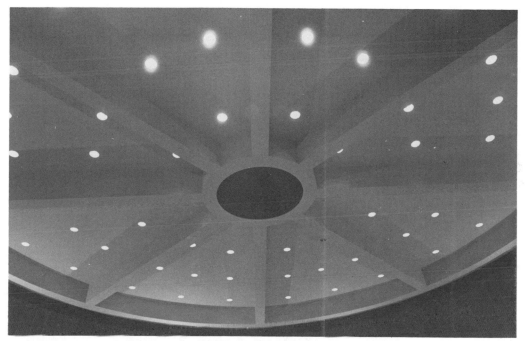

Photo V.22. *Ceiling of chamber, Wilmington, Delaware*

Photo V.23. *Exterior of chamber, Wilmington, Delaware*

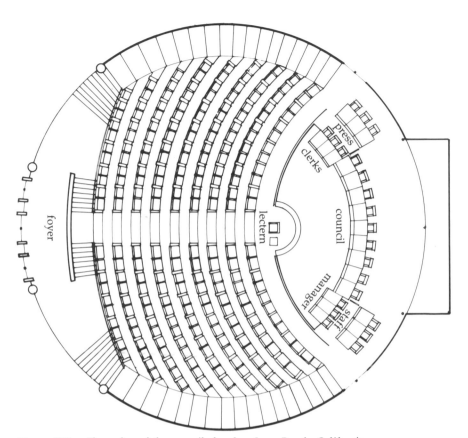

Figure V.3. *Floor plan of the council chamber, Long Beach, California*

square; hence this mandala form is not visible inside the chamber but is highly visible on the outside of the building (photo V. 23).

In two Contemporary city halls the chamber interiors are laid out in mandala form. At Santa Rosa a circular depression 50 feet in diameter is set in a 60-foot square. Half of the circle is occupied by banked seating, raked at 25 degrees in amphitheater style. A concave dais faces the audience on the other side of the depressed circle. A protective rail surrounds the circle to keep bystanders from falling into it, but during crowded meetings the rear viewing area is closed to the public because councilors feel unsafe with people standing behind and above them (photo V.24).[15] A second interior mandala is in Fort Worth. There, a 55-foot circle is depressed at the center of a 65-foot square (photoV.25). Unlike Santa Rosa, the entire circle is banked, at 10 degrees. In the manner of ancient Chinese temple cities, the sloped area is divided into four quarters, three of which are given over to audience or staff seating and one to the council's and clerk's daises. In the middle is a circular well, 27 feet in diameter and depressed 40 inches below the upper floor level. This well is informally called the pit by municipal insiders. A public lectern is the only object in the pit. Overhead, a low ceiling of waffleslab construction creates a heavy matrix of visual detail; as in Boston, this feature makes the room seem oppressive—especially compared to Santa Rosa, whose ceiling is composed of a loftier and more widely spaced lattice (photo V.24). In attempting to recreate what Edward Durrell

Photo V.24. *Council chamber, Santa Rosa, California*

Photo V.25. *Council meeting room, Fort Worth, Texas*

Stone had in mind by the Fort Worth design, an architect who worked with Stone has said:

> As I recall his thoughts it was his hope that a council meeting would be in the vein of a town hall meeting; this would include the council members and staff in a circle rather than on a stage. By creating the "pit," sightlines could be maintained without elevating the council high above the audience. He felt also that in the circle, members of the audience would have visual contact with each other as well as the council, therefore enabling them to observe feelings and responses. I think he felt that the circle created an unending link rather than the council and the people facing one another, which might indicate confrontation.[16]

In short, Stone wanted a manifestation of what we are calling joined authority. Also he expected amphitheater seating to permit the people who were present to see their own collective responses, just as Goethe described. Unintended consequences cannot, however, always be avoided. A developer who testifies frequently before the Fort Worth council confided to me that the experience of testifying in the pit is exceedingly intimidating. When standing at the lectern in the well, one feels alone and surrounded, he says, with your opponents invariably being seated behind you.[17] Curvilinearity can create problems as well as potentialities.

A Separated Room

The Contemporary chamber, then, is not the decorated square, as in the Traditional era, or the plain oblong, as in the Midcentury period; instead, it is a freely and often dramatically composed space. The room is no longer a mere container of symbolism; it itself symbolizes.

What is the location of this newly subtle, more deeply expressive civic space? In Traditional city halls, the council chamber is placed in a central location at the top of the building, reached by a grand stairway. In Midcentury municipal buildings the chamber is lowered to the inside mass of the building and is reached by elevator and corridor. Contemporary civic space, by contrast, is downstairs. In almost every instance the council chamber is located on or near the street level of modern city halls.

A symbolic interpretation of this shift might be that the council has been brought down to earth, in the sense of further secularization. More mundane explanations are, first, that this location makes the council easily accessible to the public, without disturbing the city's bureaucratic offices above, and, second, that the arrangement is useful from a security standpoint, in that the remainder of the building can be locked during nighttime council sessions. Despite this lowering of the Contemporary chamber to ground level, it still receives special treatment from the standpoints of building location and circulation. Yet these factors are manipulated quite differently from the way they are handled in Traditional city halls. The location strategy in the Contemporary period is one of *disconnecting* the chamber from the now-prolific administrative space of city halls. In this way the legislative function of government is not subjected to the unfavorable comparisons that stem from direct competition with the administrative function, as in the Midcentury model. By disconnection, comparisons are avoided. Moreover, the strategy creates opportunities for giving the legislative body an architectural status of its own, far beyond the status conveyed by internal devices, such as the ornamental corridor gates found in the Philadelphia City Hall.

Council disconnection is achieved in four ways, with some city halls employing more

Photo V.26. *Legislative foyer, Scarborough, Ontario, Canada*

Photo V.27. *Helical staircase, Raleigh, North Carolina*

than one way. One method is simply to give the council chamber specialized lobby space, thus separating the chamber itself from the rest of the interior of the city hall. This technique is Traditionalist in the sense of highlighting by means of public circulation space, but not in the dramatic manner of a grand central court or staircase. Instead, a kind of legislative foyer is created, which does not dominate the interior of the building but nevertheless provides important accentuation to the council. At Arlington the chamber is connected to the main lobby of city hall by a 19-by-40-foot foyer, which is decorated with an abstract mural. At Scarborough, a fluid 80-foot-long curvilinear space precedes the chamber entrance, which is depressed two feet below the level of the atrium lobby (photo V.26). Containing potted plants and civic exhibits, it prepares the visitor for arrival at the chamber itself, which is underground. In the circulation space of Raleigh's new city hall a helical staircase ascends from the building lobby to an upper legislative foyer, whose circular opening repeats the round configuration of the chamber itself (photo V.27).

An extravagant legislative foyer at Dallas is 39 feet wide, 65 feet long, and 30 feet high. Called the International Room, it is opulently furnished and is decorated with the flags of the thirty-two countries that maintain consular offices in Dallas. Used for official receptions, this space communicates with the chamber via glass doors on one side, while offering a fine view of the city's skyline through a window wall on the other (photo V.28; the exterior is visible in photo I.5, between the two stair towers).

A second method of achieving chamber disconnection is to make the room's internal presence in the building noticeably obvious on the outside of the structure. Disconnection is then evident from the exterior vantage point, much as the two wings of the United States Capitol separate the Senate and the House of Representatives. Another illustration is Copenhagen's city hall, mentioned in chapter II, which features an especially prominent wing given over to legislative use. Such exterior disconnection may be seen as conceptually opposite to the connecting bicameral bridges found in the capitol at Williamsburg and in the Lowell City Hall.

Examples of exterior disconnection are numerous. We have already mentioned how in Arlington, Tucson, and Wilmington the council chamber is located in a low one-story wing attached to a multistory administrative block. The public gains access to the chamber via either internal passageways or a separate street entrance. At Santa Rosa, the mandala's exterior square forms one of several wings that extrude from a relatively sprawling city-hall structure. At Raleigh, the circular chamber is clearly visible outside the otherwise rectilinear building, appearing as a protruding drumlike shape (photo V.29). The drum emerges at the intersection of two city streets and is plainly discernible to passers-by. At Fremont, the chamber space is even more noticeable outside the structure. It forms an angled mass of concrete, high on stilts, with the rest of the building extended away from it (photo V.30). The looming sides of this structure register a powerful image that can be seen for a considerable distance across open land. Fremont's status as a city was created in the 1960s by consolidating five governmental jurisdictions, and this highly visible building was deliberately designed to assert the identity of the new community.[18]

At other city halls the externally visible council chamber does not dominate the building's image but does constitute at least one of the structure's defining elements. At Brea, the council's semicircle forms a round bulge of exterior brick wall across from the main entrance to a multipurpose cultural center. At Long Beach, the circular council

Photo V.28. *International Room, Dallas, Texas*

Photo V.29. *Municipal building, Raleigh, North Carolina*

Photo V.30. *City government building, Fremont, California*

Photo V.31. *Concourse of civic center, Miamisburg, Ohio*

room is housed just underneath the fourteen-story tower of the city hall, which is intended as a landmark for the skyline of a revitalized city. With the chamber partially below ground level, its placement represents a full reversal of the earlier concept of locating the legislative space at the top of city hall. The same situation prevails even more emphatically at the tip of Tempe's inverted pyramid. A very different approach is taken at Miamisburg, whose civic center is a long, flat single-story structure with a lengthy public concourse running through it. This covered thoroughfare is 210 feet long and is pointed precisely at the doors of the council chamber (photo V.31). The administrative and judicial functions performed in spaces off to the side of the runway are handy to citizens but are placed in a status subordinate to that of the legislative activity at the terminus.

The third way that disconnection and, hence, accentuation are achieved is the aforementioned step of providing an entirely separate structure for the council. This is a legislative-building type that is even more specialized than the familiar state or national capitol, since capitol buildings usually house office space in addition to civic space. The separate council buildings typically contain the chamber alone, with councilors' offices most often being located in the city hall proper. Thus we have what might be regarded as a legislative temple, something along the lines of the bouleuteria or curiae of antiquity. Five such buildings are found in the Contemporary sample: Austin (admittedly a special case, because it was built between two existing municipal buildings), Mesa, Toronto (photo V.1), Phoenix (photo V.2), and Fairfield (photo V.32). In each of these structures there is a public lobby; and in all but Austin, the exterior of the building is noticeably different from the nearby municipal structures. Thus the earlier strategies of legislative foyer and exter-

nal visibility are, in effect, incorporated within this third technique.

Toronto is an especially powerful combination of these techniques. The massive round roof of the saucerlike council chamber—which is 130 feet in diameter—emerges out of a flat, low base containing lobbies, offices, and parking. It is largely surrounded by the two cupping, or protecting, hands of the office towers. The council chamber itself is structurally supported, not by the building's base, but by a round column, or stem, extending vertically down below it. Twenty-one feet in diameter, this pillar bears the entire weight of the council building, transmitting it down to a bed of shale 74 feet below.[19] In the main entrance lobby to Toronto's city hall, directly beneath the council building, this load-bearing column is not hidden from view. To the contrary, it is exposed at the center of the lobby and is floodlit. To further articulate the importance of the column, the area around it is sunken and rendered in dark colors. The sunken area, roped off and designated the Hall of Memory, is dedicated to the city's war dead and is decorated with plaques of unit insignia and is equipped with a book of names of the fallen (photo V.33). In contemplating the symbolism of this great column, which rises from and disappears into sacred space, a tangible *axis mundi* is inevitably brought to mind.

The fourth and final location strategy in Contemporary chambers is to center them in the ground floor's public circulation area. They are thus clearly separated off from the office sections of the building, which are located behind closed doors or are upstairs. This device surpasses merely disconnecting the legislative function from the bureaucracy; when the council chamber *is* public circulation space, the values of public accessibility and governmental openness are emphatically stressed.

At Paradise Valley the chamber consti-

Photo V.32. *Council-chamber building, Fairfield, California*

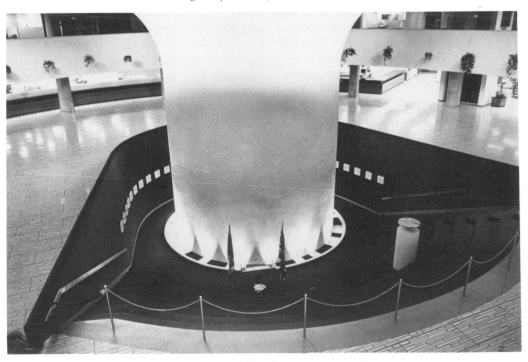

Photo V.33. *Hall of Memory, Toronto, Ontario, Canada*

tutes one side of an open room that serves as a reception and display area as well as civic space (photo V.6). The effect is a relaxed atmosphere that seems to invite citizen involvement. At Scottsdale, the sunken kiva occupies the floor of the central atrium and dominates the entire center of the building. Its openness is nothing short of total; nonetheless, the kiva itself is still a distinct spatial entity, clearly separated from the surrounding administrative offices (photo V.4). Kettering's megaphone-shaped chamber occupies the center of the triangular floor plan and is raised above the administrative (ground) floor of the building, but it can be easily reached by stairs from the foyer. The architect and the city officials alike at Kettering see this plan as symbolic both of the openness of city government and of the superiority of legislative power over administrative power. To quote from their interpretation:

> The dominant feature of the interior of the Kettering Governmental Center is the Council Chamber located in the center of the building and elevated but not enclosed . . . . The room provides the feeling of an open, receptive area, which encourages the public to communicate freely and participate in the City's decision-making process. There are no doors or walls which can be closed to the public in this space.[20]

All-or-Nothing Perforation

In Contemporary chambers such as this one, then, the issue of perforation is irrelevant because there are no walls to perforate. The Lasswellian concept that open, nondespotic space is conducive to democratic rule is realized in the extreme. In other Contemporary rooms, however, this is decidedly not the case; the opposite extreme of complete nonperforation is found. Unlike earlier rooms that tended toward some intermedi-

ate degree of perforation, Contemporary civic space is sharply bifurcated into two contrasting approaches: radically open and radically closed.

In this situation, a calculation such as gross average window area means little. (At 426 square feet, the Contemporary average lies between the Traditional one of 675 and the Midcentury one of 269.) More meaningful are separate averages for the two distinct types. For the radically open group (Fairfield, Greensboro, Miamisburg, Paradise Valley, Santa Rosa, Toronto, and Walnut Creek), the figure is 1,438 square feet; for the remaining twenty nearly closed spaces, it is a mere 63 square feet.

As for the open examples, Greensboro features a large window screen that looks out onto an interior court which is filled with plant life (photo V.8). At Santa Rosa, twenty-eight 6-by-10-foot window lights surround the mandala on all four sides (partially visible in photo V.24). At Fairfield, a mammoth angled skylight, facing west, bathes the space in the afternoon California sunlight (see photo V.32). Toronto's angled 12-foot-wide window circumscribes the entire perimeter of the round building.

In some cases, window walls are used, creating not mere holes, in the Norberg-Schulz sense, but a dematerialized wall. In the intimate Miamisburg chamber a 9-by-7 foot and a 20-by-20 foot window look out each side of the room (photo V.15). These windows face protected planted areas and provide natural light and a pleasant aspect without communicating directly to the busy street outside. At Walnut Creek, two of the four walls of the room are entirely dematerialized (photo V.9). This feature was deliberately incorporated by the architect as a way of demonstrating a philosophy of open government. At nighttime, meetings are fully visible to passers-by outside, an effect that city officials regard as suggesting open and responsible government.[21]

At the opposite extreme, the radically

closed rooms have practically no windows, or they have windows that are heavily draped. As a consequence, interior illumination is entirely artificial, and the space looks the same around the clock. At Brea, Fort Worth, Lynchburg, Mesa, and Raleigh, almost no windows are found. In Rockville and Tucson the only windows are small lights placed in the public doors. Restricted fenestration is also found in Boston, San Bernardino, and Wilmington; in the underground chambers of Scarborough and Tempe, windows are confined to the outer doors. Fremont's chamber possesses a skylight, but it communicates to the roof via a cavity above the dais; thus no one sees the outdoors, yet the dais receives accentuating light during daytime hours (photo V.16). The aboveground portion of Long Beach's drum-shaped chamber is all glass, but is completely covered by heavy opaque curtains. A similar situation obtains at Phoenix (photo V.2). The rear wall of the Dallas chamber is largely glass as well, but it was covered with blinds after an incident on the occasion of the room's first use in 1978, when a citizen who was walking across an upper hallway made an obscene gesture to the council seated below. This prompted the officials to cover the windows and to close off that corridor permanently.[22]

Turning now to perforation via doors, the Midcentury tendency toward practicality is sustained in the Contemporary era. Doors are numerous enough for safe and convenient ingress and egress but are not elaborated upon or given decorative effect. They typically consist of a simple pair of swinging 3-by-7-foot panels (for examples, see photos V.9 and V.31). Two new developments emerge with respect to Contemporary-era portals, however. One is the emergence of a vestibule—a small, closed anteroom that is windowless and is used to seal off the inside space from outside noises and light. The chambers that possess vestibules are, quite logically, the radically closed spaces. These anterooms permit the closedness to be even more extreme by establishing two walls to be perforated, not just one. Examples are found in Fort Worth, Long Beach, Lynchburg, and Phoenix. Lynchburg's vestibule, according to one councilor, imparts a womblike sanctity to the inner room.[23]

The second development is the elaboration of the private door. It no longer merely leads to corridors or offices; it now permits secluded communication to conference rooms, lounges, kitchenettes, toilets, and telephones. In other words, the private door is not merely a symbolic expression of the distinction between the governors and the governed; it is also the entryway to the councilors' private world. It may serve as a rearwards escape route in case of trouble, just as we saw in Cleveland and Madison. At Tempe and Toronto, private elevators wait behind the backdrop to whisk departing officials smoothly to safety. At Lynchburg the backdrop curtain behind the dais is parted at several points to enable quick escape (photo V.34). In another good example of Clovis Heimsath's double tracking, the space behind the Lynchburg curtain leads to back passageways and stairs to the street (photo V.35).

CONTEMPORARY SEMIFIXED FEATURES
The Dais Reigns Supreme

We recall that the most significant development in the design of semifixed features in the Midcentury room is the emergence of the dais. While the dais was unknown in Traditional chambers and was only emergent in Midcentury rooms, its presence in Contemporary spaces is almost universal. Within our sample of rooms built since 1960, all but Boston and Wilmington possess daises. The two Canadian city halls at Toronto and Scarborough use daises too, although combined with modest rostra.

In characterizing the Contemporary dais,

Photo V.34. *Council chamber, Lynchburg, Virginia*

Photo V.35. *Escape route, Lynchburg, Virginia*

it should first be remarked that this furniture ensemble remains at a relatively low elevation. The dais table itself is placed on a low platform or even on the floor of the chamber itself. The average elevation of the platform is 10 inches, about the same as in Midcentury chambers (11 inches). The highest platform is San Bernardino's 2-foot podium; more typically, the height is 6 to 12 inches. Second, skirt heights are slightly above the Midcentury norm. They vary from 30 to 60 inches, with a mean of 44 inches, compared to 39 in the earlier period. Usually this height incorporates the platform beneath, as seen in Arlington, Santa Rosa, and Lynchburg (photos V.11, V.24, and V.34). Parapets usually rise above the front edge of the top of the table, adding 2 to 9 more inches of skirt height. Such parapets can be seen in photographs of Scottsdale, Fremont, and Brea (photos V.4, V.16, and V.21).

Contemporary dais tables are 15 to 47 feet long, measured on the straight-line chord between ends, with a mean of 26 feet. With respect to form, the vast majority consist of a curved arc (e.g., Fairfield, photo V.14). A few others have rectilinear segments but are nonetheless basically concave (e.g., Greensboro, photo V.8). Some of the concave curvilinear daises describe radical horseshoe-shaped arcs, ranging in depth from 8 feet (San Bernardino) to 16 (Dallas). All are geometrically symmetrical.

The two Canadian dais systems differ from the American ones in that each of them includes four curved tables, with two concentric pairs on each side facing the center in circular fashion. At Toronto this double configuration permits the room to be used either for the twenty-two-member Toronto City Council or the area-wide Metro Council, which is made up of forty representatives (photo V.36). Other furniture at Toronto includes the mayor's rostrum, the executive secretary's desk, the executive committee's table, and various com-

missioner positions. Surely Donald and Alice Stone would be satisfied that this circular "administration of chairs" promotes group interaction and expresses equality among members.

Opportunities to undercut a sense of member equality by dais shape or skirt design are generally avoided. No San Antonio–style V-shaped dais gives special attention to the presider. Most skirt fronts are uniform in design; the only exception is in Walnut Creek, where the seating positions of elected officials are given flush skirt fronts and those of appointed officers have a 4-inch indentation (visible in photo V.9). Dais chairs tend to be equivalent in design and height for all members. Color is used as a distinguishing technique in Miamisburg, however. The presider's chair is covered in white fabric, while the councilors' chairs are done in black (photo V.15). We recall that in most cultures, white is associated with positive values and black with negative ones.

Contemporary daises provide from five to fifteen seating positions. As with Midcentury daises, the number is usually odd, with seven, nine, and eleven positions being the most common. This permits the presider to be in the central spot. As before, councilors who sit in the order of the wards or districts that they represent are usually sequenced from right to left from the presider's perspective, thus making them left to right from the audience's perspective.

Midcentury trends with respect to backdrops also continue. Contemporary backdrops tend to be rather large visual expanses, rather than sharply focused objects or designs. Broad window walls constitute the backdrop in Paradise Valley and in Walnut Creek (photos V.6 and V.9). A wide set of curtains is very popular, as seen at Brea and Phoenix (photos V.21 and V.37). In these chambers, curtains cover projection screens and can be parted when projectors are in use. Elsewhere, as in Austin and Lynchburg (photos V.7 and V.34), the cur-

Photo V.36. *Council chamber, Toronto, Ontario, Canada*

Photo V.37. *Council chamber, Phoenix, Arizona*

Photo V.38. *Council chambers, Mesa, Arizona*

Photo V.39. *Council dais, Dallas, Texas*

Photo V.40. *Dais and backdrop, Raleigh, North Carolina*

tains do not part; instead, they are used to set off a city seal. Uncovered projection screens are found also, as in Mesa and Dallas (photos V.38 and V.39). At Miamisburg a painted back wall acts as a screen (photo V.15), while at Raleigh a proscenium-style stage is created for visual displays (photo V.40). Dramatic effects can also be created by background expanses of wood (Greensboro, photo V.8), brick (Fairfield, photo V.14), unfinished cement (Fremont, photo V.16), and white plaster (Toronto, photo V.36). The most theatrical backdrop of all is at San Bernardino. There, a 19-foot seal of the city is painted in vivid colors on the back wall (photo V.41). This huge representation is covered over by a mechanically lowered screen when the back wall is being used for reflecting projected images. Adding further to the drama of the scene is a 2-foot-high circular podium, which rotates 180 degrees on its circular platform at the push of a button to permit the council to view, at exceedingly close range, the projected images.

I conclude this discussion of the Contemporary dais by commenting on its significance as a barrier. In the last chapter we learned about a tendency to minimize or even to eliminate a floor barrier that separates the governors from the governed, with the dais skirt itself becoming the only barrier in some instances. In about half of the Contemporary chambers this is precisely the case. Such a practice intimates that open communication between officials and citizens is possible, since nothing overtly separates the two by occupying the intervening floor space between them. Good examples of such open chambers are Walnut Creek, Fairfield, and Miamisburg (photos V.9, V.14, and V.15). Subtle modifications of this open pattern can restrict the spatial communication between officials and citizens to a partial degree. As we saw in Midcentury chambers, other pieces of furniture can be placed in front of the dais, such as press tables at Kettering (photo V.20), a secondary clerk bench at Fort Worth (photo V.25), and

Photo V.41. *Dais and backdrop, San Bernardino, California*

tables and a lectern at Phoenix (photo V.37). At Paradise Valley an enormous structural beam transects the overhead space in front of audience chairs, creating a subtly ethereal dividing line between the public and the official zones (photo V.42).[24]

Another technique is to extend the ends of the dais so that it nearly becomes a transchamber fence, an arrangement also encountered in Midcentury rooms. Because the wall is integral to the dais and is not isolated in space, the onlooker does not easily recognize its barricading function. Good examples are at Arlington and Dallas (photos V.11 and V.39). The base wall that surrounds Scottsdale's kiva performs a similar function (photo V.4). The Tempe dais, with its gleaming formica finish, its extended sides, and its sharply angled parapet, constitutes a particularly intimidating barrier (photo V.18). A standing joke among officials at Tempe is that this structure's hood is handy because of its ability to deflect bullets.[25]

In the remaining Contemporary rooms, overt floor barriers of some kind are found, but they are usually more subtle than earlier fences or balustrades. At Austin the barrier is massive but relatively low and is perforated by indented openings (photo V.43). A rather thin rail is used at Mesa and Long Beach (photos V.38 and V.44). In several chambers, barriers are disguised as retaining walls by placing them just in front of benches or at the base of amphitheater seating. Thus, they do not stand obviously midway between the governors and the governed; instead, they only encase the latter. Examples of retaining walls are seen at Greensboro, Boston, Fremont, and Brea (photos V.8, V.13, V.16, and V.21). A retaining rail is used at Santa Rosa (photo V.24); a retaining rope at Toronto (photo V.36).

The Adoption of the Amphitheater

The second major development in Contemporary semifixed features, in addition to the

Photo V.42. *Chamber of the town council, Paradise Valley, Arizona*

Photo V.43. *Barrier and dais, Austin, Texas*

Photo V.44. *Council chamber, Long Beach, California*

full arrival of the dais, is the adoption of the amphitheater form of public seating. As we have noted, the amphitheater possesses two characteristics simultaneously: a concave curvature, with the occupants facing inward toward a common middle ground; and a downward slope, with the benches or rows of seats banked in a decline toward that middle ground. This form, which was used in theaters of antiquity and in Gisor's National Convention hall of 1793, is found in a majority of our Contemporary rooms. Arcs of gently raked seating are found in Walnut Creek, Arlington, Fairfield, Miamisburg, Phoenix, Raleigh, San Bernardino, and Wilmington. Steeper inclines are found in Long Beach, Scarborough, Santa Rosa, and Toronto. The amphitheaters in Brea and Fort Worth slope gently but embrace three-fourths of a circle. Two other rooms, in Fremont and Mesa, are quasi-amphitheatric arrangements in that the concavity of the raked seating is attained, not by curves, but by angled straight rows.

In all of these rooms, Goethe's "noble body, shaped into unison," can fully see itself. Moreover it can easily see the council. Sight lines in gently sloped amphitheaters are essentially horizontal because of modestly raised daises. In the steeply inclined examples the audience is definitely above the officials. From the upper rim of seating, observers at Fremont look downward 6 degrees; at Santa Rosa and Scarborough, 9; at Toronto, 11; and at Long Beach, 17 (photo V.44). Such downward perspectives reverse the angle by which the public looked upon officialdom from the floors of Midcentury rooms. These perspectives superficially recreate the upstairs vistas of Traditional spaces, but now the audience is fully within the heart of the space, not banished to distant galleries.

Other chambers in the sample possess one of the two features of the amphitheater—that is, curvature or raking—but not both. Banks of seating look on the dais from various directions of surround, but on a flat floor in Greensboro, Lynchburg, Tucson, and Austin (photo V.7). Seating is declined downwards at Boston, Tempe, Dallas, and Kettering, but the rows are straight (photos V.10 and V.19). The only audience seating arrangements that possess neither amphitheatric feature are classroom-style arrangements at Scottsdale, Rockville, and Paradise Valley (photos V.17 and V.42).

In other words, the typical configuration of semifixed features in Contemporary rooms consists of a concave dais and concave seating that face each other, with the hollows of the two opposing concavities creating a roughly circular form. The Traditional concept of a private inner circle of elected officials is replaced by a grander circle of officials and citizens. The straight, head-on confrontation of the Midcentury room is replaced by essentially nonbarricaded space that separates the two arcs, the roundedness of each suggesting, not a duality of opposing camps, but linked continua of valued opinion. In some places, such as Long Beach (fig. V.3), the tips of each arc almost physically touch, binding the governors and the governed together into a symbolic whole.

Given this joined relationship, it is not surprising that the seating that is provided to citizens in the Contemporary room consists of padded and attractive theater-style chairs (note, for example, photos V.9, V.10, and V.11). The trend away from benches, which began at Midcentury rooms, is continued, with undifferentiated bench seating found in only five rooms (Boston, Kettering, Lynchburg, Scarborough, and Toronto). Other kinds of seating are plastic shell chairs fixed to pedestals (Mesa, Miamisburg, and Tucson) and free-floating wooden or metal chairs (Paradise Valley, Rockville, and Scottsdale; photos V.15, V.38, and V.42 illustrate these types).

Also, it is in keeping with the joined authority relationship that aisle arrangements facilitate and express citizen access to the dais. In most of the rooms this is the case; it is achieved either by center aisles, as illustrated by Arlington, Fairfield, and Tempe (photos V.11 and V.14 and fig. V.1), or by converging radii, as in Fremont, Fort Worth, and Tucson (photos V.16 and V.25 and fig. V.2). These aisles range from 36 to 72 inches in width; the average is 53 inches, somewhat more than in Midcentury rooms (46 inches). Chambers whose aisle figuration does not suggest easy citizen access include Walnut Creek, Raleigh, and San Bernardino, all of which lack center aisles (photos V.9, V.40, and V.41). Boston's accessibility is very low because of concrete retaining walls (photo V.13), and Wilmington's is reduced by an old-fashioned zonal gate. At Scarborough, two side aisles point toward the front adequately, but the width of the curved benches and the lack of a center aisle notably impede a sense of citizen access (photo V.45). Despite the Contemporary chamber's comparative openness, then, it is not necessarily without restrictions on movement.

The Emergence of New Nodes

We recall that nonelected officials were generally subordinated in earlier rooms, although they enjoyed some enhancement of position during the Midcentury period. The tendency toward the lessened subordination of appointed officers continues in the Contemporary era. About half the time, officials such as city managers, city attorneys, and city clerks sit at the daises themselves. Also, tables for departmental heads and stenographic personnel are often placed directly in front of the dais.

More important, however, a new development emerges after 1960 in this realm: namely, the provision of separate semifixed-feature "nodes" for nonelected officials. That is to say, they are given large, prominent, and protective pieces of furniture of their own, an honor previously bestowed only on

Photo V.45. *Amphitheater seating, Scarborough, Ontario, Canada*

presiders and councilors. In some instances these nodes are extensions of the council dais. At Arlington the dais skirt extends as a wall on each end, so as to embrace appointee enclosures that constitute an integral part of the dais ensemble (photo V.11). The enclosure on the presider's right is used by the city staff, and the one on the left is used by the city secretary. A similar arrangement is found at Tempe (photo V.18 and fig. V.1). There, the right-hand enclosure is used by the city manager, the city clerk, and the city attorney, while the left-hand node is occupied by various departmental heads. The round table between the two is occupied by lesser staff. At Long Beach, four nodes are appended to the dais, two at each end (photo V.44 and fig. V.3). On the presider's left side the front node is occupied by the city manager and the city attorney; the rear node, by staff. On the right side the city clerk and associates occupy the front node; the press, the rear. This same idea is found on a much simpler basis

at Paradise Valley, where desks are appended to each end of the dais, with the right one provided for the town manager and the clerk and the left for the town attorney and the engineer (photo V.42). At Greensboro, three straight skirted benches with protective side uprights are furnished for professional city personnel (photo V.8). These are positioned, interestingly enough, in opposition to the council dais and close to audience seating; in other words, the bureaucrats are portrayed as being on the citizens' side, so to speak. Fremont also is unusual, in that four tables are built into the well's furniture grouping at differing tabletop levels, 13 to 26 inches below the tabletop level of the dais (photo V.16). The bench to the presider's left is for the city manager, the assistant city manager, and the city attorney, while other stations are occupied by departmental heads and staff. At Kettering a set of two auxiliary benches is situated on each end of the council dais, with the right-hand set being for the city manager, the assistant city managers, the police chief, and the law director and the left-hand set being for departmental heads (photos V.19 and V.20). In accordance with the use of rounded forms at Brea, two arc-shaped noncouncil daises fit perfectly into the circle of furniture in the well of that room (photo V.21). One is used for the city manager, the city attorney, and the senior planner (on the presider's left), while the other is for the city engineer, the city clerk, and the deputy city clerk (on the presider's right). And as we have already noted, the two Canadian chambers of Scarborough and Toronto include encircled multiple daises, some of which are used exclusively by the commissioners (i.e., administrators).

Other examples of appointee nodes are even more protective and status conferring. They may even be thought of as "junior" daises, although they are not arc-shaped. At Tucson an angled, skirted table is provided for the city manager, the deputy city manager, the city attorney, staff, and reporters. It is separate from the council dais, is over 12 feet long, and is placed on a podium 13 inches lower than the council's platform (fig. V.2). Angled benches for the officials are also used at Lynchburg (photo V.34) and at Rockville, with the latter being equipped with an oak-faced skirt and a 4-inch parapet, just like its councilors' counterpart. On the circular rotating stage at San Bernardino a relatively low but sizeable administration dais directly confronts the looming high skirt of the council's dais (photo V.41). When the stage is turned so that the mayor and the council can observe images projected on the back wall, the city administrator, the city attorney, and the city clerk ingloriously swing around out of sight, with their backs to the imagery, unable to see the screen.

Public lecterns are also significantly upgraded after 1960, some to the point of becoming virtual nodes unto themselves. A box-style lectern at Brea completes the circle of official furniture; it is elegantly finished in oak, like its companion pieces, and is packed with electronic gear (photo V.46). At Santa Rosa we find a dais-shaped witness table at the center of the well; it is surmounted by a tilted reading surface (photo V.24). The lectern at Phoenix is a massive piece of furniture 52 by 53 by 44 inches, whose secondary function is to house a projection lantern (photo V.37). At Dallas the public lectern is nothing short of a technological masterpiece: it is fitted with a digital clock that shows the elapsed time; a reading lamp that shines polarized light only downward; directive speaker trumpets; and a fold-out stool for children and other short citizens (photo V.39).

Other notable lecterns include the one at Wilmington, which is part of the rostrum ensemble and has roughly the same dimensions as the clerk's own lectern. It is, however, set off to the left of the rest of the rostrum group by a space of 29 inches, just enough to establish dissociation from officialdom, reminding us of similar furniture separations at the Paris Peace talks and in Polish courtrooms. A set of two box lecterns is provided at Austin, one on each end of the dais; the arrangement is intended to separate disputing parties by a safe distance of 25 feet or so (photo V.7). This is, one might suppose, the Texas equivalent of the nine feet that separate the sword lines on the floor of the House of Commons. At Tucson, an unusual degree of protection is afforded by a 7-foot public witness node that penetrates the zonal fence (fig. V.2). Its massiveness, concavity, and access from the public zone give citizens a solid and safe bulwark from which to face officials. The public witness table at Lynchburg is deceptive in that even though it appears to be a comfortable and secure node, it is in fact not so. A high, fixed microphone requires the witness' body to be pushed well under the table in order to allow the witness to speak directly into the instrument (photo V.34).

Photo V.46. *Public lectern, Brea, California*

Yet the arms on the chair prevent the chair from sliding beneath the table; as a result, the speaker has to squat miserably on the edge of the chair, arching his or her back so as to reach the microphone. Meanwhile, administrators at the adjacent table lean back comfortably, their voices amplified by lapel-mounted lavaliere microphones.

Again, members of the press do not fare well in Contemporary rooms, yet some improvement is evident over their lowly treatment in earlier spaces. As mentioned, reporters are allowed at the administrator node in Tucson and are given a node all their own in Long Beach. A respectable press gallery is furnished at the rear of the audience benches in Scarborough; it is reached through a special lobby entrance (photo V.26). In many of the chambers, press desks are furnished, most of which are placed, not in the official zone, but well into the public zone, often intermingled with public seating. Although the press continues to suffer relatively low esteem, it is now

portrayed as a component of the broader political community.

As before, I complete this discussion of Contemporary semifixed features by commenting on chair height and right- or left-handedness as differentiating factors. Differences in chair height are at about the same degree of frequency as in Midcentury rooms. Omitting the two chambers that utilize rostra rather than daises, six show sequential gradations between the presider, the councilors, and the administrators (means of 47, 40, and 33 inches, respectively). Thirteen others have two classes of chairs, those for elected officials and those for nonelected officials (means of 43 and 34 inches, respectively). These averages are similar to what we saw in Midcentury rooms (45, 35, and 34; 41 and 34). As for handedness, city managers continue to enjoy right-hand status in a majority of cases: when seated at the dais, they are at the right hand of the mayor in six of ten cases, and when at an off-center node or table, they are on the right in eight of eleven cases. Again, the press suffers from a left-place bias, being located at the president's left in six of eleven noncentral situations.

CONTEMPORARY DECORATION AND DISPLAY

Now, what about decorative practice and the display of objects in contemporary civic space?

Modernist Decoration

In the decoration of Contemporary chambers we find, not surprisingly, the Modernist revolt in interior design practices being manifest. Detailed ornamentation and attempts to replicate Neoclassical or revivalist detailing are vigorously rejected. Thus the Contemporary chamber is far removed from the classical *genius loci* of the Traditional room. Rather than featuring elaborately decorated walls and ceilings and richly ornamented rails, doors, and lamps, the Contemporary chamber possesses clean, relatively unadorned surfaces whose basic sculpting is itself the principal source of visual interest. As in the avant-garde Midcentury chambers of Chicago and Minneapolis, walls and ceilings are themselves manipulative of the environment.

Contemporary chambers are not, however, undecorated or treated casually in their accentuating elements. Although some items are inevitably added to them over time, the rooms tend to be, according to Robert Venturi's categories, holistic ducks rather than decorated sheds. These ducks are not always heroic and original, but they do possess an internal wholeness and consistency, just as do the best Neoclassical and art-deco rooms. Too tough-minded to fall into Norberg-Schulz's *genius loci* of Romantic, they can perhaps be thought of as Cosmic—that is, integrated rational systems.

Having little applied ornamentation or few appended objects, then, the wall and ceiling surfaces of Contemporary chambers emerge clearly for visual inspection on their own terms. One sees, not a decorated overlay or an artificial façade, but the underlying structural features themselves: angled walls, as in Fairfield and Fremont; rounded surfaces, as in Brea and Phoenix; waffleslab ceilings, as in Boston and Fort Worth; sculpted ceilings, as in Tempe and Wilmington; and a massive overhead beam, as in Paradise Valley. Nor is the continuity of surfaces unnecessarily interrupted: illumination is from flush-mounted fixtures rather than from protruding or hanging lamps. In rooms with window walls, such as Miamisburg and Walnut Creek, outdoor scenes become the decoration by day, while by night, one sees expanses of dark glass. As for windowless chambers, consistency as well as continuity obtains: appearance remains unchanged over the twenty-four-hour cycle. With no visual stimuli penetrating from the outside world, designers and officials are presented with a maximized opportunity to manipulate the environment.

Before describing the character of this manipulation more fully, two aspects of nonadornment deserve special mention. First, visual plainness is augmented by a preoccupation with the technological act of projecting visual presentations of images to audiences. Hence, projection screens, video screens, grease-pencil marker boards, and tack boards are much in evidence. The surfaces of these items are perforce plain, sometimes large in area, obvious to the eye, and frequently situated just behind the dais. The huge motor-driven hinged screen above the Dallas dais is a prominent example (photo V.39). The second point regarding visual plainness is that with so little busy detail to distract the eye, decorative items that do appear on surfaces stand out more clearly than would otherwise be the case. As I mentioned earlier, the city seal is sometimes the item that is chosen for highlighting in this way. While this overt emblem of municipal authority is nothing new in council chambers, it tended previously to be swallowed up by numerous competing figurations. The Contemporary isolation of the seal on a bare field is perfectly exemplified in Toronto (photo V.36). The 19-foot backdrop seal at San Bernardino has already been mentioned (photo V.41).

Usually, however, the Contemporary backdrop is less dramatic. Also, it can be highly individualized and quite revelatory of a city's unique self-image. On Greensboro's backdrop, for example, we find a framed embroidery entitled "City Alive," stitched by members of the Junior League (photo V.8). At Boston it is not the sewing of genteel Southern women that is on display; it is an old tapestry depicting a Yankee view of the Battle of Bunker Hill (photo V.13). In the Ontario suburb of Scarborough we find a reverential portrait of the queen; in the Sun Belt Texas city of Arlington a stylized *A* logo is displayed, rendered in gold-painted plastic (photo V.11).

With the surfaces themselves more in evidence than the items displayed on them, questions of surface color and texture become especially important. One notable aspect of color in Contemporary chambers is the high contrast in hues. Unlike Traditional rooms, where dark-stained wood and pastels predominate, Contemporary civic space has surfaces that tend to consist of naturally stained or unfinished wood, stark white plasters, and brightly colored textiles. Chairs in particular are done in vivid colors, such as cherry red, goldenrod, burnt orange, and royal blue. As a result, these items of furniture stand out sharply against white walls and dark carpeting. Although it is difficult to generalize, long-wavelength colors—such as red, orange, and gold—seem to be more common than shorter-wavelength greens and blues, a point that color theorists would find significant. Consciously or un-

consciously, the coloration of Contemporary chambers seems to promote warmth, not coolness.

Also, color becomes a way of differentiating status, as we have seen in the dais chairs at Miamisburg. Fixtures in different hues designate different classes of user. At both Boston and Wilmington, for example, officials sit in brown chairs, and citizens occupy red ones. Quite frequently, in fact, audience seating is upholstered in red, ignoring the old parliamentary rule of red seating for lords but green for commoners. Also, the material that covers the chairs varies, with fancy leather going to the governors and plain fabric to the governed. At Austin, for example, the audience sits on goldenrod cloth, the clerk on blue cloth, and the council on blue leather. The color of carpeting sometimes demarcates floor zones: at Miamisburg, the carpeting is gray in the official zone but purple in the public one (photo V.15). Tabletops, too, can be differentiated by color: the council dais at Greensboro is covered in somber black, while the administration and press desks are topped in blue and orange, respectively (photo V.8).

Another environmental factor that establishes status is light. In earlier chambers the space was lit in the daytime according to the vagaries of outdoor conditions and at night by a fairly uniform level of artificial illumination. In the Contemporary room, however, the lighting, whether natural or artificial, is carefully manipulated. One overall tendency is to illuminate the official zone and dais area more brightly than the public zone, even in rooms with window walls. In windowless rooms, decorators are free to highlight by the use of spots as they choose. Moreover, they can offer a range of choices as to what lighting conditions to create for individual events, a flexibility that is made possible by a variety of lamps, rheostats, and switching circuits.

A special word should be said about television lights. Klieg lights have been obviously added to chambers built before the television era, but even in chambers that were constructed since that time, they can be very noticeable (for examples in Austin, Kettering, and Brea see photos V.7, V.20, and V.21). When these powerful lights go on, the entire scene is suddenly transformed. The physically present audience is forgotten by officials, and all attention falls on those who are bathed in the intense illumination. Unless hardened by years of television exposure, those in the spotlight become self-conscious about their behavior, for they are now actors before a mass-media audience, rather than decision makers in face-to-face governance. In this heightened power situation, elected officials reportedly dress more carefully and speak more often and longer, illustrating in an extreme way the influence that the physical setting can have on behavior.[26]

A final characteristic of the Contemporary decorative environment is texture. Modernist decorators sometimes seek to impart a warm or human quality to interior spaces by means of soft or familiar materials that are inviting to the touch. This tendency is shown in the use of deep-pile carpeting, fabric-covered walls, tall hanging curtains, exposed brick, and light-colored paneling. At Fremont, the back walls are carpeted in gold up to a level of 8 feet, thus creating the modern equivalent of wainscoting. The creative use of brick walls is illustrated at Fairfield and Miamisburg (photos V.14 and V.15). Light-colored curtains cover significant wall areas in Lynchburg and Long Beach (photos V.34 and V.44). The substantial use of wood is somewhat ironic, because it was the primary material of decoration in the Traditional era. Now, however, the formality of dark staining is eschewed in favor of treatments that reveal the grain of the wood. Examples of warm wood surfaces are the laminated beams and the unfinished ceiling at Paradise Valley (photo V.6), the

cherry paneling at Greensboro (photo V.8), the matched-grain benches at Kettering (photo V.19), and the oak lectern at Brea (photo V.46).

One tendency in the use of wood has an especially interesting implication. In several chambers, wooden battens are mounted on the walls, often on top of fabric, in order to absorb sound. These narrow strips of wood are always mounted vertically, not horizontally, and they usually extend from the floor to the ceiling. The visual effect that this gives is a greater sense of verticality, a useful aim if one is attempting to impart additional dignity to the space. Examples of such construction are in Santa Rosa, Fort Worth, and Phoenix (photos V.24, V.25, and V.37).

Surely, contradictions in chamber architecture exist, and one of the more notable is the occasional case of extreme coldness in surface texture. The plaster surfaces at Scottsdale (photo V.4), the backdrop wall at Toronto (photo V.36), and projection screens at Dallas (photo V.39) suggest, not warmth, but the antiseptic setting of a rationalist concept of rule. The exposed concrete and the thick retaining walls in Boston exude a brutal solidity (photo V.13). At Tempe the hooded, dazzlingly white formica dais, brightly illuminated from above, is not merely cold; it is fearsome (photo V.18). Although warmth tends to be characteristic of Contemporary rooms, this is not always the case.

Objects of Technology and Warmth

We recall that the Traditional chamber contained numerous historical artifacts, art objects, and ceremonial items, such as flags, gavels, and maces. The Midcentury room, by contrast, stressed not merely historico-ceremonial objects but also communication devices such as calendars, tape recorders, tally display boards, dais nameplates, and behavior-directing signs. The Contemporary model carries on these themes in some ways. Ceremonial symbols of authority are often present, such as the aforementioned municipal seals and the ever-present national, state, and city flags. Small gavels are on hand at Lynchburg and Walnut Creek, and a Bible is permanently on the lectern at Raleigh (for swearing-in purposes). Also to be seen are cultural and historical items, such as pictures of prior mayors in Fairfield, Tempe, and Tucson; a World War II ship's bell in San Bernardino; early community photographs in Walnut Creek; pioneer artifacts owned by Scarborough's founders; and Winfield Scott's bust in Scottsdale.

With respect to devices of communication—a major display theme in Midcentury rooms—a clutter of maps, blackboards, and calendars is generally out of place in the often-stark Contemporary rooms. Nameplates, however, are very common. Unlike the Midcentury tendency to utilize desk-top holders for nameplates, Contemporary nameplates are usually fixed permanently on the dais skirt or on the front rim of the parapet. In other words, the notion of designating the identity of an official has become hardened, shifting from a relatively casual and optional mode of presentation to a more formal and permanent display (see examples at Phoenix and Austin in photos V.37 and V.43). Sometimes these nameplates are not that at all; they are electric signs that put the councilors' names in lights (see Dallas and Long Beach, photos V.39 and V.44).

The use of public voting displays has been extended since 1960. Electric tally boards, showing each councilor's vote, are often mounted in public view, as at Arlington and Fremont (photos V.12 and V.16). An electric tally display at Dallas is nothing short of spectacular; 24 feet long, it is mounted behind the dais and registers the names of councilors and their votes in 3.5-inch letters (photo V.39).

Two new themes emerge in the Contemporary display of objects. One is a high-tech

stamp, a characteristic that has already been revealed by earlier discussion. When the visitor at San Bernardino witnesses preparations for an audio-visual presentation, he or she does not observe a slide projector being hauled in or a flip chart being clumsily erected. Instead, simultaneously and silently, the rotary dais platform turns 180 degrees, a giant projection screen automatically descends over the 19-foot seal, and the beam of an arc lamp leaps forth from a rear projection booth (photo V.41). At Brea, such a presentation begins with the parting of the curtain (photo V.21). On the large translucent screen behind it, slides are flashed or videotaped images are projected from a room in the rear. This permits all machines to be hidden from view; they are, however, instantly controllable from the console of the lectern as I noted earlier (photo V.46). Other high-tech aids at Brea include laser pointers, automated projection programming, and high-fidelity sound tracks.

Dallas, without question, is the most technological of chambers. An aluminum parapet on the dais shields an array of equipment that incorporates two video displays per councilor, one to show what is being projected on the backdrop screens and one to indicate the members' votes and the status of the speakers' queue (visible in photo V.10). In addition to an individual telephone, each councilor has a console on which buttons can be pushed to cast votes, to secure a place in the speaking queue, and to call personal aides. The sound that emanates throughout the chamber comes from three separate speaker systems, making voices sharp and clear at any point in the room. Thousand-watt lamps, set in the ceiling, flood various light zones at variable intensities of illumination, depending on what effect is desired. Permanently mounted television cameras record all proceedings automatically and will eventually produce a signal for public broadcast. All of this technology is controlled in an equip-

Photo V.47. *Equipment room, Dallas, Texas*

ment-packed room that is located just off the public floor, manned by a full-time electrical engineer (photo V.47).

The second new theme in the Contemporary display of objects is almost diametrically opposed to the first. It has nothing to do with technological efficiency; rather, it concerns human feelings. Objects that are found near the entries of several rooms display a warm, humane, almost homey character. The chamber at Mesa, for example, which occupies its own building, is landscaped in front with trees and shrubs. In the lobby, one finds waiting benches, two drinking fountains, potted bamboo and other plants, and a wall rug that is evocative of the desert Southwest. Also mounted nearby is a portrait of Ronald Reagan. Similarly, plants and exhibits that are displayed outside the Scarborough chamber and the comfortable furniture that is found in Dallas's International Room induce a sense of calm and warmth as one approaches the chamber (photos V.26 and V.28).

Signs of warmth and humanity can also be seen inside the chambers. Overhead

plantings and a common upright piano accompany the theatrical San Bernardino setting (photo V.41). A Christmas tree, the warmest of objects perhaps, is visible in Wilmington at holiday time. The open, lodgelike character of Paradise Valley has been mentioned earlier: sofas, coffee tables, paintings, potted plants, and hanging plants convey the intimacy and comfort of one's own living room (photo V.6). The kiva at Scottsdale also has an informal air; in fact, it was seen by architect Gonzales as a kind of community living room (photo V.4). Its loose chairs, potted plants, and trees suggest a relaxed attitude toward governance. Meanwhile, the bust of Winfield Scott, the stained glass skylights overhead, and the Paolo Soleri mobile that hangs in the atrium impart a sense of civic importance to Scottsdale's living room.

THE CONTEMPORARY AURA

The aura of Contemporary civic space, as manifested in these council chambers, may be summarized as follows. First, the growing importance of professional bureaucracy in government is manifested. Increasingly, managers and administrators are given high status. They either sit at the dais, like other governors, or possess nodes of their own. Also, architects find it necessary to disconnect the council chamber itself from the administrative block of the city hall and to give it its own sense of importance. This is achieved by the elegant foyer, visibility from the exterior of the building, central placement in public circulation space, and the creation of a separate legislative temple.

Second, a sense of subtlety prevails. Indirection and the use of less-than-obvious manipulation characterize the modern chamber. Space is sculpted, which means that the background enclosure joins the foreground mass as a source of behavioral conditioning. When this space is not perforated by windows, the visual environment is under total control. Within this environment, decoration and display tend to be simple and plain, heightening the visual impact of what is exhibited. The calculated use of color, light, and texture enables a variety of statements to be made about intended human relationships, ranging from invitations of welcome to demarcations of status and role. Yet by their nature, these statements are low-key, in the background, and largely subliminal.

Third, the Contemporary chamber embraces its occupants. Rather than separating those who are present into clearly differentiated or opposing subgroups, it symbolically draws them together into a common order within the space. Overt dividing mechanisms are generally omitted, such as the floor-mounted barrier or a long axial distance. Floorplans are often curvilinear, even perfectly round. Concave daises face concave audience seating in a mutually open and receptive configuration. The combina-tion of raked banks of seats and low dais podiums permits the governed to be on a horizontal plane with the governors, or even above them. Short separating distances, rounded or angled ceilings and walls, and curvilinear floor plans add to the sense of an intimate community. Then too, the provision of substantial public lecterns, public aisles "aimed" at the dais, and permanent nameplates and tally boards underscores the notion of responsible officials who are accountable to an informed and participating public.

Finally, the substance of this subtle embrace is, at the same time, simultaneously harsh and tender. In some instances this duality is shown in contrasts between chambers: for example, between an intimidating Boston or Tempe, at one extreme, and a homey Scottsdale or Paradise Valley at the other. Yet also the ambivalence is found within the same rooms, as in Dallas, Long Beach, and San Bernardino, among others. Contemporary civic space is, inescapably, contradictory. On the one hand, it revives the large spatial size of Traditional rooms, is capable of presenting overwhelming official furniture, overpowers us with technology and media projection, and is even capable of humiliating us without knowing why, as in the witness table at Lynchburg. On the other hand, the Contemporary model offers soft and comfortable seating, permits the audience to see itself as "animated by one spirit," pleases the eye with window walls and atria, invites the touch with warm colors and textures, presents a kind of civic living room, and reassures us subconsciously with a mandala in the floor plan and an *axis mundi* puncturing the ceiling. Architectural expressions of governmental authority have simultaneously become both more ominous and more seductive.

VI The Social Meaning of Civic Space

In this book, I have examined the physical designs of seventy-five city-council chambers. My purpose has been to uncover, by means of architectural study, changing patterns of authority in democratic governance. The organizing thesis of the study has been that three principal categories of chamber design emerge from the welter of detail and individuality. These are the Traditional model, the dominant design from 1865 to 1920; the Midcentury one, the form favored from 1920 to 1960; and the Contemporary one, popular from 1960 onward.

I now conclude this volume with, first, an analysis of what the chambers tell us about what Merriam would call the miranda and credenda of our democratic political culture. Second, I consider the implications of this study for future research on architecture and society.

THE IDEAS THAT THE CHAMBERS EXPRESS

The descriptive findings of our study are summarized in the comparisons presented in table VI.1 and in the generic floor plans shown in figure VI.1. These summaries reveal the dramatic changes in chamber design that have occurred over the three eras.

The Traditional chamber is a large, boxlike square space, dominated by a massive elevated node of central focus, or rostrum, whose persona is that of unquestioned unilateral authority. Surrounding the rostrum are individual aldermanic desks, emphasizing that democratic governance centers on the representation of separate constituencies. The fact that the desks face the rostrum and not the audience suggests

that the authority relationships that count are those between the representatives and the presiding officer. Meanwhile, members of the public, separated from these officials by a high balustrade, are seated on benches around the periphery of the floor or in upstairs galleries, making them outside spectators to the governing process. The importance and the dignity of this process are architecturally stated by a grand staircase leading to the chamber; outsized and enhanced public portals; a high and ornate ceiling; formalistic decoration and wood paneling; and a rich trove of ceremonial and cultural objects.

The Midcentury chamber, by contrast, is smaller, has lower ceilings, and is laid out on a long rectangular floor plan. Even more consistently boxlike than its predecessor, its ceiling is flat. Officials and the public face each other along the major axis of the box, in an oppositional relationship. At one end of the space is the dais, mounted on a low platform. Behind this concave skirted table are seated the members of the council and the presiding officer, presenting themselves as a corporate body, rather than as individual representatives. At the other end of the room, separated by a thin rail and a public lectern, are blocks of audience chairs, squarely facing the dais in straight rows. In short, officials and citizens face each other in direct confrontation. Factors surrounding this confrontation—that is, the chamber's location, its doors, its decoration, and its objects—suggest a relatively pedestrian, utilitarian secular space.

Finally, the Contemporary chamber, like the Midcentury one, is fitted with a dais, a platform, audience chairs, convential door-

TABLE VI.1
All Chambers: Summary of Comparisons

| | SPATIAL COMPOSITION | |
Traditional Chambers	Midcentury Chambers	Contemporary Chambers
A Large Box	A Long Box	A Sculpted Enclosure
Large-volume spaces	Smaller-volume spaces	Intermediate-volume spaces
Low public-seating capacity	Medium public-seating capacity	High public-seating capacity
Chunky, squarish floor plans	Rectangular floor plans	Variously-shaped floor plans
Flat, perpendicular walls	Flat, perpendicular walls	Angled, canted, or rounded walls
Flat, horizontal floors	Flat, horizontal floors	Inclined or banked floors
High, configured ceilings	Low, flat ceilings	Sculpted ceilings of varying height
Public located around and apart from officials	Public located at one end of room and officials at the other end	Public and officials joined in a uniting form

An Exalted Room	Just Another Room	A Separated Room
On top floor of city hall	On intermediate floors of city hall	On ground floor of city hall
Reached by rotunda or court and grand staircase	Reached by lobbies, stairwells, elevators, and corridors	Reached by separating foyers, vestibules, and plazas
Symmetrically centered in building's floor plans	Located at any point in building or floor plans	Visible from outside of building or located in separate building

Generous Perforation	Reduced Perforation	All-or-Nothing Peforation
Numerous large windows	Fewer and smaller windows	Either window walls or no natural light permitted
Public doorways out-sized and enhanced	Public doorways smaller and plainer	Public doors totally utilitarian
Private doors for officials	Segregated doors for officials	Safe passage to officials' lounge

Traditional Chambers	FIXED FEATURES Midcentury Chambers	Contemporary Chambers
The Rostrum	The Dais	
Attention focused on presiding officer	Attention focused on council as a corporate body	
Presiding done behind massive bench	Presiding done from middle of concave table or dais	
Bench rests on elevated podium	Dais rests on floor or low platform	
Front of bench configured and protective	Front of dais consists of opaque skirt and parapet, concavely formed	
Presider framed against ceremonial chairs and backdrops	Dais chairs functional and equivalent; dais backdrops relatively simple and plain.	
Aldermanic Desks	Dais Seating	
Individual desks provided for each member	Councilors sit side by side around a common dais surface	
Desks face each other or rostrum	Councilors face the public, rather than themselves or the presiding officer	
Strict Segregation	Lessened Segregation	Obscured Segregation
Elevated public galleries segregated from floor	Public seated on floor at one end of room	Public seated in banked curve around officials
Fencelike floor barrier surrounds officials	Floor barrier diminished in importance	Floor barrier replaced by dais skirt
Casual Treatment of Others	Interest Shown in Others	Studied Treatment of Others
Bench seating for public	Individual seating for public	Amphitheater seating for public
A minimal lectern, if any	A consequential lectern	A sophisticated lectern
Simple tables for nonelected officials	Enhanced positions for nonelected officials	Protected positions for nonelected officials
Press in official area near rostrum	Press more centrally located in room	Press placed near audience seating

Table VI.1—*continued*

	DECORATION AND DISPLAY	
Traditional Chambers	Midcentury Chambers	Contemporary Chambers
Classic Decoration	Eclectic Decoration	Modernist Decoration
Formal embellishment of surfaces	Mixture of decorative styles and degrees	Decoration by structure, texture, color, light
Rich ornamentation throughout room	Mixture of ornamentation and utilitarian plainness	Surfaces relatively clean and clear
Cultural Displays	Functional Displays	Ambivalent Displays
Ceremonial objects and historico-artistic artifacts	Objects of communication, e.g., nameplates and directive signs	High-technology equipment and objects of warmth

ways, a lectern, and a limited number of ceremonial and cultural objects. Yet the room differs in significant ways. Instead of being boxlike, it constitutes a freely sculpted space. The room's nonperpendicular angles, flowing curves, and roundness on occasion bring together, in encircling fashion, a concave dais, on the one hand, and an amphitheater-style bank of public seating on the other. The concave hollows of the dais and the seating face each other across an open, unimpeded space. The open, trusting, and joined relationship that is suggested by this configuration is not a confrontation of the governors and the governed; it is a circular conferring of those who are dealing with the affairs of the common community. The decor of Contemporary civic space is simple, unadorned, and subtle; the environment is fully controlled, is often windowless, and transmits a combination of high-tech stimuli, on the one hand, and warm mood cues on the other.

What, then, does this architectural evolution tell us about the changes in North American political culture? As I admitted in chapter I, the use of architecture as an index of political culture is most unusual in the study of political culture. This study's premise is that unlike the more common surveys of political attitudes, architecture can—because of the durability of buildings—give us "readings" of the past as well as of the present. Moreover, this methodology has the advantage of taking us straight to the heart of the political culture—that is, to the values that are reposited in the habits of mind of those who rule by legitimated governmental authority. The ceremonial nature of civic space means that the "text" of what we are reading reveals these values of rule in more vivid and concentrated form than would be the case in purely utilitarian space, such as the back rooms and private offices of the public administration. The fact that this study of civic space has included detailed empirical comparisons—across numerous examples of one category of civic space—gives us the opportunity to uncover insights that would be missed by a noncomparative, small-sample, less-rigorous study.

We begin our analysis of this text with a highly concrete architectural change that has been noted: the replacement of rostrum and aldermanic desks by the dais. This shift, which began in the Midcentury era and was

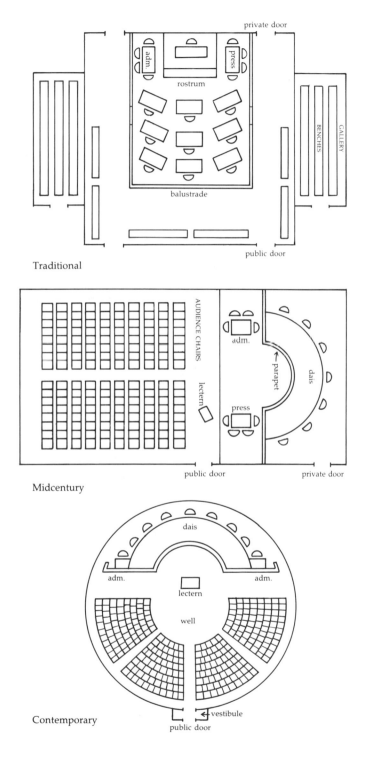

Traditional

Midcentury

Contemporary

Figure VI.1. *Generic floor plans*

completed in the Contemporary period, is almost total. The change constitutes a radical structural modification of chamber layout and cannot be attributed to a municipality's form of government. Both rostrum and dais appear in strong- and weak-mayor cities, in manager and nonmanager cities, and in municipalities where the council members are elected by district, at large, or by a combination of the two. Something deeper than legal powers or electoral arrangements is being manifested.

My interpretation is that this physical transformation expresses to us two fundamental and intertwined long-term trends in democratic governance. One is a trend away from personalistic rule; the other is a downgrading of geographic representation. The first notion is reflected in the shift in central focus from the rostrum's individual presiding officer to the council's corporate existence; the second idea corresponds to the move from separated aldermanic desks to the common dais table. Both trends can be noted in municipal governance and in the broader polity as well. Whereas once we were accustomed to boss-led machines and individualized leadership as the hallmark of city government, today we think more commonly in terms of the administration and of council policy. More broadly, as Max Weber so brilliantly analyzed, authority in the modern era is not derived from personal charisma; it is "routinized," controlled by rules and reasons, and lodged in ongoing institutions.[1]

Geographic representation also appears to be on the wane, relatively speaking. In the past, travel times were such that the legislative representative needed to possess ample autonomy and discretion in order to reflect local interests in the distant capital. Now, with modern communications and jet aircraft, the legislator is not so much an ambassador from afar as he is a political actor who happens to enjoy substantial access to the political process by virtue of occupying a

legislative seat. Growing social and economic interdependency within the society, meanwhile, makes national and even international issues more important than sectional controversies. Politics today is not so much a contest between regions of a geographic area as it is a contest between rival economic interests, opposing ideological positions, and competing ethnic and racial subgroups of the population.[2]

A second chamber transformation that is significant concerns the place of the public in democratic governance. The relevant architectural shifts are: adoption of the turnabout, whereby elected officials face the public, rather than having their backs to citizens; the movement of citizen visitors from the galleries to the floor; the furnishing of the public with individual chairs, rather than benches; the addition of proportionately more seating capacity as time goes on; the introduction and development of a public lectern; the downgrading or removal of upright barriers that segregate citizens and officials; and a swinging of the floor angle of vision from upwards at the rostrum to horizontally toward the dais and then, finally, downward from the amphitheater. These changes generally convey concepts of promoting popular sovereignty and democratic rule, of viewing the people as individuals rather than an undifferentiated mass, and of establishing the moral equality of the rulers and the ruled.

To appreciate the significance of these changes, let us review the place of the public in each era. In the Traditional chamber a ruling circle of governors confers internally as the public observes from afar. Within the chamber, officials, in comparison with citizens, are given fancier furniture, greater comfort, more room, more individual attention, and more visual emphasis. The relationship between the two sides is clearly asymmetrical; the scene is one of inferiors in the presence of superiors.

In the Midcentury room the relative status of the public is substantially uplifted by a substantial diminishment of this asymmetry. The governors are placed at one end of a longitudinal space; the governed, at the other. This bilateral relationship symbolizes the idea that government derives its power from the people and in turn is required to be accountable to the people for its exercise. The rulers are empowered, but their power is also checked or at least confronted. Those to whom the responsibility is entrusted are clearly identified, as are those to whom they are accountable. This is classic democratic doctrine, and the Midcentury model captures it perfectly.

In the Contemporary chamber, an upgraded and uplifted public is no longer so clearly identified. Seated in an amphitheater, the citizens see themselves as a collective body which is involved in the process of governance. The lectern from which they speak may be used by administrators as well as citizens. The walls and the ceiling of the space are configured in a way that embraces both parties at once. The concave hollows of the dais, on the one side, and the amphitheater, on the other, face each other in an open and trusting pattern. In short, all occupants of the space are brought together, joined in the common enterprise of governance. Citizens and officials, rather than being differentiated from each other or opposed to each other, are drawn into an intimate community.

This joined architectural design does not express the classic democratic doctrine of accountable representative government. Instead, by bringing citizens into the circle of governance itself, it projects what might be called the citizen-participation ideal. According to this ideal, citizens do not merely vote or run for office to control their destinies; they become actively and directly involved in the very processes of governance. Citizen participation has its pros and cons, its advocates and detractors.[3] It can be costly in time and money, but under the right con-

ditions, deliberate public involvement can encourage processes of open dialogue and foster a sense of civic responsibility. Citizen participation can also create false expectations and mislead the public on its true role in policy making. The nobility of the concept in terms of fulfilling the potentialities of citizenship can be buried by an empty, hypocritical ritualism that only masks the powerlessness of the ordinary citizen. The Contemporary chamber, then, expresses a noble ideal, but it also offers itself as a setting for the callous corruption of that ideal.

My concerns about the manipulation of civic life arise from what might be thought of as shifts in the strategy of authority over the three eras. In the Traditional chamber the strategy was one of creating a sense of awe in the hearts of those who entered. Size, height, grandeur, formality, ornateness, quality of workmanship, and artistic richness were used to overwhelm the visitor and to establish a sense of the great importance and dignity of the proceedings that transpired within. This is shown, for example, in high coffered ceilings; elaborately decorated doors, windows, and furniture; imperious rostra, with their carved front tiers and elaborate backdrops; and a panoply of artistic and ceremonial objects.

In the Midcentury model, by contrast, we encounter less height, less formality, functional ceilings and furniture, and a clutter of utilitarian objects and directional signs. Authority is exerted, not by inspiring awe, but by telling us directly what to do or by working out reasonable agreements by compromise and in accordance with the law. The room's aura is relatively relaxed, attuned to efficiency and economy, and concerned with the here and now. It is not burdened with monumental stairways, outsized portals, dim portraits, dust-catching statues, irrelevant maces, and gavel-striking blocks. Authority is "legal-rational," as Weber would describe it.

The Contemporary chamber utilizes a

very different strategy of authority. It barely asserts authority at all—at least not openly. Instead of demanding obedience or proposing reasonableness, it presents itself as inherently attractive and desirable. The Contemporary room seduces, rather than frightens; invites, rather than imposes; comforts, rather than commands. It achieves this by curved smooth lines, comfortable and colorful seating, ground-floor convenience, pleasant lobbies and anterooms, warm-textured surfaces, and homey potted plants. The visitor is assured the opportunity to see well because of raked seating, to hear well because of high-fidelity sound systems, and to feel well by virtue of complete climate control. Elitist fine art is replaced by egalitarian technology. Windows are no longer for architectural decoration or for cooling off the room on a hot night; instead, they are image-producing walls of glass, if they exist at all. Subtlety has replaced overtness as the mode of transmitting mood cues, and "looking good" has overcome solid craftsmanship as the standard of quality—whether in terms of designer fabrics and colors or the latest in technological hardware.

Even in the more intimidating Contemporary rooms the source of anxiety is obscure rather than blatant. Boston's concrete retaining walls, ostensibly to keep citizens from falling to the floor, segregate them effectively from the proceedings. Tempe's formica dais, seemingly the latest thing in design and materials, constitutes a gleaming fortress that is psychologically capable of deflecting bullets. Lynchburg's public witness desk, presumably a boon to the comfort and status of its occupant, makes people squat humiliatingly before the dais. In short, control is quietly exerted in the Contemporary room, perhaps more ominously than in earlier eras when authority was candidly superior or openly confronted.[4]

A final textual reading concerns the treatment, over the three eras, of the legislative function and its relation to the rest of government. As I noted in chapter II, city halls that were built prior to the Civil War did not necessarily set aside a specialized space devoted only to the deliberations of the city council. But during the Traditional era, council chambers became one of the most emphasized parts of the city hall. They were located in a strategic section of the upper floors of the building, reached by an open staircase that dominated the building's rotunda or inner court. In the Midcentury period, as we have seen, the chamber's key position was downgraded to being just another room of the building. Then, in the Contemporary period, the chamber was reemphasized again by preceding it with impressive anterooms, making it visible on the outside of the building, placing it within public circulation space, or creating a separate legislative temple.

My analysis of this development is that during the Traditional period, no reason existed *not* to give the council preeminence. The legislative function was, after all, the most powerful and obvious function of municipal government at that time. Only later did the unique status enjoyed by an elected council become endangered by the arrival of modern bureaucracy. As time went by, administrative offices and rooms for records and equipment took up more and more space in city hall. Such encroachment was gradual, and not until the latter half of the twentieth century was the council's identity and prestige seriously threatened. By 1960 the professional bureaucracy was so obviously the dominant force at city hall that elected officials and their collaborative architects found it necessary to compensate for this by introducing the special devices of the disconnection and the enhancement of the legislative function.

The rise of bureaucratic power and the corresponding loss of legislative prerogative is a widely recognized historical transition in modern government. Thus, while the point is nothing new, the close correspondence of this known trend with its architectural manifestation, which I have traced in this book, confirms the validity of my methodology. The rise of bureaucratic influence is furthermore manifested inside the chamber. Before 1920 the bureaucrats were given casual furniture treatment in the form of simple tables and chairs located behind the elected officials. Over the next four decades the semifixed features of administrators were made more substantial and were moved forward to a position of greater visibility. Then, after 1960, nonelected officials came to enjoy positions at the dais itself or were granted nodelike daises of their own. In addition to coming to terms with the lay public in their ritual space, legislators now had to do so with the experts and professionals as well.

IMPLICATIONS FOR FUTURE RESEARCH

The antecedents of this study are the ruminations of Paul Goodman on the meaning of legislative floor plans and articles by John Hazard and Allan Greenberg on the symbolism of courtroom design. In this book, although I have gone beyond these pioneering efforts, I have by no means exhausted the subject; indeed, an almost unlimited amount of future research seems possible on the symbolism of formal rooms.

Many other kinds of civic space could be studied, for one thing. These would include national parliamentary chambers, state capitol chambers, legislative committee rooms, the hearing rooms of regulatory bodies, official reception areas, and the public offices of heads of state or other important governmental officials. Also, attention could be given to temporarily created ritual spaces, such as stages for inaugural ceremonies and state funerals, and purely ceremonial places, such as enclosed monuments and shrines. Future studies could, moreover, explore not merely the meaning of era of construction as

an explanatory variable but also differences between cultural settings of the same era. Legislative or judicial space could be compared between nations, for example. Also, committee and hearing rooms could be investigated from the standpoint of differing subject-matter jurisdictions, and offices and reception areas of officials could be looked at from the perspective of contrasting political styles.

In this book, I offer a varied set of conceptual tools for those who might wish to engage in such additional inquiry. One such tool is our very notion of civic space. I also propose specific categories for the collection and analysis of data—namely, the composition of space, the arrangement of semifixed features, the patterns of decoration, and the character of portable objects.

A number of conceptual notions are also offered as guidance to interpretation. These have been derived from diverse literatures in anthropology, sociology, political science, psychology, linguistics, art history, architecture, and environmental design. The concepts include the dichotomies of sacred/profane, solid/void, front/back, up/down, left/right, sociopetal/sociofugal, and cohesive/differentiating; the abstract forms of square, circle, mandala, cross, and *axis mundi*; the architectural elements of enclosure, mass, ceiling, dome, pit, stair, door, window, and canopy; the spatial ideas of explicitness, perforation, centrality, opposition, path, and boundary; the feature design ideas of semifixed object, interpersonal distance, node, landmark, and edge; and the decorative elements of rhythm, symmetry, texture, and warmth.

Also offered by our study is a methodological approach. Suggested by the work of Amos Rapoport, the method calls for the direct examination of large numbers of examples of a certain category of civic space. The category in which comparisons are made is chosen with a view to eliminating the effects of irrelevant variables and to introducing true comparability to the investigation. Also called for is rigorous observation, careful measurement, thorough note taking, prolific photography, and extensive interviewing of users and, if possible, builders.

Rooms are not merely objective or impersonal spaces; they are places that constitute human domains and that carry subjective meaning. Hence a sound methodology must insist on humility and respect for others' understanding as the task of interpretation is approached. Vast collections of data and large samples must be studied over a considerable time; and from this extensive effort the student must be prepared to extract relatively few overarching conclusions. Such conclusions, even at that, will not constitute scientific findings; they will be tentative generalizations, subject to continuous refinement and reconsideration.

If further applications of such a methodology are made, I would argue, we can greatly exceed our current level of insight in this realm of the confluence between architecture and politics. We can leave behind, for example, Lasswell's oversimplified association of openness with democracy and closedness with despotism. Also, we can overcome the antiestablishment biases of writers such as Milne, who are obsessed with public architecture's stabilizing function. The same is true with students of public architecture such as Piñón, who insist that governmental structures merely legitimize corrupt authority. If nothing else, we have learned from this book that state-sponsored space can take multiple forms, can express diverse concepts of authority, and can project varying proclivities toward authenticity and/or manipulation.

Let us now consider the implications of this study for research in fields other than architecture. The principal conclusion of this book is that the council chambers that I studied fall into three categories, each of which embodies a concept of political authority. These are imposed authority, where

power is unilaterally asserted by superiors over inferiors; confronted authority, where the power asserted by superiors is checked by inferiors; and joined authority, where the power asserted is either shared with inferiors or is reasserted in a more subtle way. This third approach could open the way to the truly democratic community; also it could imply the manipulative aspects of impression management, behavioral modification, or cooptation as Philip Selznick conceptualized it.[5]

That my readouts of North American political culture via the council chamber would yield this set of ideas about political authority should not surprise us, if we think for a moment about parallel notions that have guided Western political life over the past few centuries. Indeed, three great ideas from the history of Western political ideas parallel quite closely our three chamber types. First, the unilateralism of the Traditional model calls to mind the notion of monarchic rule by virtue of divine right. Philosophic concepts such as the state and sovereignty, espoused by such thinkers as Jean Bodin and Thomas Hobbes, have much in common with our architecturally expressed ideas of the unquestioned authority of governmental officialdom and the subservient status of the general public. Second, the aura of our Midcentury room parallels ideas that cluster around the broad notion of constitutional government. Limited state power and individual rights, checks of parliament upon the king, and a Madisonian separation of powers correspond to the configuration of officials confronted by citizens. Third, the Contemporary chamber can be linked to the twin ideas of political community and direct democracy. Jean Jacques Rousseau's concept of the General Will and progressivism's faith in direct democracy through initiative, referendum, and recall correspond to the ethos of joined authority. More contemporary parallels include totalitarian people's republics and U.S.–style citizen participation. In short, our three models of political authority do not stand in intellectual isolation. They can be traced to equivalent earlier streams of political thought.

Can our triad of ideas concerning authority offer suggestions for future research that extend beyond the analysis of the underlying political culture? Do the notions of imposed authority, confronted authority, and joined authority have relevance for analysis in other social realms? Let us consider this possibility by exploring other conceptual parallels.

In 1925 the social theorist Mary P. Follett suggested that "there are three main ways of dealing with conflict: domination, compromise, and integration." Her notion of domination, it would seem, could be linked to imposed authority. Compromise, for its part, can be thought of as the logical outcome of confronted authority. Integration, by which Follett means discovering new options through a revaluation of interests, could potentially occur in the context of joined authority.[6] Two contemporary authors in the field of political economy also offer comparable frameworks. Charles E. Lindblom maintains that social control is primarily achieved by three methods: authority, exchange, and persuasion. The first method utilizes direct compulsion; the second, voluntary agreement between parties; and the third, a revision of preferences by education or propaganda. John Kenneth Galbraith argues that there are three types of power: condign—the ability to inflict punishment in the event of noncompliance; compensatory—the ability to offer rewards in return for cooperation; and conditioned—the ability to persuade and educate others. The parallels between these triads and our own are intriguing.[7]

One can also consider successive schools of thought in various academic disciplines in this light. Classic management theory, as espoused by Frederick Winslow Taylor and Henri Fayol, calls for an imposed type of unilateral exercise of managerial control. Neoclassical theorists, such as Chester I. Barnard and Herbert A. Simon, visualize management as an executive balancing act whereby incentives are distributed among competing requirements so as to maximize the cooperation of employees. Joined authority is then represented by the human-relations school of management and its successor schools, which argue that cooperation is best induced by allowing workers to fulfill their potential as creative participants in the management process itself. In the field of public administration, too, we encounter a remarkable mirroring of ideas. Imposed authority is comparable to the merit-system model of Alexander Hamilton, whereby the most able and the best trained are sought out to administer the state, without further legitimization. Confronted authority coincides with the politics/administration dichotomy of Woodrow Wilson, whereby administrators are strictly accountable to legislators. Joined authority suggests Andrew Jackson's faith in the common man as an administrator and, more recently, the active commitment to shared power and equitable policy identified with the so-called New Public Administration.

The parallels do not end with intellectual constructs. They also extend to stages or steps in the unfolding of history. On a world scale, three great forms of politicoeconomic organization that have emerged since feudalism match our triad. Mercantilism constituted an imposed economic policy on behalf of the sovereign. Capitalism, which replaced mercantilism, contemplates open confrontation among competing producers. Corporatism, a system popular in fascist countries during the 1930s and now gaining renewed favor among intellectuals, structures the participation by all sectors of society in the making of policy but at the same time exerts governmental control on both the processes of consultation and their outcomes. Another grand historical parallel is contrasting approaches to world social and economic change. Colonialism, the device of the nineteenth century, involved imposing metropolitan power on peripheral areas. Subsequent revolutionary movements for national independence created violent confrontation between imperialists and nationalists. More subtle economic and cultural hegemony that has been achieved by international investment and multinational business corresponds to a kind of joined authority.

Still more examples of correspondence are found in the history of American public policy. Time and time again, successive shifts of approach in a specific policy area seem to coincide with our triad. In the area of business policy, for example, the trusts and monopolies of the late nineteenth century imposed their will unilaterally on the marketplace. Subsequent antitrust laws have attempted to lessen economic concentration and to foster competitive confrontation in each market. The rise of modern advertising and mass-media broadcasting then permitted the manipulation of consumer demand to become the key to business success, in the manner of Lindblom's persuasion.

In public welfare, one might liken paternalistic charity to imposed authority, the client-rights movement to confronted authority, and negotiated action plans or service coproduction to joined authority. Similarly, in labor policy, one can point successively to the employer's unchallenged exploitation of a nonunion work force; the bilateralism of collective bargaining; and the fluid processes of labor mediation. In the field of business/government relations the triadic parallels are the unilateral governmental regulation of the firm; negotiated settlements with politically powerful corporations; and a united industrial policy based on mutual interest.

These numerous parallels—in such wide-ranging realms as the history of political ideas, the conceptual frameworks of com-

mentators, the schools of thought of academic disciplines, the stages of world history, and finally, the development of public policy—suggest indeed that this study of council chambers has yielded a social meaning beyond the symbolism of public architecture. The very tangible nature of architecture has, perhaps, uncovered for us a conceptual organizing tool of widespread applicability in studying the intangible social world. This tool is obviously not original, but its simultaneous presence in so many realms has perhaps not been as clear as it could have been. Without claiming that the sequence of imposing, confronting, and joining has some mysterious universality or structural importance, let us be content to propose that the further deployment of this framework as a research tool be attempted in other areas.

This triad is, after all, a very simple and elemental one. Its internal logic involves a basic dialectic whereby those who are in power merely act in their own interest. First, they initially assert power over others, whether as monarchs, managers, mercantilists, colonialists, monopolists, philanthropists, employers, or regulators. Second, this act thereby stimulates the introduction of a counterresponse by those who are thus controlled, for example, by parliaments, employees, capitalists, revolutionaries, competitors, litigants, unions, or the regulated. Third, those in power do not stand idly by in the face of this counterresponse; instead, they take steps to neutralize it. These steps are either a demonstrated willingness to share power or a pretended willingness to do so. The result, to repeat our selective examples, is such enterprises as people's republics, quality circles, neofascist corporatism, economic imperialism, seductive advertising, client coproduction, labor mediation, and industrial policy. Whether one is content with what joined authority produces is a question to be pondered: Is it an evolutionary step to be sought or resisted?

Appendix: Proposals for Civic Space

The following comments are addressed to architects and city officials who are concerned with the construction of new city halls or with the renovation of old ones. I offer a brief set of my own personal suggestions on the design of city-council chambers that stem from my interest in these rooms as expressions of political values. Certainly I have no expectation of building democratic values via architecture in the spirit of a latter-day John Ruskin, but I would like to offer some design suggestions that comport with the notions of public responsiveness and accountability, reject devices of intimidation and deception, and preserve links to the past. While my own values will clearly shape these recommendations, civic space is highly utilitarian as well as highly symbolic; hence the exercise of personal preference is limited by practicalities, as Canter pointed out in regard to designing a kitchen. If the reader is interested in pursuing my prescriptive suggestions in greater detail than developed here, I have published a short monograph on planning the council chamber and an article specifically directed to the chamber of the small municipality.[1]

I have noted that more recent chambers tend to downplay the individual leader, such as the mayor or the council president. While the era of bosses is appropriately behind us, effective leadership remains indispensable in the modern polity. It is my belief that the present-day council chamber can go too far in portraying leadership as collective. Clearly it would be a mistake to build new chambers that would contain majesterial rostra that glorify the presider. Yet some rather simple, practical things can be done to reassert the idea of individual leadership in civic space and thereby clarify the lines of responsibility for municipal actions.

One thing that can be done is to provide a special chair. At Miamisburg, we recall, the mayor's chair is white, while councilors are seated in black chairs of the same design. There is no reason why the presider's chair could not also have a higher back. It would not have to be of a totally different design, as in Bay City or Worcester; it could simply be a few inches higher. Presiders' chairs in Toronto, Phoenix, and San Bernardino exemplify what can be done. Another device to accentuate the chairperson is to give the central position at the dais some special architectural emphasis. One way to achieve this is to make the center of the dais convex, while the dais as a whole remains concave. This is what was done, in effect, in the most recent modification at Annapolis. A simpler and probably equally effective approach is to make the center position both raised in horizontal surface and forward in its vertical face—in short, to create a presiding officer's quasi node at the center of the dais so that it protrudes from the rest of the furniture. This method is used in various ways at Sacramento, Denver, and Duluth.

Also, something could be done architecturally to reestablish the concept of geographical representation. This is a point of particular importance in communities where ethnic minorities are attempting to secure political power by electing their own representatives from electoral districts in which they constitute a majority of the population. It is possible, of course, to revive the old aldermanic desk-rostrum pattern. But steps to enhance the importance of district representation can also be taken in a dais-type configuration. One solution is to form a dais by a row or arc of individual aldermanic-style desks. In this way, each councilor is more clearly identified as a separate member of the council by his or her separate piece of furniture. Arrangements in Bay City, Annapolis, and Denver reflect this idea.

In the integrated dais, efforts could also be made to identify more clearly which district or ward a member is representing. Electric name signs, such as those integrated into the skirt at Dallas or placed on the top of the dais in Long Beach, could state in large numerals the district being represented. These numerals could perhaps be taller than the letters used for the councilor's name. Also vote-tally display boards could prominently list the voter's district number; in most such displays, only the names are given.

Practical steps could also be taken to make Contemporary chambers more honest and less hypocritical with respect to citizen involvement. The basic objective here is to make it clear that governmental officials alone are responsible for the decisions made by the government, and no one else. This can be done without sanctifying authority, as the Traditional model does. Also, there is no need to ask modern architects to eliminate spatial sculpting or amphitheater seating and to readopt the box. Three rather simple features in a chamber can do much to stress the responsibility of the council and preserve the notion that citizens can and should participate, while also holding the councilors accountable for their actions. One measure is to place some kind of upright barrier on the floor between the council and the audience. Without resorting to the classic balustrade or solid wall, an open rail or hanging rope or chain will serve this purpose. The simple rail approach is exemplified in nineteenth-century brass at Philadelphia and in nonelaborated iron at Long Beach. A hanging rope is used with effectiveness in Pittsburgh and Los Angeles, and a chain in Cincinnati.

Another device is to make sure that the council is raised on a platform of some kind. A revived Roman *suggestus* is one possibil-

ity. The platform need not be more than six or twelve inches high, just enough elevation to accommodate one or two steps. This height will not create radically upward sight lines for the audience, but it will articulate unmistakably who is in charge. Moreover, I urge that such ascendency not be achieved by a hidden platform, such as one that extends behind the dais only. When the dais skirt absorbs the podium's height, the council appears to be elevated and thus more august to the observer; but the eye does not immediately discern why this is so. Such manipulative visual impressions should be avoided.

Finally, the public lectern can be shifted from its usual location inside the official zone or at the zonal boundary to well within the public zone. Then it truly becomes a *public* lectern, belonging to the citizens for their independent use, and not one primarily for the administrators and other insiders.

Let us now consider the relations between the legislative function and the bureaucracy. Attempts to highlight the council's importance by means of foyers, external visibility, separate temples, and the like should be strongly encouraged in the age of the modern administrative state. Otherwise, in view of the office nature of most of the city hall, the crucial importance of the legislative process to democratic governance is downplayed in the popular mind.

Inside the chamber itself, design and furniture arrangements should give the unmistakable impression that administrators are subordinate in authority to elected officials. It is in this realm that considerable improvement in Contemporary trends could be made, because all too frequently the senior nonelected officials are given status comparable to that of the elected representatives. City managers, city attorneys, city clerks, and other nonelected officers should not sit at the dais next to council. They may be clustered with elected officials, but at the same time they must be clearly subordinate to them. This can be achieved by placing their writing surfaces several inches lower or by locating the administrators' desks clearly apart from the dais.

The overall aura that a chamber projects should be consciously considered. The dignity and majesty of New York's elaborate baldachin, San Francisco's oak paneling, Trenton's proud murals, Milwaukee's reredos backdrop, and Schenectady's church-like sanctity stir the soul, even in the late twentieth century. The relaxed clutter of some Midcentury civic space, on the other hand, does not inspire. The Contemporary chamber, with its impression management, comforts more than it inspires.

The temptation to be reactionary in one's prescriptions is difficult to resist. The old seems better than the new; then why not return to it? That is impossible, of course; we must think of new ways in which civic space can be inspirational, in accordance with present times and circumstances.

I propose, first, that cities that now have beautiful older civic space do their best to preserve it. Care must be taken not to remodel rooms of ritual in a manner that violates their underlying purpose. We must put a permanent ban on dropping ceilings, painting over fine paneling, and inserting a modern dais in a nineteenth-century setting. Civic spaces that have already been violated architecturally should be returned to their original condition; in this regard the cities of Baltimore, Bay City, Cambridge, New York, Peoria, Providence, and Schenectady should be congratulated for their restoration programs. Other cities should be given credit for keeping older spaces nicely intact, such as Buffalo, both Charlestons, Cleveland, Kansas City, Los Angeles, Lowell, Madison, Milwaukee, Oakland, Pasadena, Philadelphia, Saint Paul, San Francisco, and Springfield. While these rooms are clearly out of date in the era of Modern architecture, they are innately impressive and dignified on their own terms and can serve their commu-

nities well. They should be treasured by their citizens.

Second, I propose that architecturally undistinguished chambers be appropriately remodeled so as to introduce thematic unity and a sense that they are important places. The clutter can be removed, matching and substantial furniture can be built, and care can be taken with decorative details so as to impart the notion that the space deserves respect. Particular attention should be paid to selecting a relatively small number of wall hangings and to reducing the obtrusiveness of communications gear through the use of miniaturized and remotely operated equipment. The city of Annapolis exemplifies what can be done in an appropriate upgrading program.

Finally, I recommend that in constructing new city halls, close attention be given to symbolized values, as well as to contemporary design fads. While individual architects must be free to be artistically creative and responsive to the design impulses of their own generation, they should also consider the broader expressive implications of civic space for democratic political life. This was done by Eugene W. Betz in Kettering, Edward Durrell Stone in Fort Worth, Bennie M. Gonzales in Scottsdale, and Viljo Revell in Toronto, with generally if not wholly laudable results.

Without sacrificing Contemporary trends of simplicity, subtlety, and sculpted space, it is possible to give special attention to certain key issues in modern chambers. One is intimacy. The flexibility of sculpted space permits the physical distances between the occupants to be minimized, even while maintaining differentiations that underscore accountability. Another issue is perforation. Surely the sense of openness that is created by window walls projects an image that is more advantageous to the municipality than are any psychological gains that may be achieved by the closed room's impression management. Another issue is technology:

while the latest sound, light, projection, security, and television systems should obviously be employed, there is no need to flaunt technological sophistication before the lay citizen. The city's duly conferred legal powers, not its acquired hardware, should be the source of its authority. Also of importance is the question of intimidation and hidden coercion: these qualities should be ruled out as being morally unacceptable. No democratically governed community should permit San Antonio's V-shaped dais with gooseneck microphones, Lynchburg's humiliating witness chair, or Tempe's formica fortress.

Last is the matter of the expression of humanity's deeper longings. More critical to humanitarian civic space than all the newest gimmicks, designer fabrics, and potted plants in the world is a sense of connectedness with one's origins and the universal aspirations of humankind. Designers should not hesitate to introduce showcases of historical artifacts (as at Charleston), a lithograph of the young city as it once was (as in Alexandria), or the bust of a founder (as in Scottsdale). The yearning for what is aesthetically beautiful exists also at this level of need, hence the fine oil painting, the ancient tapestry, the graceful staircase, or the beautifully polished wood must always be welcome. Then finally come the mystical archetypes—the circles, the mandalas, the occuli, and the *axes mundi*. If they are planned in too calculating a way, esoteric artificiality results. But we should not stifle such deep impulses in the architect's mind if they should emerge on their own. When they do, let us celebrate the mystery of what is wrought.

Notes

CHAPTER I. THE NOTION OF CIVIC SPACE

1. The description is based on an illustration included in Geoffrey Broadbent, "Revolutionary France," *Architectural Design*, profile 23 (on Neoclassicism), vol. 49, nos. 8 and 9 (London, 1979): 22. An illustration of the previous assembly of the Estates General, convened in 1614, is found in A. R. Myers, *Parliaments and Estates in Europe to 1789* (London: Thames & Hudson, 1975), p. 103.

2. R. K. Gooch, *Parliamentary Government in France: Revolutionary Origins, 1789–1791* (New York: Russell & Russell, 1960), chap. 1. Also see J. A. Laponce, *Left and Right: The Topography of Political Perceptions* (Toronto: University of Toronto Press, 1981), pp. 47–52. Laponce cites evidence to the effect that prior to 1789 the extreme right and left positions in assembly halls had become the accustomed places for the most vigorous debaters, but apparently this practice was not translated into ideological seating positions until this incident.

3. Gisors's National Convention space, as well as his similar Assembly Hall for the Council of 500, which was built in the Bourbon Palace in 1795, are illustrated in Broadbent, "Revolutionary France," pp. 22–23. For further discussion and illustration of the Bourbon Palace see Ferdinand Boyer, *Le Palais-Bourbon sous la Révolution et l'Empire* (Paris: Jean Schemit, 1936); and Jean Marchand, *Le Palais Bourbon* (Paris: Librairie Hachette, 1962).

4. Robert R. Taylor, *The Word in Stone: The Role of Architecture in the National Socialist Ideology* (Berkeley: University of California Press, 1940). Note also Barbara M. Lane, *Architecture and Politics in Germany, 1918–1945* (Cambridge, Mass.: Harvard University Press, 1968), chaps. 6–8.

5. Taylor, *Word in Stone*, pp. 130–37 (see photographs of the rooms hereafter described). Additional description of the Reich Chancellery is found in Gerald Blomeyer, "Architecture as a Political Sign System," *International Architect* 1, no. 1 (1979): 54–61.

6. Taylor, *Word in Stone*, p. 140; and Charlotte L. Stuart, "Architecture in Nazi Germany: A Rhetorical Perspective," *Western Speech* 37 (Fall 1973): 256.

7. In this phrase, Churchill was probably echoing Montesquieu's words: "At the birth of societies, the rulers of republics establish institutions; and afterwards the institutions mold the rulers." The address is reprinted in full in *Winston S. Churchill, His Complete Speeches, 1897–1963*, ed. Robert Rhodes James (New York: Chelsea House, 1974), vol. 7, pp. 6869–73.

8. Kenneth R. MacKenzie, *The Palace of Westminster* (Norwich, Eng.: Jarrold & Sons, 1977), p. 57. For added details on the Commons chamber see Michael Rush and Malcolm Shaw, eds., *The House of Commons: Services and Facilities* (London: George Allen & Unwin, 1974); and Bryan H. Fell and Kenneth R. MacKenzie, *The Houses of Parliament*, 13th ed. (London: Eyre & Spottiswoode, 1977).

9. Materials for this incident are drawn from the following press sources: *New York Times*, 17 Jan. 1969; *Times* (London), 17 Jan. 1969; *Time*, 24 and 31 Jan. 1969; *U.S. News & World Report*, 27 Jan. 1969.

10. Sources for these ideas will be given when they are discussed in greater detail in chap. 2.

11. Again, this literature will be fully cited later.

12. Charles E. Merriam, *Political Power* (New York: Collier Books, 1964), chap. 4.

13. William E. Connely proposes that political language—he calls it the terms of political discourse—be used to assess the underlying structure of political culture; see *The Terms of Discourse* (Lexington, Mass.: D. C. Heath, 1974).

14. Bill Kinser and Neil Kleinman, "History as Fiction," from *The Dream That Was No More a Dream* (1969); passage excerpted in James E. Combs and Michael W. Mansfield, eds., *Drama in Life: The Uses of Communication in Society* (New York: Hastings House, 1976), pp. 402–3.

15. Juan Pablo Bonta, *Architecture and Its Interpretation: A Study of Expressive Systems in Architecture* (London: Lund Humphries, 1979).

While indexes originate directly from reality but have no senders, or emitters, Bonta defines signals as expressions that are intentionally emitted by senders.

16. Amos Rapoport, "Vernacular Architecture and the Cultural Determinants of Form," in *Buildings and Society: Essays on the Social Development of the Built Environment*, ed. Anthony D. King (London: Routledge & Kegan Paul, 1980), pp. 283–305.

17. The published outcome of this project is William L. Lebovich, *America's City Halls* (Washington, D.C.: Preservation Press, 1984).

18. Edward Relph, *Place and Placelessness* (London: Pion, 1976), pp. 54–55.

19. Robert J. Braidwood, Halet Cambel, and Wulf Schirmer, "Beginnings of Village-Farming Communities in Southeastern Turkey: Çayönü Tepesi, 1978 and 1979," *Journal of Field Archaeology* 8 (1981): 249–58. A personal communication received from Professor Braidwood, dated 2 July 1985, elaborates on the ground-plan forms.

20. Frank Frost Abbott, *A History and Description of Roman Political Institutions*, 3d ed. (New York: Biblio & Tannen, 1963), pp. 226–27.

21. Clifford Geertz, *Negara: The Theatre State in Nineteenth-Century Bali* (Princeton, N.J.: Princeton University Press, 1980), pp. 109–13.

22. Paul Goodman, *Utopian Essays and Practical Proposals* (New York: Random House, 1952), pp. 168–72.

23. John N. Hazard, "Furniture Arrangement as a Symbol of Judicial Roles," *ETC: A Review of General Semantics* 19 (July 1962): 181–88.

24. Allan Greenberg, "Commentary: Symbolism in Architecture," *Architectural Record* 165 (May 1979): 114–16.

25. Michel Ameller, *Parliaments: A Comparative Study on the Structure and Functioning of Representative Institutions in Fifty-Five Countries*, 2d ed. (London: Cassell, 1966), pp. 122–25. Valentine Herman, in collaboration with Françoise Mendel, *Parliaments of the World: A Reference Compendium* (Berlin and New York: DeGruyter, 1976), pp. 257–66. Other items with a cross-parliamentary focus are Kurt Peschel, "Council Chambers of the Great Parliaments," *Parliamentary Affairs* 14 (1961): 518–33; and P. F. Thorne, "Accommodation in a Legislature," *Parliamentarian* 45 (1964): 260–68.

26. Samuel C. Patterson, "Party Opposition in the Legislature: The Ecology of Legislative Institutionalization," *Polity* 4 (Spring 1972): 344–66;

Donald Stone and Alice Stone, "The Administration of Chairs," *Public Administration Review* 34 (Jan.–Feb. 1974): 71–77.

27. Irene S. Rubin, "An Anthropological View of City Councils," *Proceedings, Conference on the Small City and Regional Community*, vol. 1, ed. Robert Wolensky and Edward Miller (Stephens Point: Foundation Press, University of Wisconsin, 1978), pp. 154–61.

28. Cortus T. Koehler, "City Council Chamber Design: The Impact of Interior Design upon the Meeting Process," *Journal of Environmental Systems* 10, no. 1 (1980): 53–79.

29. Nikolaus Pevsner, *A History of Building Types* (Princeton, N.J.: Princeton University Press, 1976), chaps. 2, 3; Ernest J. Kump, "Town and City Halls," chap. 22 in *Forms and Functions of Twentieth Century Architecture*, vol. 3, ed. Talbot Hamlin (New York: Columbia University Press, 1952), pp. 782–813.

30. Fell and Mackenzie, *Houses of Parliament*; Colin Cunningham, *Victorian and Edwardian Town Halls* (London: Routledge & Kegan Paul, 1981).

31. "Neo-Classicism," *Architectural Design*, profile 23, vol. 49, nos. 8 and 9 (London, 1979), especially "Introduction," by Geoffrey Broadbent, and "Roman America," by William Chaitkin. Also note Henry-Russell Hitchcock and William Seale, *Temples of Democracy: The State Capitols of the USA* (New York: Harcourt Brace Jovanovich, 1976); and James Marston Fitch, *American Building: The Historical Forces That Shaped It*, 2d ed. (Boston, Mass.: Houghton Mifflin, 1966).

32. On U.S. city halls the best source is Lebovich's *America's City Halls*; also see Charles King Hoyt, *Public, Municipal, and Community Buildings* (New York: McGraw-Hill, 1980). On courthouses see Richard Pare, ed.: *Court House: A Photographic Document* (New York: Horizon Press, 1978); idem, "Court Houses: County Symbols," *Historic Preservation* 29 (Oct. 1977): 31–37; and *One Hundred Courthouses: A Report on North Carolina Judicial Facilities*, 2 vols., Robert P. Burns, project director (Raleigh: North Carolina State University Graphics, 1978).

33. John Ely Burchard and Albert Bush-Brown, *The Architecture of America: A Social and Cultural History* (Boston, Mass.: Little, Brown, 1961); Donald Drew Egbert, *The Beaux-Arts Tradition in French Architecture* (Princeton, N.J.: Princeton University Press, 1980). For a revisionist view of the Beaux-Arts tradition see Robert

Hughes, "An Architecture of Grandeur: The Beaux-Arts Tradition Reconsidered," *Horizon* 18, no. 1 (Winter 1976): 64–69.

34. Ada Louise Huxtable, "The Public Building," *New York Times Magazine*, 10 Nov. 1974, pp. 86–87, 89; Lois Craig, "The Boston City Hall and Its Antecedents," *AIA Journal* 69 (Sept. 1980): 46–52; idem, *The Federal Presence: Architecture, Politics, and National Design* (Cambridge, Mass.: MIT Press, 1978); Robert Peck, "How to Make Friends with a Federal Building or Two," *Nation's Cities*, July 1977, pp. 6–8; Daniel Patrick Moynihan, "Civic Architecture," *Architectural Record* 142 (Dec. 1967): 107–30.

CHAPTER II. IDEAS PERTINENT TO CIVIC SPACE

1. Jack Goody, "Religion and Ritual: The Definitional Problem," *British Journal of Sociology* 12 (June 1961): 142–64.

2. "A Death in Due Time," in *Rite, Drama, Festival, Spectacle: Rehearsals toward a Theory of Cultural Performance*, ed. John J. MacAloon (Philadelphia: Institute for the Study of Human Issues, 1984), pp. 151–52.

3. An unusually clear definition of *symbol* is offered by Peter F. Smith: "Reduced to its simplest, a symbol is a phenomenon (object, sound, smell or tactile sensation) which has a meaning additional to that which is communicated by its superficial configuration or stimulus profile. It stands for a 'landscape' of meaning without a precise horizon. Because of the contrast between the relative simplicity of the object and the potential complexity of the meaning towards which it points, the experience of symbols evokes an emotional reaction. Indeed one of the things which distinguishes a symbol from a sign is the involvement of the emotions. Most of these reactions remain out of reach of consciousness, but can nevertheless take a decisive influence upon mood and behavior" ("Architecture, Symbolism and Surrealism," *Architectural Design* 48, no. 2 [1978]: 150).

4. Dan Sperber, *Rethinking Symbolism* (Cambridge, Eng.: Cambridge University Press, 1975).

5. A good general source on the dramatist approach is Combs and Mansfield, *Drama in Life*. The quotation is from Hugh Dalziel Duncan, *Communication and Social Order* (London: Oxford

University Press, 1962), p. 295.

6. George Herbert Mead, *Mind, Self and Society from the Standpoint of a Social Behavioralist*, ed. Charles W. Morris (Chicago: University of Chicago Press, 1934); E. Gordon Ericksen, *The Territorial Experience: Human Ecology as Symbolic Interaction* (Austin: University of Texas Press, 1980).

7. Erving Goffman, *The Presentation of Self in Everyday Life* (Garden City, N.Y.: Doubleday Anchor Books, 1959), pp. 22, 229.

8. Émile Durkheim, *The Elementary Forms of the Religious Life* (London: George Allen & Unwin, 1915; republished in 1926).

9. Mircea Eliade, *The Sacred and the Profane: The Nature of Religion* (New York: Harcourt Brace Jovanovich, 1959).

10. Paul Wheatley, *The Pivot of the Four Quarters* (Chicago: Aldine, 1971); see especially chap. 5, "The Ancient Chinese City as a Cosmo-Magical Symbol."

11. Lord Raglan, *The Temple and the House* (London: Routledge & Kegan Paul, 1964).

12. Edwyn Bevan, *Symbolism and Belief* (1938; reprint, Port Washington, N.Y.: Kennikat, 1968).

13. Laponce, *Left and Right*, chap. 4; Barry Schwartz, *Vertical Classification: A Study in Structuralism and the Sociology of Knowledge* (Chicago: University of Chicago Press, 1981).

14. A translation of Robert Hertz's 1909 article appears in Rodney Needham, ed., *Right and Left: Essays on Dual Symbolic Classification* (Chicago: University of Chicago Press, 1973). Laponce, *Left and Right*, chaps. 2, 3. Other writings by Laponce on this topic include "In Search of the Stable Elements of the Left-Right Landscape," *Comparative Politics* 4 (July 1972): 455–75; "Spatial Archetypes and Political Perceptions," *American Political Science Review* 69 (Mar. 1975): 11–20; and "The Use of Visual Space to Measure Ideology," in *Experimentation and Simulation in Political Science*, ed. Laponce and Paul Smoker (Toronto: University of Toronto Press, 1972).

15. Sean Wilentz, ed., *Rites of Power: Symbolism, Ritual, and Politics since the Middle Ages* (Philadelphia: University of Pennsylvania Press, 1985), p. 8.

16. Murray Edelman, *The Symbolic Uses of Politics* (Urbana: University of Illinois Press, 1964), pp. 95–99.

17. Harold D. Lasswell, in collaboration with Merritt B. Fox, *The Signature of Power: Buildings,*

Communication, and Policy (New Brunswick, N.J.: Transaction Books, 1979), pp. 18, 32, 84–85. An earlier publication to come from his study is "The Signature of Power," *Society* 14 (Nov.–Dec. 1976): 82–85.

18. David Milne, "Architecture, Politics and the Public Realm," *Canadian Journal of Political and Social Theory* 5 (Winter–Spring 1981): 131–46.

19. Flavio Conti, *Shrines of Power* (Boston, Mass.: Harcourt Brace Jovanovich, 1977); Richard C. Trexler, *Public Life in Renaissance Florence* (New York: Academic Press, 1980), pp. 49–50.

20. Helio Piñón, "Ideologia y lenguaje en las arquitecturas del poder," *Arquitecturas bis* 12 (Mar. 1976): 19–25; Lisbet Balslev Jørgensen, Hakon Lund, and Hans Edvard Nørregård-Nielsen, *Denmarks Arkitektur: Magtens bolig* (Copenhagen: Gyldendal, 1980).

21. Carl G. Jung, *Man and His Symbols* (Garden City, N.Y.: Doubleday, 1964).

22. Clare Cooper, "The House as Symbol of the Self," in *Designing for Human Behavior: Architecture and the Behavioral Sciences*, Jon Lang, Charles Burnette, Walter Moleski, and David Vachon, eds. (Stroudsburg, Pa.: Dowden, Hutchinson & Ross, 1974), pp. 130–46.

23. John G. Neihardt, *Black Elk Speaks: Being the Life Story of a Holy Man of the Oglala Sioux* (London: Barrie & Jenkins, 1932; reprint, University of Nebraska Press, 1961), pp. 198–200. On the kiva see Frank Waters, *Masked Gods* (Chicago: Swallow Press, 1950), pp. 173–77. For additional discussion of the symbolism of the circle see Bruno Munari, *Discovery of the Circle* (New York: George Wittenborn, 1966).

24. Edward F. Edinger, *Ego and Archetype* (New York: G. P. Putnam, 1972); Aniela Jaffe, "Symbolism in the Visual Arts," in Jung, *Man and His Symbols*, chap. 4; J. E. Cirlot, *A Dictionary of Symbols* (New York: Philosophical Library, 1962), p. 193; Roger G. Kennedy, *American Churches* (New York: Stewart, Tabori & Chang, 1982), chap. 2.

25. Olivier Marc, *Psychology of the House* (London: Thames & Hudson, 1977).

26. Jaffe, "Symbolism in the Visual Arts," pp. 244–45; and Marc, *Psychology of the House*, p. 89.

27. Note the following articles, all from the *International Journal of Symbology*: Robert J. Blanch, "The Origins and Use of Medieval Color Symbolism," vol. 3, no. 3 (1972), pp. 1–5; Faye J. Goldberg and John R. Stabler, "Black and White Symbolism in Japan," vol. 4, no. 3 (1973), pp. 37–

46; Peggy Porter Kaplan, "The Symbolism of Color," vol. 6, no. 1 (1975), pp. 1–9.

28. Gary T. Moore, "Knowing about Environmental Knowing: The Current State of Theory and Research on Environmental Cognition," *Environment and Behavior* 11 (Mar. 1979): 33–70. Early examples of this literature are Joachim F. Wohlwill, "The Physical Environment: A Problem for a Psychology of Stimulation," *Journal of Social Issues* 22 (Oct. 1966): 29–38; and Kenneth H. Craik, "The Comprehension of the Everyday Physical Environment," *Journal of the American Institute of Planners* 34 (Jan. 1968): 29–37.

29. Kevin Lynch, *The Image of the City* (Cambridge, Mass.: Harvard–MIT Joint Center for Urban Studies, 1960).

30. Charles H. Burnette, "The Mental Image and Design," in *Designing for Human Behavior*, pp. 169–82.

31. Kent C. Bloomer and Charles W. Moore, *Body, Memory, and Architecture* (New Haven, Conn.: Yale University Press, 1977).

32. General references in semiotics are David Robey, ed., *Structuralism: An Introduction* (Oxford, Eng.: Clarendon Press, 1973); Umberto Eco, *A Theory of Semiotics* (Bloomington: Indiana University Press, 1979); and Ladislav Matejka and Irwin R. Titunik, eds., *Semiotics of Art* (Cambridge, Mass.: MIT Press, 1976). Treatments from an architecture vantagepoint are Charles Jencks and George Baird, eds., *Meaning in Architecture* (New York: George Braziller, 1969); Geoffrey Broadbent, "A Plain Man's Guide to the Theory of Signs in Architecture," *Architectural Design* 47, nos. 7 and 8 (1977): 476–82; and Jon Lang, "Symbolic Aesthetics in Architecture: Toward a Research Agenda," *EDRA* 13 (1982): 172–82.

33. Peter D. Eisenman, "Notes on Conceptual Architecture," in *Environmental Design Research*, ed. Wolfgang F. E. Preiser (Stroudsburg, Pa.: Dowden, Hutchinson & Ross, 1973), pp. 319–23.

34. Donald Preziosi, *The Semiotics of the Built Environment: An Introduction to Architectonic Analysis* (Bloomington: Indiana University Press, 1979).

35. James Holston, "On Reading and Writing Streets: Political Discourse in Two Models of Brazilian Urbanism" (ms., Yale University, Department of Anthropology).

36. Dennis Doxtater, "Spatio-Symbolic Oppositions in Ritual and Architecture," *Design Studies* 4 (Apr. 1983): 124–32.

37. Diana Agrest and Mario Gandelsonas,

"Semiotics and the Limits of Architecture," in *A Perfusion of Signs*, ed. Thomas A. Sebeok (Bloomington: Indiana University Press, 1977), pp. 90–120; see also their "Critical Remarks on Semiology and Architecture," in *Semiotica* 9, no. 3 (1973): 252–71. Other relevant articles by Gandelsonas are "From Structure to Subject: The Formation of Architectural Language," *Oppositions* 17 (Summer 1979): 1–29; and "Semiotics as a Tool for Theoretical Development," in *Environmental Design Research*, pp. 324–30.

38. Erwin Panofsky, *Studies in Iconology: Themes in the Art of the Renaissance* (New York: Oxford University Press, 1939; reprint, New York: Harper & Row, 1972), chap. 1. In a later edition, Panofsky calls the third stratum "Iconology" (see *Meaning in the Visual Arts: Papers in and on Art History* [New York: Doubleday, 1955], pp. 31–32).

39. Barbara Maria Stafford, *Symbol and Myth: Humbert de Superville's Essay on Absolute Signs in Art* (Cranbury, N.J.: University of Delaware Press, 1979), pp. 43–44.

40. B. A. Uspensky, "'Left' and 'Right' in Icon Painting," *Semiotica* 13, no. 1 (1975): 33–39.

41. E. McClung Fleming, "Artifact Study: A Proposed Model," *Winterthur Portfolio* 9 (June 1974): 153–61; reprinted in *Material Culture Studies in America*, ed. Thomas J. Schlereth (Nashville, Tenn.: American Association for State and Local History, 1982), pp. 162–73, with quotation at pp. 172–73.

42. Cornelis J. Van der Ven, *Space in Architecture* (Assen, the Netherlands: Van Gorcum, 1980); N. N. Patricios, "Concepts of Space in Urban Design, Architecture and Art," *Leonardo* 6, no. 4 (Autumn 1973): 311–18; Robert Grinnell, "The Theoretical Attitude towards Space in the Middle Ages," *Speculum* 21 (Apr. 1946): 141–57.

43. Philip Thiel, "Notes on the Description, Scaling, Notation, and Scoring of Some Perceptual and Cognitive Attributes of the Physical Environment," in *Environmental Psychology: Man and His Physical Setting*, ed. Harold M. Proshansky, William H. Ittelson, and Leanne G. Rivlin (New York: Holt, Rinehart & Winston, 1970), pp. 602–7; Rikard Küller, *Architecture for People: Explorations in a New Human Environment* (New York: Holt, Rinehart & Winston, 1980), p. 93.

44. Louis Hammer, "Architecture and the Poetry of Space," *Journal of Aesthetics and Art Criticism* 39 (Summer 1981): 381–88, with quotation at p. 382.

45. Steven Kent Peterson, "Space and Anti-Space," *Harvard Architectural Review* 1 (Spring 1980): 88–113.

46. Rudolf Arnheim, *The Dynamics of Architectural Form* (Berkeley: University of California Press, 1977), pp. 210, 253–54.

47. Charles Moore and Gerald Allen, *Dimensions: Space, Shape, and Scale in Architecture* (New York: Architectural Record Books, 1976), p. 51; C. M. Deasy, *Design for Human Affairs* (New York: Wiley, 1974), p. 45.

48. Steen Eiler Rasmussen, *Experiencing Architecture* (New York: Wiley, 1959), pp. 33–37; Christian Norberg-Schulz, "Place," *AAQ* 8, no. 4 (1976): 3–10.

49. Christian Norberg-Schulz, *Genius Loci: Towards a Phenomenology of Architecture* (New York: Rizzoli, 1979).

50. Christian Norberg-Schulz, *Space and Architecture* (New York: Praeger, 1971), with quotation from p. 45.

51. James Marston Fitch, *American Building: The Environmental Forces That Shape It*, 2d ed. (Boston, Mass.: Houghton Mifflin, 1972), p. 25.

52. Norberg-Schulz, *Genius Loci*, p. 67.

53. "Interior Volume," in Symposium on "The Major Space," *Progressive Architecture* 46 (June 1965): 155–65.

54. Arnheim, *Dynamics of Architectural Form*, chap. 3.

55. René Smeets, *Signs, Symbols and Ornaments* (New York: Van Nostrand Reinhold, 1973); Arnheim, *Dynamics of Architectural Form*, p. 217.

56. Robert Venturi, Denise Scott Brown, and Stevens Izenour, *Learning from Las Vegas*, rev. ed. (Cambridge, Mass.: MIT Press, 1977).

57. Charles Jencks, *The Language of Post-Modern Architecture* (New York: Rizzoli, 1977), p. 131.

58. Joseph R. Gusfield, *Symbolic Crusade: Status Politics and the American Temperance Movement* (Urbana: University of Illinois Press, 1966), taken from Combs and Mansfield, *Drama in Life*, p. 247.

59. Arnheim, *Dynamics of Architectural Form*, p. 269.

60. Phyllis Ackerman, "The Symbolic Sources of Some Architectural Elements," *Journal of the Society of Architectural Historians* 12, no. 4 (Dec. 1953): 3–7; W. R. Lethaby, *Architecture, Nature and Magic* (London: Gerald Duckworth, 1956); see also E. Baldwin Smith, *The Dome: A Study in the History of Ideas* (Princeton, N.J.: Princeton University Press, 1950).

61. Lily Ross Taylor, *Roman Voting Assemblies*

(Ann Arbor: University of Michigan Press, 1966).

62. R. E. Wycherley, *How the Greeks Built Cities* (London: Macmillan, 1949); D. S. Robertson, *A Handbook of Greek and Roman Architecture*, 2d ed. (Cambridge, Eng.: Cambridge University Press, 1943).

63. Richard J. A. Talbert, *The Senate of Imperial Rome* (Princeton, N.J.: Princeton University Press, 1984), chap. 3.

64. William L. MacDonald, *The Pantheon: Design, Meaning, and Progeny* (Cambridge, Mass.: Harvard University Press, 1976). Sigfried Giedion also sees the Pantheon as revolutionary; note his *Architecture and the Phenomena of Transition: The Three Space Conceptions in Architecture* (Cambridge, Mass.: Harvard University Press, 1971).

65. Adolf Reinle, *Zeichensprache der Architektur: Symbol, Darstellung und Brauch in der Baukunst des Mittelalters und der Neuzeit* (Zurich: Artemis, 1976). The quote, at p. 2, was translated from the German by Amanda Sandell.

66. E. Baldwin Smith, *Architectural Symbolism of Imperial Rome and the Middle Ages* (Princeton, N.J.: Princeton University Press, 1956), chaps. 4 and 6; Reinle, *Zeichensprache*, pp. 288–91, 336–39.

67. Anthony Vidler, "The Writing of the Walls," *Artforum* 9 (Dec. 1980): 37–40.

68. Elizabeth Read Sunderland, "Symbolic Numbers and Romanesque Church Plans," *Journal of Architectural Historians* 18 (Oct. 1959): 94–103.

69. Rasmussen, *Experiencing Architecture*, p. 115.

70. Rudolf Wittkower, *Architectural Principles in the Age of Humanism* (London: Alec Tiranti, 1952); Christian Norberg-Schulz, *Intentions in Architecture* (Rome: Universitetsforlaget, 1963), p. 124.

71. Andrew L. Drummond, *The Church Architecture of Protestantism* (Edinburgh: T. & T. Clark, 1934).

72. Brad Fisher, "Ecclesiology and the Deep Chancel: From Cambridge to New York," *Historical Magazine of the Protestant Episcopal Church* 47, no. 3 (1978): 313–31.

73. Roger G. Barker, *Ecological Psychology: Concepts and Methods for Studying the Environment of Human Behavior* (Stanford, Calif.: Stanford University Press, 1968). Barker's work is reviewed by Richard Price in "Behavioral Setting Theory and Research," in *The Human Context: Environmental Determinants of Behavior*, ed. R. H.

Moos (New York: Wiley, 1976), pp. 213–47.

74. Guy Ankerl, *Experimental Sociology of Architecture* (The Hague: Mouton, 1981).

75. John W. Black, "The Effect of Room Characteristics upon Vocal Intensity and Rate," *Journal of Acoustical Society of America* 22, no. 2 (Mar. 1950): 174–76; Tom Porter and Byron Mikellides, *Color for Architecture* (New York: Van Nostrand Reinhold, 1976), pp. 13–17; Faber Birren, "Reactions of Body and Eye," *AIA Journal* 58, no. 3 (Sept. 1972): 35–39.

76. David E. Campbell, "Interior Office Design and Visitor Response," *Journal of Applied Psychology* 64 (Dec. 1979): 648–53; Paula C. Morrow and James C. McElroy, "Interior Office Design and Visitor Response: A Constructive Replication," *Journal of Applied Psychology* 66, no. 5 (1981): 646–50; Duncan Joiner, "Social Ritual and Architectural Space," in *Environmental Psychology*, 2d ed., pp. 224–41; Clovis Heimsath, *Behavioral Architecture: Toward an Accountable Design Process* (New York: McGraw-Hill, 1977), pp. 91–96.

77. Edward T. Hall, *The Silent Language* (New York: Doubleday, 1959) and *The Hidden Dimension* (London: Bodley Head, 1969). For a detailed discussion of the distance ranges see Hall, "Silent Assumptions in Social Communications," in *Disorders of Communication*, Research Publication 42, Association for Research in Nervous and Mental Disease (1964), pp. 41–55; reprinted in *People and Buildings*, ed. Robert Gutman (New York: Basic Books, 1972), pp. 136–51. Hall's work is discussed further by Irwin Altman in *The Environment and Social Behavior* (Monterey, Calif.: Brooks Cole, 1975).

78. Hall, *Hidden Dimension*, chap. 9; Fred I. Steele, "Problem Solving in the Spatial Environment," in *EDRA* 1 (1970): 127–36; Humphry Osmond, "Function as the Basis of Psychiatric Ward Design," *Mental Hospital* 8 (Apr. 1957): 23–29.

79. Robert Sommer, *Personal Space: The Behavioral Basis of Design* (New York: Spectrum–Prentice-Hall, 1969); Alton J. De Long, "Seating Position and Perceived Characteristics of Members of a Small Group," *Cornell Journal of Social Relations* 5, no. 2 (1970): 134–51. For a further discussion of this literature see Corwin Bennett, *Spaces for People: Human Factors in Design* (New York: Prentice-Hall, 1977).

80. Raymond G. Studer and David Stea, "Architectural Programming, Environmental Design, and Human Behavior," *Journal of Social Issues* 22

(Oct. 1966): 127–36, quote at p. 127.

81. Oscar Newman, *Defensible Space* (New York: Macmillan, 1972); Mayer Spivak, "Archetypal Place," *Architectural Forum* 140 (Oct. 1973): 44–49; S. D. Joardar and J. W. Neill, "The Subtle Differences in Configuration of Small Public Spaces," *Landscape Architecture* 68 (Nov. 1978): 487–91; Robert Sommer, *Tight Spaces: Hard Architecture and How to Humanize It* (New York: Prentice-Hall, 1974); Tim R. V. Davis, "The Influence of the Physical Environment in Offices," *Academy of Management Review* 9, no. 2 (Apr. 1984): 271–83.

82. Leanne G. Rivlin and Marilyn Rothenberg, "The Use of Space in Open Classrooms," in *Environmental Psychology*, pp. 479–84; Robert W. Marans and Kent F. Spreckelmeyer, *Evaluating Built Environments: A Behavioral Approach* (Ann Arbor, Mich.: Survey Research Center and Architectural Research Laboratory, 1981); Johnathan King and Robert W. Marans, *The Physical Environment and the Learning Process: A Survey of Recent Research* (Ann Arbor, Mich.: Survey Research Center and Architectural Research Laboratory, 1979), pp. 15, 16.

83. Maurice Broady, "Social Theory in Architectural Design," *Arena* (London) 81 (Jan. 1966): 149–54, reprinted in *People and Buildings*, pp. 171–85. An attempt to reassert the determinism approach is David J. Giber's "Psychological Effects of Prison Architecture and Environmental Design" (Ph.D. diss., Duke University, 1980). Giber surveyed inmates of a prison and found a statistically significant relationship between perceptions of the setting (e.g., the quality of the maintenance of the cells) and work effectiveness in prison industries.

84. Robert Gutman, "The Social Function of the Built Environment," in *The Mutual Interaction of People and Their Built Environment: A Cross-Cultural Perspective*, ed. Amos Rapoport (The Hague: Mouton, 1976), pp. 37–49, quote at p. 45.

85. Jon Lang, "The Built Environment and Social Behavior: Architectural Determinism Reexamined," *Via* 4 (1980): 147–53.

86. Lars Lerup, *Building the Unfinished: Architecture and Human Action* (Beverly Hills, Calif.: Sage, 1977), pp. 23, 71.

87. David Canter, *The Psychology of Place* (New York: St. Martin's Press, 1977); Canter, Peter Stringer, et al., *Environmental Interaction: Psychological Approaches to Our Physical Surrounding* (New York: International Universities Press, 1975).

88. Canter, *Psychology of Place*, pp. 121, 124–25, and *Environmental Interaction*, pp. 147, 210–13.

89. Amos Rapoport, *Human Aspects of Urban Form* (Oxford, Eng.: Pergamon Press, 1977).

90. Amos Rapoport, *The Meaning of the Built Environment: A Non-Verbal Communication Approach* (Beverly Hills, Calif.: Sage, 1982), quoted at p. 67. Another statement of Rapoport's position is found in John B. Calhoun, ed., *Environment and Population: Problems of Adaptation* (New York: Praeger, 1983), pp. 200–201.

91. Amos Rapoport, "Sociocultural Aspects of Man-Environment Studies, in *Mutual Interaction of People and Their Built Environment*, pp. 7–35.

CHAPTER III. THE TRADITIONAL CHAMBER: IMPOSED AUTHORITY

1. Lebovich, *America's City Halls*, pp. 16–24.

2. Lee H. Nelson and Henry A. Judd, "An Architectural Study of Old Town Hall" (duplicated consultant study, July 1965).

3. "Baltimore City Hall," *Contract Interiors* 137 (Oct. 1977): 78–85.

4. "Alterations to the City Hall at Albany, N.Y.," *American Architect* 117 (June 1920): 809–15; "The Aldermanic Chamber: A Preservation Plan for the Cambridge City Council Chamber" (duplicated consultant study, Sept. 1979). On the Cincinnati chamber, note Charles T. Goodsell, "Civic Space and Urban Image: Council Chambers in Cincinnati and Cleveland," *Urban Resources* 1 (Spring 1984): 9–14.

5. Loring P. Rixford, "The City Hall of San Francisco," *Architect* 20 (Nov. 1906): 385–403; Thomas S. Hines, "The Paradox of 'Progressive' Architecture: Urban Planning and Public Building in Tom Johnson's Cleveland," *American Quarterly* 25, no. 4 (1973): 426–47. On Cleveland see Goodsell, "Civic Space and Urban Image."

6. For more on how the Charterite movement affected the Cincinnati chamber see Goodsell, "Civic Space and Urban Image."

7. If Küller is correct in saying that more intense enclosure is obtained in either relatively empty or relatively crowded spaces, these rooms must be psychologically "close" indeed.

8. Interview with Mayor Anne R. Hachtel, 10 Aug. 1982.

CHAPTER IV. THE MIDCENTURY CHAMBER: CONFRONTED AUTHORITY

1. Lebovich, *America's City Halls*, pp. 30–35.

2. "New City Hall, Pasadena: Distinctive Southern California Type of American Architectures," *Riverside Plastite Progress* 3, no. 1 (Oct. 1927): 3–14; John Bakewell, Jr., "The Pasadena City Hall," *Architect and Engineer* 93, no. 3 (June 1928): 35–39.

3. "Saint Paul City Hall and Ramsey County Courthouse," *American Architect* 143 (July 1933): 3–14; note also vol. 17, no. 1 (n.d.) of *Ramsey County History*, devoted entirely to the building and its history.

4. Barrie Scardino, "A Legacy of City Halls for Houston," *Houston Review* 4, no. 3 (Fall 1982): 154–64.

5. A. Theodore Brown, *The Politics of Reform: Kansas City's Municipal Government, 1925–1950* (Kansas City, Mo.: Community Studies, 1958), chap. 2.

6. George P. Hales, *Los Angeles City Hall* (Los Angeles, Calif.: Board of Public Works, 1928).

7. The old Chicago council chamber is pictured in David Lowe, *Chicago Interiors: Views of a Splendid World* (Chicago: Contemporary Books, 1979), pp. 114–15.

8. Interview with Estelle Dvorin, 17 Mar. 1983.

9. Interview with William B. Bradley, 4 Sept. 1982.

CHAPTER V. THE CONTEMPORARY CHAMBER: JOINED AUTHORITY

1. Burchard and Bush-Brown, *Architecture of America*, pp. 389, 507.

2. Ibid., pp. 371, 392–93, 430, 427–74.

3. "Toronto City Hall: Continuing Controversy," *Architectural Record* 138 (Nov. 1965): 165–72; "Singular Symbol for Toronto," *Architectural Forum* 123 (Nov. 1965): 15–23. For materials on the Toronto international competition see *Journal of the Royal Architectural Institute of Canada* 35 (Oct. 1958): 358–71. On the importance of Toronto City Hall as an urban symbol see Trudi Elizabeth Bunting, "An Empirical Analysis of Symbolic Urban Imagery: A Case Study of the New City Hall in Toronto" (Master's thesis, De-

partment of Geography, University of Western Ontario, 1967).

4. Sibyl Moholy-Nagy, "Boston's City Hall," *Architectural Forum* 130 (Jan.–Feb. 1969): 38–53; "The New Boston City Hall," *Architectural Record* 145 (Feb. 1969): 133–44; Ellen Perry Berkeley, "More Than You May Want to Know about the Boston City Hall," *Architecture Plus* 1 (Feb. 1973): 72–77, 98; Craig, "Boston City Hall and Its Antecedents," pp. 46–52.

5. Peter Papdemetriou, "Angling for a Civic Moment," *Progressive Architecture* 60 (May 1979): 102–5; John Pastier, "Bold Symbol of a City's Image of Its Future," *AIA Journal* 67 (May 1978): 112–17.

6. "Scottsdale's New Civic Center," *Architectural Record* 149 (Mar. 1971): 119–24.

7. "Fremont Civic Center," *Architectural Record* 152 (Dec. 1972): 93; "City Hall for Santa Rosa," *Architectural Record* 147 (Jan. 1970): 102–3; "Terraced City Hall," *Progressive Architecture* 53 (Apr. 1972): 94–96 (on Santa Rosa); "Good Decisions and Good Design Provide a Small Town with a Distinguished Civic Center," *Architectural Record* 151 (June 1972): 101–4 (on Fairfield); "High Tech Images," *Progressive Architecture* 55 (Feb. 1974): 66–71 (on San Bernardino).

8. Lebovich, *America's City Halls*, p. 36.

9. Letter from V. Glenn Cootes, City of Austin, dated 15 June 1982.

10. Interview with Gene Randall, City of Arlington, 24 Feb. 1983.

11. Interview with Bennie M. Gonzales, 16 Feb. 1983.

12. Interview with Eugene W. Betz on 14 Sept. 1983. Betz emphasized that the roof window permitted persons outside the building to know when the council was in session at night. This idea parallels the effect of the Traditional chamber's ceremonial windows along the front of the building.

13. Some graphics-design literature contends that round forms can be equated with femininity; squared configurations, with masculinity. This point is sometimes considered germane to corporate logo design.

14. Telephone conversation with Henry White of Corbonell and Associates, 3 Jan. 1983.

15. Letter from Kenneth R. Blackman, city manager of Santa Rosa, dated 26 Apr. 1983.

16. Letter from Preston M. Geren, Geren Associates, dated 23 Mar. 1983. Some quotation

marks have been removed from the original text.

17. Interview with Tom E. Purvis, Purvis and York, 24 Feb. 1983.

18. Interview with Charles K. McClain, Fremont's city manager, 18 Mar. 1983.

19. Hedley E. H. Roy, "Toronto City Hall and Civic Square," *Journal of the American Concrete Institute* 62 (Dec. 1965): 1481–1502.

20. Submittal to America's City Halls Program by the City of Kettering, Ohio, 27 Aug. 1981, pp. 14–15. A practical problem has arisen from this theoretically admirable arrangement, however. During the course of council meetings, citizens go downstairs after the conclusion of their personal item on the agenda and talk loudly and excitedly within easy earshot of the continuing meeting. In an attempt to solve this problem, electrically lit "Silence" signs have been installed.

21. Letter from Thomas G. Dunne, city manager of Walnut Creek, Calif., dated 14 Sept. 1982; also interview with Mr. Dunne, 22 Mar. 1983.

22. Interview with William David Grubbs, City of Dallas, 25 Feb. 1983.

23. Interview with Joseph F. Freeman, city councilor, City of Lynchburg, 11 Nov. 1982.

24. Feng Shui, the ancient Chinese art of placement and harmony in interior design, would no doubt regard this beam as emitting an overwhelming weight on the space below it. This would have the consequence of cutting off the flow of *ch'i*, which means cosmic breath or human energy. The ability of ch'i to flow properly through rooms is a principal aim of Feng Shui practitioners (see Sarah Rossbach, *Feng Shui: The Chinese Art of Placement* [New York: E. P. Dutton, 1983], pp. 115–16).

25. Interview with Jack T. Hofmann of Ahern, MacVittie and Hofmann, 16 Feb. 1973. The Greensboro and Tucson daises do indeed have this capacity, as they are fitted with bullet-proof glass behind the skirt.

26. Interview with Leon F. Shore, city manager of College Park, 25 Nov. 1983.

CHAPTER VI. THE SOCIAL MEANING OF CIVIC SPACE

1. Max Weber, *The Theory of Social and Economic Organization*, trans. A. M. Henderson and Talcott Parsons (New York: Free Press, 1947), chap. 3.

2. In cities, racial and ethnic groups often live in separate neighborhoods, which has made geographic representation once more important within the municipal context. The reappearance of district voting systems in many cities has not been accompanied by a return to the aldermanic desk, however. A deeper shift in the political culture toward pan-territorial, nonsectional politics seems to be reflected.

3. For summaries of the argument see Mary G. Kweit and Robert W. Kweit, *Implementing Citizen Participation in a Bureaucratic Society* (New York: Praeger, 1981); and Richard M. Buttistoni, *Public Schooling and the Education of Democratic Citizens* (Jackson: University Press of Mississippi, 1985), chap. 2. For participative and otherwise elevated interpretations of the notion of "citizenship," note the special issue of *Public Administration Review*, vol. 44 (Mar. 1984).

4. As we recall from chapter I, Koehler's research on council chambers in California showed reduced communication in rooms with curvilinear floor plans, a finding that is not inconsistent with the concern just expressed.

5. Philip Selznick, *TVA and the Grass Roots: A Study in the Sociology of Formal Organization* (Berkeley: University of California Press, 1949).

6. Mary P. Follett, "Constructive Conflict," first published in 1926 and reprinted in *Dynamic Administration*, ed. Henry C. Metcalf and Lyndall Urwick (New York: Harper, 1942).

7. Charles E. Lindblom, *Politics and Markets: The World's Political-Economic Systems* (New York: Basic Books, 1977); John Kenneth Galbraith, *The Anatomy of Power* (Boston, Mass.: Houghton-Mifflin, 1983).

APPENDIX. PROPOSALS FOR CIVIC SPACE

1. Charles T. Goodsell, "Planning a Council Chamber," *Management Information Service Report* 15, no. 12 (Dec. 1983; International City Management Association, 1120 G. St., N.W., Washington, D.C. 20005); idem, "Designing a Democratic Council Chamber for the Small Municipality," *Municipal Management* 7 (Summer 1984): 19–21.

Selected Bibliography

Ackerman, Phyllis. "The Symbolic Sources of Some Architectural Elements." *Journal of the Society of Architectural Historians* 12, no. 4 (Dec. 1953): 3–7.

Agrest, Diana, and Mario Gandelsonas. "Critical Remarks on Semiology and Architecture." *Semiotica* 9, no. 3 (1973): 252–71.

———. "Semiotics and the Limits of Architecture." In *A Perfusion of Signs*, edited by Thomas A. Sebeok. Bloomington: Indiana University Press, 1977.

Altman, Irwin. *The Environment and Social Behavior.* Monterey, Calif.: Brooks Cole, 1975.

Arnheim, Rudolf. *The Dynamics of Architectural Form.* Berkeley: University of California Press, 1977.

Barker, Roger G. *Ecological Psychology: Concepts and Methods for Studying the Environment of Human Behavior.* Stanford, Calif.: Stanford University Press, 1968.

Bennett, Corwin. *Spaces for People: Human Factors in Design.* New York: Prentice-Hall, 1977.

Bevan, Edwyn. *Symbolism and Belief.* 1938. Reprint. Port Washington, N.Y.: Kennikat, 1968.

Blomeyer, Gerald. "Architecture as a Political Sign System." *International Architect* 1, no. 1 (1979): 54–61.

Bloomer, Kent C., and Charles W. Moore. *Body, Memory, and Architecture.* New Haven, Conn.: Yale University Press, 1977.

Bonta, Juan Pablo. *Architecture and Its Interpretation: A Study of Expressive Systems in Architecture.* London: Lund Humphries, 1979.

Broadbent, Geoffrey. "Introduction." *Architectural Design* (profile 23 [on Neoclassicism]) 49, nos. 8 and 9 (London, 1979), pp. 2–3.

———. "A Plain Man's Guide to the Theory of Signs in Architecture." *Architectural Design* 47, nos. 7 and 8 (1977): 476–82.

———. "Revolutionary France." *Architectural Design* (profile 23 [on Neoclassicism]) 49, nos. 8 and 9 (London, 1979): 20–25.

Broady, Maurice. "Social Theory in Architectural Design." *Arena* (London) 81 (Jan. 1966): 149–54. Reprinted in *People and Buildings*, edited by Robert Gutman, pp. 171–85. New York: Basic Books, 1972.

Burchard, John Ely, and Albert Bush-Brown. *The Architecture of America: A Social and Cultural History.* Boston, Mass.: Little, Brown, 1961.

Burnette, Charles. "The Mental Image and Design." In *Designing for Human Behavior: Architecture and the Behavioral Sciences*, edited by Jon Lang, Charles Burnette, Walter Moleski, and David Vachon, pp. 169–82. Stroudsburg, Pa.: Dowden, Hutchinson & Ross, 1974.

Burns, Robert P., ed. *One Hundred Courthouses: A Report on North Carolina Judicial Facilities.* 2 vols. Raleigh: North Carolina State University Graphics, 1978.

Campbell, David E. "Interior Office Design and Visitor Response." *Journal of Applied Psychology* 64 (Dec. 1979): 648–53.

Canter, David. *The Psychology of Place.* New York: St. Martin's Press, 1977.

———, Peter Stringer, et al. *Environmental Interaction: Psychological Approaches to Our Physical Surrounding.* New York: International Universities Press, 1975.

Chaitkin, William. "Roman America." *Architectural Design*, profile 23 (on Neoclassicism), vol. 49, nos. 8 and 9 (London, 1979), pp. 8–15.

Combs, James E., and Michael W. Mansfield, eds. *Drama in Life: The Uses of Communication in Society.* New York: Hastings House, 1976.

Conti, Flavio. *Shrines of Power.* Boston, Mass.: Harcourt Brace Jovanovich, 1977.

Cooper, Clare. "The House as Symbol of the Self." In *Designing for Human Behavior: Architecture and the Behavioral Sciences*, edited by Jon Lang, Charles Burnette, Walter Moleski, and David Vachon, pp. 130–46. Stroudsburg, Pa.: Dowden, Hutchinson & Ross, 1974.

Craig, Lois. "The Boston City Hall and Its Antecedents." *AIA Journal* 69 (Sept. 1980): 46–52.

———. *The Federal Presence: Architecture, Politics, and National Design.* Cambridge, Mass.: MIT Press, 1978.

Craik, Kenneth H. "The Comprehension of the Everyday Physical Environment." *Journal of the American Institute of Planners* 34 (Jan. 1968): 29–37.

Cunningham, Colin. *Victorian and Edwardian Town Halls.* London: Routledge & Kegan Paul, 1981.

Deasy, C. M. *Design for Human Affairs.* New York: Wiley, 1974.

Doxtater, Dennis. "Spatio-Symbolic Oppositions

in Ritual and Architecture." *Design Studies* 4 (Apr. 1983): 124–32.

Drummond, Andrew L. *The Church Architecture of Protestantism.* Edinburgh: T. & T. Clark, 1934.

Duncan, Hugh Dalziel. *Communication and Social Order.* London: Oxford University Press, 1962.

Edelman, Murray. *The Symbolic Uses of Politics.* Urbana: University of Illinois Press, 1964.

Edinger, Edward F. *Ego and Archetype.* New York: G. P. Putnam, 1972.

Egbert, Donald Drew. *The Beaux-Arts Tradition in French Architecture.* Princeton, N.J.: Princeton University Press, 1980.

Eisenman, Peter D. "Notes on Conceptual Architecture." In *Environmental Design Research,* edited by Wolfgang F. E. Preiser, pp. 319–23. Stroudsburg, Pa.: Dowden, Hutchinson & Ross, 1973.

Eliade, Mircea. *The Sacred and the Profane: The Nature of Religion.* New York: Harcourt Brace Jovanovich, 1959.

Fisher, Brad. "Ecclesiology and the Deep Chancel: From Cambridge to New York." *Historical Magazine of the Protestant Episcopal Church* 47, no. 3 (1978): 313–31.

Fitch, James Marston. *American Building: The Environmental Forces That Shaped It.* 2d ed. Boston, Mass.: Houghton Mifflin, 1972.

————. *American Building: The Historical Forces That Shaped It.* 2d ed. Boston, Mass.: Houghton Mifflin, 1966.

Fleming, E. McClung. "Artifact Study: A Proposed Model." *Winterthur Portfolio* 9 (June 1974): 153–61.

Goffman, Erving. *The Presentation of Self in Everyday Life.* Garden City, N.Y.: Doubleday Anchor Books, 1959.

Goodman, Paul. *Utopian Essays and the Practical Proposals.* New York: Random House, 1952.

Goodsell, Charles T. "The City Council Chamber: From Distance to Intimacy." *Public Interest* 74 (Winter 1984): 116–31.

————. "Civic Space and Urban Image: Council Chambers in Cincinnati and Cleveland." *Urban Resources* 1 (Spring 1984): 9–14.

————. "Designing a Democratic Council Chamber for the Small Municipality." *Municipal Management* 7 (Summer 1984): 14–21.

————. "Planning a Council Chamber." *Management Information Service Report* 15, no. 12 (Dec. 1983).

Greenberg, Allan. "Commentary: Symbolism in Architecture." *Architectural Record* 165 (May 1979): 114–16.

Grinnell, Robert. "The Theoretical Attitude towards Space in the Middle Ages." *Speculum* 21 (Apr. 1946): 141–57.

Gusfield, Joseph R. *Symbolic Crusade: Status Politics and the American Temperance Movement.* Urbana: University of Illinois Press, 1966.

Gutman, Robert. "The Social Function of the Built Environment." In *The Mutual Interaction of People and Their Built Environment: A Cross-Cultural Perspective,* edited by Amos Rapoport, pp. 37–49. The Hague: Mouton, 1976.

————. ed. *People and Buildings.* New York: Basic Books, 1972.

Hales, George P. *Los Angeles City Hall.* Los Angeles, Calif.: Board of Public Works, 1928.

Hall, Edward T. *The Hidden Dimension.* London: Bodley Head, 1969.

————. "Silent Assumptions in Social Communications." In *Disorders of Communication.* Research Publication 42, Association for Research in Nervous and Mental Disease (1964), pp. 41–55. Also in *People and Buildings,* edited by Robert Gutman, pp. 136–51. New York: Basic Books, 1972.

————. *The Silent Language.* New York: Doubleday, 1959.

Hammer, Louis. "Architecture and the Poetry of Space." *Journal of Aesthetics and Art Criticism* 39 (Summer 1981): 381–88.

Hazard, John N. "Furniture Arrangement as a Symbol of Judicial Roles." *ETC: A Review of General Semantics* 19 (July 1962): 181–88.

Heimsath, Clovis. *Behavioral Architecture: Toward an Accountable Design Process.* New York: McGraw-Hill, 1977.

Hitchcock, Henry-Russell, and William Seale. *Temples of Democracy: The State Capitols of the USA.* New York: Harcourt Brace Jovanovich, 1976.

Hoyt, Charles King. *Public, Municipal, and Community Buildings.* New York: McGraw-Hill, 1980.

Hughes, Robert. "An Architecture of Grandeur: The Beaux-Arts Tradition Reconsidered." *Horizon* 18, no. 1 (Winter 1976): 64–69.

Jaffe, Aniela. "Symbolism in the Visual Arts." In *Man and His Symbols,* by Carl G. Jung, chap. 4. Garden City, N.Y.: Doubleday, 1964.

Jencks, Charles. *The Language of Post-Modern Architecture.* New York: Rizzoli, 1977.

————, and George Baird, eds. *Meaning in Archi-*

tecture. New York: George Braziller, 1969.

Joiner, Duncan. "Social Ritual and Architectural Space." In *Environmental Psychology: Man and His Physical Setting,* 2d ed., edited by Harold M. Proshansky, William H. Ittelson, and Leanne G. Rivilin, pp. 224–41. New York: Holt, Rinehart & Winston, 1976.

Jung, Carl G. *Man and His Symbols.* Garden City, N.Y.: Doubleday, 1964.

King, Anthony D., ed. *Buildings and Society: Essays on the Social Development of the Built Environment.* London: Routledge & Kegan Paul, 1980.

Koehler, Cortus T. "City Council Chamber Design: The Impact of Interior Design upon the Meeting Process." *Journal of Environmental Systems* 10, no. 1 (1980): 53–79.

Kump, Ernest J. "Town and City Halls." In *Forms and Functions of Twentieth Century Architecture,* vol. 3, edited by Talbot Hamlin, pp. 782–813. New York: Columbia University Press, 1952.

Lane, Barbara M. *Architecture and Politics in Germany, 1918–1945.* Cambridge, Mass.: Harvard University Press, 1968.

Lang, Jon. "The Built Environment and Social Behavior: Architectural Determinism Reexamined." *Via* 4 (1980): 147–53.

———. "Symbolic Aesthetics in Architecture: Toward a Research Agenda." *EDRA* (Environmental Design Research Association) 13 (1982): 172–82.

———, Charles Burnette, Walter Moleski, and David Vachon, eds. *Designing for Human Behavior: Architecture and the Behavioral Sciences.* Stroudsburg, Pa.: Dowden, Hutchinson & Ross, 1974.

Laponce, J. A. "In Search of the Stable Elements of the Left-Right Landscape." *Comparative Politics* 4 (July 1972): 455–75.

———. *Left and Right: The Topography of Political Perceptions.* Toronto: University of Toronto Press, 1981.

———. "Spatial Archetypes and Political Perceptions." *American Political Science Review* 69 (Mar. 1975): 11–20.

Lasswell, Harold D. "The Signature of Power," *Society* 14 (Nov.–Dec. 1976): 82–85.

———, in collaboration with Merritt B. Fox. *The Signature of Power: Buildings, Communication, and Policy.* New Brunswick, N.J.: Transaction Books, 1979.

Lebovich, William L. *America's City Halls.* Washington, D.C.: Preservation Press, 1984.

Lerup, Lars. *Building the Unfinished: Architecture and Human Action.* Beverly Hills, Calif.: Sage, 1977.

Lynch, Kevin. *The Image of the City.* Cambridge, Mass.: Harvard–MIT Joint Center for Urban Studies, 1960.

MacAloon, John J., ed. *Rite, Drama, Festival, Spectacle: Rehearsals toward a Theory of Cultural Performance.* Philadelphia: Institute for the Study of Human Issues, 1984.

MacDonald, William L. *The Pantheon: Design, Meaning, and Progeny.* Cambridge, Mass.: Harvard University Press, 1976.

Marans, Robert W., and Kent F. Spreckelmeyer. *Evaluating Built Environments: A Behavioral Approach.* Ann Arbor, Mich.: Survey Research Center and Architectural Research Laboratory, 1981.

Marc, Olivier. *Psychology of the House.* London: Thames & Hudson, 1977.

Milne, David. "Architecture, Politics and the Public Realm." *Canadian Journal of Political and Social Theory* 5 (Winter–Spring 1981): 131–46.

Moore, Charles, and Gerald Allen. *Dimensions: Space, Shape, and Scale in Architecture.* New York: Architectural Record Books, 1976.

Moore, Gary T. "Knowing about Environmental Knowing: The Current State of Theory and Research on Environmental Cognition." *Environment and Behavior* 11 (Mar. 1979): 33–70.

Morrow, Paula C., and James C. McElroy. "Interior Office Design and Visitor Response: A Constructive Replication." *Journal of Applied Psychology* 66, no. 5 (1981): 646–50.

Moynihan, Daniel Patrick. "Civic Architecture." *Architectural Record* 142 (Dec. 1967): 107–30.

Munari, Bruno. *Discovery of the Circle.* New York: George Wittenborn, 1966.

Myers, A. R. *Parliaments and Estates in Europe to 1789.* London: Thames & Hudson, 1975.

Needham, Rodney, ed. *Right and Left: Essays on Dual Symbolic Classification.* Chicago: University of Chicago Press, 1973.

Norberg-Schulz, Christian. *Genius Loci: Towards a Phenomenology of Architecture.* New York: Rizzoli, 1979.

———. *Intentions in Architecture.* Rome: Universitetsforlaget, 1963.

———. "Place." *AAQ* (Architectural Association Quarterly) 8, no. 4 (1976): 3–10.

———. *Space and Architecture.* New York: Praeger, 1971.

Osmond, Humphry. "Function as the Basis of

Psychiatric Ward Design." *Mental Hospital* 8 (Apr. 1957): 23–29.

Panofsky, Erwin. *Meaning in the Visual Arts: Papers in and on Art History.* New York: Doubleday, 1955.

———. *Studies in Iconology: Themes in the Art of the Renaissance.* New York: Oxford University Press, 1939. Reprint. New York: Harper & Row, 1972.

Pare, Richard. "Court Houses: County Symbols." *Historic Preservation* 29 (Oct. 1977): 31–37.

———. ed. *Court House: A Photographic Document.* New York: Horizon Press, 1978.

Patricios, N. N. "Concepts of Space in Urban Design, Architecture and Art." *Leonardo* 6, no. 4 (Autumn 1973): 311–18.

Patterson, Samuel C. "Party Opposition in the Legislature: The Ecology of Legislative Institutionalization." *Polity* 4 (Spring 1972): 344–66.

Peterson, Steven Kent. "Space and Anti-Space." *Harvard Architectural Review* 1 (Spring 1980): 88–113.

Preziosi, Donald. *The Semiotics of the Built Environment: An Introduction to Architectonic Analysis.* Bloomington: Indiana University Press, 1979.

Proshansky, Harold M.; William H. Ittelson; and Leanne G. Rivlin, eds. *Environmental Psychology: Man and His Physical Setting.* New York: Holt, Rinehart & Winston, 1970. 2d ed., 1976.

Raglan, Lord. *The Temple and the House.* London: Routledge & Kegan Paul, 1964.

Rapoport, Amos. *Human Aspects of Urban Form.* Oxford, Eng.: Pergamon Press, 1977.

———. *The Meaning of the Built Environment: A Non-Verbal Communication Approach.* Beverly Hills, Calif.: Sage, 1982.

———. "Sociocultural Aspects of Man-Environment Studies." In *The Mutual Interaction of People and Their Built Environment,* edited by Amos Rapoport, pp. 7–35. The Hague: Mouton, 1976.

———. "Vernacular Architecture and the Cultural Determinants of Form." In *Buildings and Society: Essays on the Social Development of the Built Environment,* edited by Anthony D. King. London: Routledge & Kegan Paul, 1980.

———. ed. *The Mutual Interaction of People and Their Built Environment: A Cross-Cultural Perspective.* The Hague: Mouton, 1976.

Rasmussen, Steen Eiler. *Experiencing Architecture.* New York: Wiley, 1959.

Reinle, Adolf. *Zeichensprache der Architektur:* *Symbol, Darstellung und Brauch in der Baukunst des Mittelalters und der Neuzeit.* Zurich: Artemis, 1976.

Relph, Edward. *Place and Placelessness.* London: Pion, 1976.

Roy, Hedley E. H. "Toronto City Hall and Civic Square." *Journal of the American Concrete Institute* 62 (Dec. 1965): 1481–1502.

Schlereth, Thomas J., ed. *Material Culture Studies in America.* Nashville, Tenn.: American Association for State and Local History, 1982.

Schwartz, Barry. *Vertical Classification: A Study in Structuralism and the Sociology of Knowledge.* Chicago: University of Chicago Press, 1981.

Smeets, René. *Signs, Symbols and Ornaments.* New York: Van Nostrand Reinhold, 1973.

Smith, E. Baldwin. *Architectural Symbolism of Imperial Rome and the Middle Ages.* Princeton, N.J.: Princeton University Press, 1956.

Sommer, Robert. *Personal Space: The Behavioral Basis of Design.* New York: Spectrum-Prentice-Hall, 1969.

———. *Tight Spaces: Hard Architecture and How to Humanize It.* New York: Prentice-Hall, 1974.

Steele, Fred I. "Problem Solving in the Spatial Environment." *EDRA* 1 (1970): 127–36.

Stone, Donald, and Alice Stone. "The Administration of Chairs." *Public Administration Review* 34 (Jan.–Feb. 1974): 71–77.

Stuart, Charlotte L. "Architecture in Nazi Germany: A Rhetorical Perspective." *Western Speech* 37 (Fall 1973): 253–63.

Studer, Raymond G., and David Stea. "Architectural Programming, Environmental Design, and Human Behavior." *Journal of Social Issues* 22 (Oct. 1966): 127–36.

Talbert, Richard J. A. *The Senate of Imperial Rome.* Princeton, N.J.: Princeton University Press, 1984.

Taylor, Lily Ross. *Roman Voting Assemblies.* Ann Arbor: University of Michigan Press, 1966.

Taylor, Robert R. *The Word in Stone: The Role of Architecture in the National Socialist Ideology.* Berkeley: University of California Press, 1940.

Thiel, Philip. "Notes on the Description, Scaling, Notation and Scoring of Some Perceptual and Cognitive Attributes of the Physical Environment." In *Environmental Psychology: Man and His Physical Setting,* edited by Harold M. Proshansky, William H. Ittelson, and Leanne G. Rivlin, pp. 602–7. New York: Holt, Rinehart & Winston, 1970.

Uspensky, B. A. "'Left' and 'Right' in Icon Painting." *Semiotica* 13, no. 1 (1975): 33–39.

Van der Ven, Cornelis J. *Space in Architecture.* Assen, the Netherlands: Van Gorcum, 1980.

Venturi, Robert; Denise Scott Brown; and Stevens Izenour. *Learning from Las Vegas.* Rev. ed. Cambridge, Mass.: MIT Press, 1977.

Vidler, Anthony. "The Writing of the Walls." *Artforum* 9 (Dec. 1980): 37–40.

Wheatley, Paul. *The Pivot of the Four Quarters.* Chicago: Aldine, 1971.

Wilentz, Sean, ed. *Rites of Power: Symbolism, Ritual, and Politics since the Middle Ages.* Philadelphia: University of Pennsylvania Press, 1985.

Wittkower, Rudolf. *Architectural Principles in the Age of Humanism.* London: Alec Tiranti, 1952.

Wohlwill, Joachim F. "The Physical Environment: A Problem for a Psychology of Stimulation." *Journal of Social Issues* 22 (Oct. 1966): 29–38.

Index